The Fragmentation of Policing in American Cities

Toward an Ecological Theory
of Police–Citizen Relations

Hung-En Sung

Criminal Justice, Delinquency, and Corrections
Marilyn D. McShane and Frank Williams, Series Editors

PRAEGER

Westport, Connecticut
London

Library of Congress Cataloging-in-Publication Data

Sung, Hung-En, 1968–
   The fragmentation of policing in American cities : toward an ecological theory of police–citizen relations / Hung-En Sung.
       p. cm.—(Criminal justice, delinquency, and corrections, ISSN 1535–0371)
   Includes bibliographical references and index.
   ISBN 0–275–97321–2 (alk. paper)
   1. Police–community relations—United States. I. Series.
   HV7936.P8S86   2002
   363.2′3′0973—dc21   2001034614

British Library Cataloguing in Publication Data is available.

Copyright © 2002 by Hung-En Sung

All rights reserved. No portion of this book may be
reproduced, by any process or technique, without
the express written consent of the publisher.

Library of Congress Catalog Card Number: 2001034614
ISBN: 0–275–97321–2
ISSN: 1535–0371

First published in 2002

Praeger Publishers, 88 Post Road West, Westport, CT 06881
An imprint of Greenwood Publishing Group, Inc.
www.praeger.com

Printed in the United States of America

The paper used in this book complies with the
Permanent Paper Standard issued by the National
Information Standards Organization (Z39.48–1984).

10 9 8 7 6 5 4 3 2 1

To my loving parents

Contents

Series Foreword	ix
Preface	xi
Introduction	1
1 Police–Citizen Relations	19
2 The Residential Organization of American Metropolises	43
3 The Ecology of Police–Community Relations: Hypotheses	69
4 Data, Variables, and Analytical Strategy	97
5 Testing the Theory	111
6 Conclusion and Discussion	133
References	155
Index	167

Series Foreword

This book marks the beginning of a new series of scholarly monographs, *Criminal Justice, Delinquency, and Corrections*. We are pleased to once again be facilitating the publication of new and innovative works in the field. Aside from writing on our own research agendas, the opportunity to work with colleagues, especially those publishing for the first time, is truly one of the most rewarding experiences in this profession. We look forward to assisting many others through this very exciting and gratifying process.

In this study, Hung-En Sung takes an interesting and unique approach to the study of community policing by integrating data from an ecological perspective into his argument for a model that will more broadly encompass the realities of the law enforcement environment. His work brings together contemporary community policing findings, traditional police attitudes toward community research, recently revived community disorganization approaches, and variables from past and present ecological models. This represents a timely reflection on the current state of policing that will be of interest to students, scholars, practitioners, community activists, policymakers, and consumers of law enforcement. We are proud to launch this new series with Dr. Sung's important contribution to criminal justice.

Marilyn D. McShane
Frank P. Williams III
School of Juvenile Justice and Psychology
Prairie View A & M University
Prairie View, Texas

Preface

Police research has time and again been a practice of pouring new wine into old skins. Millions of grant dollars are regularly spent in gathering new and ever-richer information, only to analyze it with aged and simplistic conceptual categories. New data do not necessarily lead to creative insights because their collection and analysis are too often guided by dated views of crime and society. Being an exceedingly concrete government service, policing is repeatedly examined and debated in terms of effectiveness, propriety, and fairness, but it rarely inspires theoretical imagination. It usually confronts us as an urgent social problem to be solved, and not as an object of scientific knowledge. As a result, we frequently lack adequate conceptual tools for maximizing the usefulness of our data. This book is a bold attempt to make fresh insight for policymakers and police researchers.

A theory of police and policing is an ambitious undertaking. While the ecological theory expounded in this book purports to be general, it is at the same time partial. It is partial because it explains the complex problem of police–citizen interactions from a specific perspective and does not seek to substitute alternative theories. To the contrary, I am aware of the need for hypotheses from psychology and legal and political theories to complement our understanding of police–citizen interactions. Furthermore, not even the ecological approach presented in these pages has made sufficient use of the rich tradition initiated by the Chicago

School of Urban Sociology a century ago. There is much left to be explored. However, I believe that the proposed theoretical model can explain a substantial amount of variance not accounted for by other hypotheses.

I argue for the plausibility and fruitfulness of analyzing police–citizen exchanges through the lenses of urban political economy. There would be no need for policing if there are no differences in people's income and spending, education and employment, and political involvement. Formal constructs such as social power and moral respectability and theoretical continuums such as marginality and centrality are devised to depict the ecology of police–citizen interactions. They may contribute to our knowledge of policing, but surely need more adjustments and better measurement in order to have a lasting impact in the field.

I also challenge the basic assumptions of current police reform, which focus on the disorganization of high-crime neighborhoods without placing the problem in the broader historical and structural context. Efforts to mobilize community resources without altering the distribution of social power and moral respect across neighborhoods may result in the fragmentation of police services, which undermines the democratic ideals of justice and equality. Policing is, after all, an institution with coercive authority that exercises its discretion, as this book argues, under the constraints and possibilities originated in the web of dominance–subordination relations among metropolitan neighborhoods. What the government and the market have failed to achieve cannot be accomplished by reinventing the work of a handful of police officers, however radical or deliberate.

I am privileged to have benefited from the support of many mentors and friends throughout the course of this project. David Bayley, David Duffee, Graeme Newman, Alissa Worden, and Robert Worden read the first draft of the manuscript and provided valuable comments and challenging questions that led to significant revision of parts of the book. Their generosity deserves more specific acknowledgment. David Bayley's no-nonsense work on police and public policy kindled my interests in policing. The framework of this project was directly influenced by David Duffee's community analysis of criminal justice practices; without his enthusiasm and encouragement this book would not be conceived. Graeme Newman's experiments in examining crime and justice with unorthodox ideas motivated me to undertake this theoretical task. When my ideas were taking shape, Alissa Worden reminded me that this research was both relevant and important. Toward the end of the process, she encouraged me to disseminate the results. I am also indebted to Robert Worden in many ways. His familiarity with police literature as well as his expertise in research methods were of enormous help to me during the analysis of the Police Service Study data. More important, his guidance and companionship have been a wonderful source of professional enrichment.

Marilyn McShane, the series editor, offered helpful comments on an earlier version of the draft and devoted time and energy to improve the manuscript. Suzanne Staszak-Silva of Praeger Publishers, through her friendliness and efficiency, has made the process of academic publishing a much less intimidating and more enjoyable experience. To both of them I am deeply grateful. Finally, I thank my wife, Sheila Chen, for her patience and understanding through it all.

This book is dedicated to my parents, Hsin-Yung and Hsiu-Yun Sung. Without my mother's determination to provide her children with the best education she could afford, I would never have had the opportunity to study and help to alleviate today's social problems. Without my father's optimism and example, I would probably never believe that human failures can be corrected, and difficulties overcome.

Introduction

"Community policing" has become the synonym of policing in America. It is praised as the renaissance to revive past treasures in the art of serving urban needs, and revered at the same time as the enlightenment in the science of maintaining law and order in a free society. Strong rhetorical and budgetary support for community policing has come from the highest ranks of civilian authorities, including the nation's president.

Current police reform shares the neoconservative belief that bureaucratic agencies tend to become monuments to governmental indifference and inefficiency in the long run, and that the way to prevent it from fossilization is for local citizens to reclaim their right to manage their own lives. The effectiveness and legitimacy of policing in a democratic society have essentially depended upon the approval and participation of the people, at least in theory. Disillusioned with the proven ineffectiveness of traditional methods of doing business (e.g., random motorized patrol, rapid response to calls, increased number of officers, etc.), police executives and scholars have brought about innovations centered on *police–community reciprocity*. This new philosophy advocates for the return of civil society through new forms of citizen participation at the community level, and views the police and the public as co-producers of crime prevention and expects the police to learn from and be accountable to their partner: the community (Body-Gendrot, 2000; Skolnick & Bayley, 1986).

Amidst this widespread enthusiasm, however, some solitary voices crying for caution have been heard. As a steady stream of findings from outcome evaluations has started to shed light on different achievements and failures of the first community policing programs implemented in the United States, a healthy skepticism sprouts among police practitioners and scholars. Tough questions arose from these evaluation studies: Why do some officers remain stubbornly ambivalent toward, and doubtful of, police efforts to change crime and neighborhood relations (Lurigio & Skogan, 1994)? How can we explain the inability of the police to mobilize residents or to reduce fear of crime in those most needy areas (Grinc, 1994; Skogan, 1990)? Why is it practically impossible for ordinary citizens to mature out of the secondary roles of eyes and ears, or cheerleaders, of the police, and become effectively involved in planning and decision making (Buerger, 1994)? These and many other observations tell us how much we expect from the magic of community policing, yet at the same time, how little we actually know about how the neighborhood as a human system relates to the work of police and vice versa.

Reform and *innovation* are subjective terms. Nobler standards can lead to improvements in delivering justice and order, but exaggerated expectations can also foster disillusion and cynicism. If current police reform keeps focusing on the attractiveness of the broken window theory without placing it in the social and political context that first creates broken windows, efforts to eliminate disorder and incivilities in urban communities may result in the reappearance of lawlessness and social conflict in another and more serious form. The disjunction between political expectations and social reality can lead to an insistence that the police solve problems beyond their capacities. Thus in a very real sense, the police—charged with monitoring and controlling society's failures—will remain a permanent object of societal criticism and resentment. What the market and the state cannot do, neither can the police. After all, police are a key component of the market-state complex. This view requires a realistic appraisal of the actual services to the public that American police departments deliver day after day and suggests that policing be understood in historical perspective and structural context. Such an analytical exercise will first challenge several recurring myths about policing and crime: (1) decreases in crime are associated to police effectiveness; (2) broken windows are the exogenous cause of the spiral of community decay; and (3) police-initiated programs alone can be viable tools to reverse the trend of community disorganization. Accurate explanations lead to realistic expectations and reveal the range of actual changes that the public might reasonably expect.

Police expert David A. Klinger has recently expressed his astonishment at the lack of any "systematic attempt to specify how and why patterns of policing vary across communities" and urges more scientific inquiry

Introduction

into the influence of community characteristics, such as levels of crime, on the delivery of police services (1997, p. 278).[1] This is not only a question of poor research design; it also reveals our insecurity to reduce this particular social phenomenon to some general logical skeleton capable of carrying "beautiful empirical flesh" (Stinchcombe, 1987, p. 5). Lawrence Sherman, another police scholar, pointed out 20 years ago that "theoretically the community level should be given the most attention" in police studies (1980, p. 94). Yet as of today, there is no *place-oriented* theory of police to guide *place-oriented* strategies of crime control such as community and problem-oriented policing. Police studies in America have been indicted for being predominantly *atheoretical*, of focusing narrowly on theorizing street-level interactions, and of ignoring how police maintain the vertical and horizontal distribution of groups in a broader social space (Manning, 1997). For community policing to avoid the caricature of promoting a "cheap, certain, and relatively easy solution" based on wishful thinking and sporadic anecdotal successes (Buerger, 1994), it must be both backed by a cogent theoretical argument and rooted in a solid empirical foundation. Too many hypotheses about group processes and collective behavior that have modeled much of the community policing philosophy have been formulated without benefit of empirical research. These wishful assumptions have been echoed by many as articles of faith, but tested by few.

The goal of this book is to fill this gap by visualizing "community" as the unit of analysis for police thinking and research and by constructing an ecological theory of police–citizen relations that acknowledges policing as a product of power relations among communities. This systematic explanation of policing across neighborhoods provides a foundation for rethinking theory and policy. It is based on the reanalysis of a classic set of data: The study of police–citizen interactions in 60 neighborhoods conducted jointly by the Workshop in Political Theory and Policy Analysis at Indiana University and the Center for Urban and Regional Studies at the University of North Carolina at Chapel Hill. The recoding and reanalysis of these comprehensive data allowed me to test a theoretical framework developed from current police research and urban studies that acknowledges the importance of urban political economy in shaping police–citizen relations. Through clearly defined concepts and logically consistent propositions one can argue why residential segregation lies at the heart, and is an essential part, of police work in the United States.

THE GEOGRAPHY OF RESIDENTIAL DISTRIBUTION AND POLICE ORGANIZATION

Urban life has been the prime object of study among American sociologists since the early years of the 20th century. Cities and their neighborhoods evoke curiosity. Families and individuals become neighbors when they come to share values and norms, and to relate to specific institutions and agencies in common endeavors. Patterns and outcomes of these interactions exert important effects on multiple aspects of human life, ranging from children's cognitive development (Entwisle, Alexander, & Olson, 1994) and life satisfaction (Fernandez & Kulik, 1981), to sexual activity (Brewster, Billy, & Grady, 1993) or even adult fertility (Billy & Moore, 1992). Moreover, the residential environment has become a central domain of quality-of-life experiences; positive residential environments enhance life satisfaction and the individual's overall sense of well-being. Wider routines develop in places of residence where one's concrete daily needs are satisfied through an informal network of people supplying life-sustaining products and services. It provides a sense of physical and psychological security that comes with a familiar and dependable environment and an important reference for identity, for its residents and for others. Neighborhoods thus become unique units of social/spatial organization in which individuals and families participate in the larger society through their daily rounds.

In recent decades, the neighborhood has surfaced as the focus of social policy and urban planning. Class inequality and racism materialized in urban communities as dilapidated housing, poor schools, and welfare dependence grew widespread. These social maladies are thus diligently fought at this level through governmental programs. A rich body of exchanges and research findings stemmed from these experiences. Participants in these policy discussions raised their concerns over external political interests and uncontrolled market forces that bear on policy feasibility (White, 1987). The unintended consequences of seemingly well-intended programs such as urban renewal on residents of lower-class neighborhoods have frustrated policy planners and angered the public. Contextual constraints and outside forces (e.g., corporate interests or changing global economy) can easily defeat good intentions and distort outcomes. Past failures in revitalizing urban neighborhoods should alert us to the significance of ecological interference in the forging of police–community contacts, which involve activities by and control of ordinary citizens. It has become evident that geographic identity and spatial location are social constructions evolved in and through relations of dominance and subordination. Therefore, we must reflect on police–citizen relations from the perspective of all participants (Wilson, 1968), look into the role of land use and population characteristics in facilitating uncivil or illicit activities (Green, 1996), and assess how the neighborhood levels of deviance reduce police strategic choices (Klinger, 1997).

Despite the pervasive image of the "good old days" of policing when the public valued and respected police officers who knew the good guys from the bad guys, and were allowed to do their jobs without too many questions from the grateful public, such "good old days" never existed. During the past 150 years, efforts to use police to solve social problems in disadvantaged places have always turned out to be broken dreams. In fact, police work has always been associated with public anger and resentment.

In retrospect, we can now assert that the rise of modern urban police performed two basic social functions during periods of drastic demographic transformations in American cities. First, the development of the police force responded to a growing intolerance for incivilities and unconventional behaviors attributed to the immigrants and the urban poor (Monkkonen, 1992). Since the second half of the 19th century, white Anglo-Saxon Protestant (WASP) residents occupying metropolitan areas fought, retreated, and resettled in a succession of struggles for the social hygiene of their habitats. Police forces were created to participate in these battles as rear-guard armies representing the worldviews of the WASP establishment regrouped in strategic areas of the cities. Second, the creation of urban police was a response to the industrialization and urbanization that had deleteriously affected the moral and institutional fabric of the inner city. The twisted, narrow, and darkened streets of urban slums where an underworld of thieves, drunkards, malcontents, and prostitutes lurked were a breeding ground for the breakdown of God-fearing morals. The deployment of police patrol in public places was to add force to the weakening social control capabilities of family, school, church, and other voluntary organizations. Urban policing reflected the deep-seated fear many had toward the threat of indigents and strangers. Fear of dangerous groups and fear of riots and disorders prevented many officers from exercising restraint in transactions with disadvantaged groups to such a point that, at the turn of the century, police mistreatment of the immigrant population became a major issue in many big cities such as New York (Reiss, 1971). Since these earliest days, the modern municipal police have inextricably been connected with stories of class conflict and ethnic rivalry and mandated to maintain an order that has never ceased to be contested.

At the very beginning, police administrators decided that street crime and disorder would be suppressed or deterred if officers patrolled small areas—their beats—with sufficient regularity and visibility. The whole city was therefore broken down into numerous patrol areas with officers assigned to each of them. Police behavior and misbehavior varied enormously from beat to beat from the inception of this spatial work organization in the 19th century. Prior to the Progressive reform, patrolmen offered little resistance to the temptation of running protection rackets and licensing gambling and prostitution, which flourished in the burgeoning sections of major cities. The moral integrity of high-ranking police managers was no better than that of their subordinates. Wildly partisan, police executives flirted with city political machines and did not hesitate to make public their political allegiance by encouraging citizens to vote for particular candidates and by fixing ballot boxes. The quick surrender to the bribes from the vice industries together with the complacent willingness to be manipulated by local politicians eventually corrupted large municipal police departments, such as that of New York City, to the core. This first police–community encounter left a lasting impact on American police thinking. Under the assumption that familiarity with the community encourages corruption, commanding officers in precincts were often rotated and patrolmen were also transferred with greater frequency. Reformers equaled the covetous elements of the underworld and the unprincipled urban elite with the community and found the antidote to police corruption in isolating the force from citizen input. Officers were required not to live or to become involved in businesses in the areas they patrolled and to restrict informal ties with the general public. Even casual conversations with the citizenry were strongly discouraged in some police departments (Sparrow, Moore, & Kennedy, 1990). This philosophy of professionalization through separation and some of its ensuing isolationist practices have survived nearly to the present day.

Two gross fallacies were implicit in this quarantine approach to combat police corruption and misconduct. First, it excluded the majority of ordinary citizens who had neither lured the police into any inappropriateness nor ever wanted them to do so. What seems to have been perilously jeopardized is the political legitimacy of police work, a vital buffer against social unrest in a democratic society that only a fair degree of civilian support can provide. This mistake would exact heavy cost in later decades. Second, when reformers sought to neutralize unwelcome environmental influences by reducing the intensity of formal and informal contacts with local residents, problem citizens became the police's main clients. Offenders and suspects were *the* citizens that patrol officers interacted with on a daily basis. When open and direct communication between police and the law-abiding public diminishes, hearsay, stereotypes, myths, and prejudices are internalized as shared commonsense. Real people are thus replaced by their shadows, their distorted images, in this delicate and often stormy relationship. The idea of achieving police professionalism at the expense of citizens' involvement in the negotiation of their own neighborhood order did not change until the late 1970s and early 1980s, when the importance of "neighborhood people" was resuscitated in criminological literature and criminal justice policymaking.

Despite being cut off from direct community input, policing in America remains largely a territorially organized enterprise, mainly because of its decentralized nature. The responsibility of providing comprehensive police services rests with county and municipal governments as "a massive patchwork of distinct police organizations delineated by political boundaries" (Klinger, 1997, p. 281). Police policies and practices are determined at the top and flow down in the form of rules and orders, although the actual operational decision making is extremely decentralized and highly discretionary. Even though all police departments maintain an elaborate vertical structure, most police work takes place outside the direct monitoring of supervisors. In each of these numerous individual agencies, the patrol work, which has always been the spine of modern policing, is further subdivided into smaller and manageable sections—usually known as "beats"—to which patrol units are typically assigned. Assigned to a patrol beat, officers are granted legal authority and moral dominion over a territory. Patrol officers act as sovereigns of their beats (Crank, 1998). In larger cities, patrol beats tend to be grouped to form divisions or precincts that are linked to a superordinate administrative structure. The collections of patrol beats possess the social stability that defines the police occupation as a system of human groups and subcultural norms circumscribed by territorial and temporal boundaries. The correspondence that exists between the context of neighborhood formation and the context of police work-group formation underscores the reason why the role of community ecology is fundamental for explaining police–citizen relations.

The neighborhood-based division of labor in urban policing produces and maintains distinct and stable patrol work groups in police departments. Despite the administrative vicissitudes that make each of the thousands of urban police departments a unique agency, officers working patrol in any district constitute a clearly identifiable entity unto themselves. Most officers patrol the same sets of beats with the same colleagues on an almost daily basis. Patrol involves driving, walking, or bicycling around assigned beats. The continuity of patrol groups within jurisdictional territories is rarely disrupted. That the patrol of urban areas occurs in the context of neighborhood-based work groups indicates that policing in America has always geared toward the community: its people and the places they live. The stability and autonomy of patrol work groups allow officers to immerse themselves in the districts they are in charge of and devise rules to handle local problems relatively unaffected by direct outside influence. Different interpretations of police work develop according to the unique structural characteristics of different patrol districts. In the long run, different approaches to crime control and service delivery emerge in different places.

THE GEOGRAPHY OF LAW AND ORDER

Public opinion and popular culture have always portrayed certain urban enclaves, if not their occupants, as suspicious and dreadful. Clifford R. Shaw and Henry D. McKay (1942) first proposed the *kind-of-places* explanation to counteract the dominant *kind-of-people* argument for the breakdown of community order. Since then social scientists point to the deficit in social organization and the distorted opportunity structure as the main causes of deviation from socially approved lifestyles. Yet the *kind-of-people* hypothesis still receives wider acceptance among the general audience and political leadership. Being tough on crime is consistently equated to imposing drastically punitive sanctions against specific kinds of individuals rather than devising long-term comprehensive measures to restore the prosperity and sustainability of crime-stricken neighborhoods. Law enforcement, as a government institution accountable to the empowered constituencies, ignores the geographic organization of fortunes and misfortunes in favor of the prevalent *kind-of-people* view of crime and justice in which the restoration of individual rights remains the priority for social engineering. Yet police work begins where people and place converge.

Residence in a "marked" neighborhood is often used by the police as a general indicator for identifying potential offenders. Varying social conditions—the presence of danger in the community, the political complexion of the community, the demographic dissimilarity of the population—all contribute to the conception of the criminal held by the police. Based on this judgment, they develop rules about what deviance should be handled and how crime should be processed in accordance with the wealth, education, respectability, and conventionality of local residents. Persons encountered in a bad neighborhood are likely to be treated as possessing the moral liability of the area itself through the process of ecological contamination (Smith, 1986). This stereotype can generate stable expectations among law enforcement agents regarding what control tactics are appropriate in a particular neighborhood. The guiding as well as the constraining influence of the community context can be seen not only in individual police behavior but also in general police strategies and citizen attitudes toward police practices. To a white suburbanite, the most immediate image of police work is usually derived from TV news and drama series or from the less pleasant experience of a traffic violation stop. But a nonwhite slum resident may easily think of police as arrogant agents of an oppressive world. Police–community relations thus diverge into fixed patterns over time and vary considerably from one neighborhood context to the next.

Very few would dispute the view that the patrolman's conception of the police role varies with the character of the community. However, this truism is never elaborated into a coherent theory and is rarely put to empirical test. Past studies of policing highlighted the central relevance of structural attributes in determining the quality of police–citizen interactions. For instance, Reiss (1971) reported that encounters in high-crime black areas generally attracted larger crowds and thus presented a more serious challenge to police authority solely by reason of higher residential density in these neighborhoods. Policemen were more likely to resort to coercive tactics to assert their authority in situations involving large audiences because of the more serious problem of control. It was also observed that police serving small communities were more responsive to, and consequently less autonomous from, their constituents who had more direct access to the department to communicate their demands and complaints (Brown, 1988). If both the population density and territorial size could become so central to the making of policing style, how equally critical, if not more important, would structural traits such as ethnic and class compositions impact on police–citizen relations?

POLICE BEHAVIOR AS MACRO-LEVEL PHENOMENON

The concept of police behavior has grown in width and depth as the scientific study of policing matures over time. It means more now than it once did. The majority of past ethnographic studies addressing police conduct as behavioral patterns of individual patrol officers resulted from complex interaction among the status properties of those involved (e.g., race, age, and sex) and their personality traits (e.g., capacity to empathize with human suffering), value systems (e.g., readiness to resort to coercive means), and occupational environment (e.g., social isolation and paramilitary bureaucratic organization of work). Researchers spent a great amount of time talking and listening to officers at length about their personal lives and their perceptions of local problems. These in-depth observations and interviews were often supplemented with the administration of systematic surveys to collect standardized information that allows statistical comparisons of key variables.

Since the mid-1960s the systematic observation of police services entered the scene and settled as the research method of choice among police scholars. Trained observers are sent to ride or walk along with officers on patrol with the purpose of recognizing and noting relevant information concerning the occurrence of any incident or routine. Observation and recording of police work are done using explicit procedures that permit replication and rules are followed that allow the use of the logic of scientific inference. The introduction of systematic observation of police patrol produced an important array of detailed data, which was subsequently analyzed and published in numerous books and professional journals. Police–citizen encounters became the unit of analysis, which dominated later research discourse.

The transition from the description of individual officers' mind-sets and departments' administrative outcomes to the measurement of actual exchanges between patrolmen and citizens has enormously enriched police reflection and inquiry and represented a vital breakthrough. The analysis of police–citizen encounters allowed a vivid visualization of police work, permitting direct access to circumstantial conditions such as the nature of the incident and the demographic characteristics of the parties involved, which had not been known in earlier literature. It also elevated the discussion about police to a higher level of abstraction. Police–citizen *encounters* are an analytical entity of higher order in which police behavior acquires a new meaning and is no longer seen as an outcome of decision making by individual officers but as a process of transactions that occur among the patrolmen, victims, suspects, bystanders, and other participants. Officers act and react in a concrete situation in which one has to keep in control, invoke the law if necessary, and ultimately administer justice, whatever "justice" implies at that precise moment. This broadening in the operational definition elevates the construct of police behavior from the realm of individual psychology to that of social psychology. Nevertheless, limited within the analytical scope of psychology, police behavior is still mainly perceived as being initiated by discrete officers. Limited by the data and methods of analysis, police studies have so far been fundamentally psychological, either cognitive, social, or organizational. Psychological approaches highlight the personality outlooks and individual actions, and centers on the examination of selected attributes and behavior patterns associated with discrete participants of an encounter, ignoring situational exigencies generated by structural relations among institutions and social groups. Despite its intuitive appeal, social psychological research has demonstrated that the causal relationship that exists between people's attitudes and their behavior ranges from moderate to negligible (Worden, 1996).

In his widely acclaimed treatise *Varieties of Police Behavior*, James Q. Wilson (1968) unpretentiously advanced a new conceptualization of "behavior" that had not been properly recognized yet. When Wilson turned to empirical data to develop his now famous "styles" of policing, his analysis focused on a collectivist view of police conduct. Defined as "the operational code of the department" (p. 140), the style of police behavior was theoretically conceived as the way most patrolmen of a department carry out their duties and empirically measured as the aggregate administrative outcomes. Wilson coded and compared administrative records pertaining to eight diverse police departments serving eight cities and abstracted three ideal types of police behavior (i.e., watchman style, service style, and legalistic style). The purpose was to describe the strategic philosophy that reigned in a specific police department as well as the overall tone of police services a determined community received. Note that "behavior" here does not denote the activity of individual officers but the organizational output of an entire department in response to environmental exigencies. It inaugurates the sociology of police.

How does the sociological "behavior" differ from the psychological "behavior" in the study of criminal justice in general? It challenges us to view criminal justice behavior as a "social fact" in the grand tradition of Emile Durkheim (1964 [1895]). What exactly does analyzing policing as a "social fact" entail? When seen as a social fact or institution, policing becomes ways of acting, thinking, and feeling, external to the individual officer and endowed with a power of coercion by means of which these manners of acting, thinking, and feeling control every individual officer. This analytical approach does not deny the plausibility of active individual participation in the construction of the police–citizen reality. It simply maintains that causes and outcomes of police service delivery are, in large measure, external to specific individuals and thus can be meaningfully examined at a higher level of aggregation and abstraction. Societal expectations that do not appear directly relevant to constituencies of community predict, to a large extent, police decisions and citizen demeanors in specific street-level encounters. The normative and perceptual categories that contribute to how the police are involved in the definition of community are not expectations of individuals interacting on the street but expectations institutionalized in structural relations and cultural understandings (Duffee, Fluellen, & Roscoe, 1999). These expectations, assimilated into police subculture, are also shared by parents in their evaluations of school districts or real-estate developers in their assessment of land values and growth potentials. The most relevant societal expectations that are built into the structure and traditions of city life are those regarding the spatial ordering of power and respect.

There is no doubt that police–citizen relationships could be relevantly interpreted if the sequential exchanges of actions and reactions in face-to-face contacts are fully investigated. But this micro-level perspective should be balanced and complemented with macro-level analyses in order to avoid outright subjectivism and individualism in the study of police behavior and the public response it encounters. Unfortunately, current police research is disproportionately biased toward a micro-level approach and can only be corrected with renewed macro-level theoretical formulations and empirical testing. One of the lasting consequences resulting from the dominance of social psychology in the analysis of deviance and its control has been the neglect of community-building mechanisms operating in neighborhoods, which in turn, have often supported governmental interventions that only seek to control individuals (Duffee, 1990).

Eight years after Wilson's research on the varieties of police behavior, Donald Black launched an elegant and intensely debated theoretical speculation about the varying application of law in *The Behavior of Law* (1976). In it, Black proposed a scientific, that is, testable, theory of law. This attempt at bringing law into the scrutiny of empirical examination was based on the premise that as a natural phenomenon, law can be scrupulously quantified. Law behaves, according to Black, because as a changing aspect of social reality, it varies in time and space. Law can be validly regarded as a quantitative variable as it increases and decreases from one setting to another, from one historical epoch to another. Police discretion, seen from this perspective, constitutes the law in action *par excellence*. Any increment in the volume of criminal law invocation or any systemic drop in enforcement changes its quantity. By emphasizing the nature of law as an aspect of social reality and its relationships to other dimensions of social life, any individualistic explanation is forcefully removed from the model. As Black explains,

Theory of this kind predicts and explains social life without regard to the individual as such.... It neither assumes nor implies that he is, for instance, rational, goal directed, pleasure seeking, or pain avoiding. It has no concept of human nature. It has nothing to do with how an individual experiences reality. It has nothing to say about the responsibility of an individual for his own conduct or about its causes. Theory of this kind, then has nothing to do with the psychology of law. (p. 7)

Black's methodological dogmatism echoes Wilson's acceptance of bureaucratic organizations and residential communities as agents and recipients of police behavior. Both authors tackle the analysis of the legal process beyond the seduction of psychological reductionism and refuse to be confined by the particularistic treatment of police services; instead, they explain the behavior of the police as a social institution of control. Later on, Richard J. Lundman (1980) defines police behavior from a sociological perspective as the collection of encounters and decisions routinely characteristic of the patrol experience in large urban areas, and suggests that further conceptual elaboration should focus on extra-individualistic forces or events. As such, the goal of macro-level research is not so much to explicate the use of discretion by individual officers, although it can, but to isolate characteristics of communities, cities, or even societies that lead to varying rates of law enforcement or under enforcement. The collective properties of groups, classes, organizations, and institutions that directly or indirectly participate in the forging of police–community relations are to be systematically theorized and tested. This paradigmatic shift offers new promises to police research and policymaking. But lamentably this thread of scientific inquiry has been largely restricted by a self-imposed moratorium among police scholars; with a few sporadic exceptions, very few police researchers have followed.

In the preface of the second edition of his seminal work, Wilson urged his colleagues to begin using residential neighborhoods as the prime unit of analysis to investigate the dynamics of alternative police styles. Studying municipal police departments led him to consider the eight small- and medium-sized cities as meaningful units of aggregation for police study. The general conclusion that urban policing styles are mainly determined by organizational culture and departmental leadership cannot be adequately assessed without taking into account the original design and sample choice. Aggregates as large as counties or cities are inappropriate for the estimation of the effects of structural environment on police behavior due to their internal heterogeneity. Patrol officers serve and come into contact with citizens within ecological units much smaller than cities or towns. Neighborhoods possess a range of mechanisms for making demands on police and other governmental agencies and should be accorded corresponding attention. Hence Wilson maintained, "I know of very few efforts to discover whether different neighborhoods in a large city receive differing kinds of police services" (1978, p. vii).

The most appropriate level of aggregation for the ecological study of police is the residential neighborhood.[2] Each neighborhood experiences its own distinctive style of policing because rather than letting each officer create and follow his or her own guidelines, patrol and service norms are largely set and enforced by collective means. Patrol work groups develop informal rules on the use of coercive force (Hunt, 1985; Waegel, 1984), the making of arrest decisions (Walsh, 1986), the processing of criminal cases (Waegel, 1981), and other routines that serve the individual needs of the officers as they mediate conflicting demands of police bureaucracies and community. The freedom of patrol officers to devise and act upon whatever rules they see fit is large, but not unlimited. Many police–citizen encounters involve more than one officer; even when only one officer is handling a situation, his behavior and decisions are officially or unofficially checked and reviewed through written reports, radio contacts, and locker-room conversations. It is simply impossible for patrol officers to manage encounters within their districts without some sort of corporate normative guidelines operating. Inexplicably, more than 20 years have passed since Wilson's remarks were made, neighborhood study of police is still comparatively neglected. Micro-level analyses monopolize the field, despite the fact that most police researchers were trained in the macro disciplines of sociology and political science.

We should not precipitate into a foolish "individual versus aggregate" kind of debate, which blatantly overlooks the complementarity that exists between the study of group phenomena and the examination of individual events or persons. Each analytical approach has its own merits and answers to a unique set of questions. What we have is not a tree- or-wood dilemma but a tree-and-wood possibility. The reality of police– public interactions is composed of micro-events that foster and are fostered by macro-trends, and is understood in this treatise as taking the form it does because of the stratification and segregation that characterizes American metropolises, which are independent of the motives or personality of particular officers or citizens. The goal of the present work is to specify a formal model to account for macro variations in police–community relations.

THE NEED FOR A MODEL

Why should police–citizen relations be explored through the explicit specification of a theoretical model? Some might see the use of abstract models objectionable on the grounds that formal propositions involve such dramatic simplifications of the complexity of the real "cop world" that they cannot possibly deepen our knowledge in this regard. I offer three brief counterarguments to such objections.

First, the fact that models constitute simplifications of complexity is not in and of itself a shortcoming, but a virtue. This is precisely what a good theory of policing should accomplish: to get to the heart of the complex problem of police–citizen relations by identifying the key causal linkages. Second, the essential structure of a formal model of police is to create a thought experiment of police behavior; that is, one is forced to specify the underlying assumptions of the model, the conditions that are treated as parameters, and the ways in which the mechanisms work. Even though experiments are essential to give plausibility to any causal claims made about police or citizen behaviors, in real-life situations it is extremely hard to construct experimental conditions to unravel the web of causal mechanisms (as the Kansas City Patrol Experiment or the Minneapolis Domestic Violence Experiment has demonstrated). But the crucial question to ask of a formal theory is not whether it is true, but whether it is useful in increasing our explanatory capacity (Stinchcombe, 1987). Finally, lurking behind every causal explanation is a tacit formal model. All explanatory arguments of criminal justice behavior contain assumptions about social organization and human decision making, claims about the conditions under which the explanations hold, and expectations about how the various intervening mechanisms fit together. Ignoring implicit assumptions is definitely more dangerous than formal modeling, which not only enhances the depth of our understanding of the abstract arguments themselves, but also makes it much easier to identify their weaknesses and reconstruct them in light of empirical findings.

Although only rarely can models provide full answers to policy questions, they are still indispensable in the quest for better solutions to current police problems. What models of police–citizen relationships can achieve, if developed and used with care, is to provide evidence that, together with other sources of information, may be used in arguments supporting a certain conclusion or recommendation. A good model is just one type of evidence among others, not the end of the debate over how police and the public contribute to the maintenance of law and order in the community, much less the ultimate authorities to make such judgment.

DATA USED IN THIS STUDY

In order to assess whether the formulated conceptual framework can take root and grow in the empirical world, it is required that abstract constructs be validly translated into empirical measures to test the hypothesized relationships among variables. This task is particularly challenging given the multiplicity of structural factors and social forces articulated in an ecological theory of policing. Most police data focus on specific dimensions of policing (e.g., expenditures, use of deadly force, public perceptions, etc.) and are rarely cross-jurisdictional in scope. Collecting and coding information from the police and the policed, as well as from the social environment of their interactions, is a labor-intensive, time-consuming, and often unbearably expensive enterprise. As a result, no police data have ever been collected solely for the purpose of theory testing. In the study of crime and justice, existing data that were collected for the purposes of a prior study are usually used to pursue a pure theoretical interest distinct from the original work. As a matter of fact, some of the most influential criminological theories proposed in the past few decades were originated from or confirmed with secondary empirical analyses (e.g., Cohen & Felson, 1979; Sampson & Laub, 1993).

An initial or preliminary assessment of the ecological hypotheses proposed in this book was conducted using data from the 1977 Police Services Study (PSS). Although more than 20 years have lapsed since the original collection and American society has experienced some changes in ideological predilection (particularly in regard to crime and justice) as well as in the demographic composition of the big metropolises, this comprehensive set of computerized information on police services remains unrivaled in size and scope. The enduring relevance of race and class (two social factors that guided PSS's design of information gathering) in American policing have greatly prolonged the active life of the data. In fact, they were still used in research articles published in first-rank criminology journals 20 years after its collection (e.g., Worden & Shepard, 1996). Despite a few recent studies reporting the declining significance of race in mediating police–citizen relations (Sampson & Bartusch, 1999; Weitzer, 2000) and longitudinal national polls detecting important ethnic and racial differences in public perceptions of police and policing (Ludwig, 2000), some of these perceptual and attitudinal gaps were even more prominent than those found in the turbulent decade of the 1960s (Chambers & Newport, 2000). Familiar names such as

Rodney King, Abner Louima, and Amadou Diallo attest how race and ethnicity still play a critical role in the police politics of metropolitan regions, which remain as segregated as, if not more segregated than, they were in 1977 (Jargowsky, 1997; Massey & Denton, 1993).

Although efforts at collecting new police data have never ceased since 1977, none of these research projects generated information as wide-ranging in details and extensive in magnitude as the PSS data. Take, for example, the Project on Policing Neighborhoods (POPN) conducted during 1996 and 1997, a direct descendant of the PSS in terms of data collection philosophy and methodology and arguably the largest in scale in recent times (Mastrofski et al., 1998; Mastrofski, Parks, Reiss, & Worden, 1998, 1999). Initiated by a group of scholars previously involved in PSS, POPN is a state-of-the art undertaking to explore what policing was like in Indianapolis, Indiana, and St. Petersburg, Florida, by gathering massive observation, survey, and interview data from police officers and citizens in 24 neighborhoods. Yet even this magnificent endeavor fell short of providing empirical materials as ideal as the PSS data for testing neighborhood-based theories. Given the small number of neighborhoods sampled, which makes multivariate comparisons of neighborhoods extremely difficult, POPN is likely to produce, primarily, studies based on individual-level findings or simple comparisons of police departments and neighborhoods.

What is then so unique about the PSS data set? Hailed as the richest and most complete study of police work (Walker, 1992), the PSS data have nurtured a generation of police scholars. The entire study spanned from 1974 to 1980 and a crucial part of the project consisted of an in-depth examination of 24 police departments and 60 neighborhoods. Intensive on-site data collection was conducted in the summer of 1977 by researchers in three Standard Metropolitan Statistical Areas (SMSAs): Rochester, New York; St. Louis, Missouri; and Tampa–St. Petersburg, Florida. Departments were selected in each SMSA to yield a sample that would reflect a rough cross-section of organizational arrangements and service conditions for urban policing in the United States. The objective was not to obtain a representative sample reflecting the entire population of American police forces, but to maximize the variance of police services in urban and suburban residential areas.

Data were gathered from various sources and in various ways and can be analyzed separately or linked together to give a richer set of information for analysis. Although some were coded from official agency records, most were assembled through instruments specifically designed and independently administered. Trained observers systematically monitored patrol work in 60 neighborhoods. These neighborhoods were defined on the basis of police beat boundaries, census block groups, and enumeration districts, and selected to reflect the residential conditions under which each department plans and delivers services. Two structural factors, ethnicity and family income, served as the principal selection criteria, most neighborhoods being either predominantly white or nonwhite.

Information was obtained from police officers' encounters observed during selected shifts, telephone interviews with citizens, and observational data of general patrol shifts. The first set of data consisted of a description of police–citizen encounters involving 7,200 hours of in-person observation of more than 500 officers. Fifteen shifts were sampled in each of the 60 neighborhoods. A total of 5,688 police–citizen encounters involving more than 10,000 citizens were coded. Variables provide valuable details about the officer's role in the encounter and their demeanor toward citizen(s) involved, including how the encounter began, police actions during the encounter, and services requested by the citizen. The second data file, containing victimization and demographic information, was a survey of a random sample of neighborhood residents. Approximately 200 residents per neighborhood were interviewed by telephone with a total of 12,022 interviews completed. There were up to 172 items surveyed per interview, including respondent characteristics and household victimizations. The last section of data included a detailed recounting of 949 eight-hour patrol shifts or fractions thereof, including variables describing the shift, the officers, the events occurring during an observed shift, the total number of encounters, and officer attitudes on patrol styles and activities. All these data can be aggregated to the community level to obtain indicators of area characteristics for each of the 60 neighborhoods. The magnitude and the richness of the PSS data make it the best available to evaluate neighborhood-based theories of policing.

NOTES

1. I take the liberty of using the terms "district," "neighborhood," and "community" almost interchangeably without reference to the fact that, obviously, they are not synonymous.

2. There is a growing interest on the relevance of locating even smaller geographic units, or "hot spots," that produced the most calls to police (LeBeau & Coulson, 1996; Sherman, Gartin, & Buerger, 1989). Although these micro-units possess singular strategic relevance for the implementation of special enforcement operations, usually against vice and drug offenses (see Green, 1996), their adequacy for the explanation of police patrol styles and police public relations is evidently inadequate. Rather than having their own internal structural consistency, hot spots are addresses, housing complexes, or street blocks that depend on wider surroundings to acquire their criminal significance. Most of these and other defining traits of crime hot spots are, above all, signs of lower quality of life in broader neighborhoods.

CHAPTER 1

Police–Citizen Relations

Most salient problems in American policing revolve around police–community relations. Rather than a euphemism for police–race relations as some have suggested (e.g., Walker, 1992), police–citizen relations hinge on the political foundations of state authority. The ideal of democratic governance has given *community* a central place in the discussion and evaluation of policing. Effectiveness, in terms of catching criminals and clearing crimes, is recognized as *not* being the only purpose of law enforcement. As the roots of the American criminal justice system are deep in an ideology of personal freedom and the fundamental worth and dignity of people, police activities are required to be controlled by higher principles of due process of law, fairness, and propriety. Citizen complaints of police brutality, corruption, or charges of discriminatory practices inexorably erode the political legitimacy of the state. Police–citizen relations reflect, in the last instance, the character of the political system.

An overview of the operational characteristics that distinguish the organization of American police forces will unpack the meaning of *community* entailed in current police rhetoric. As in other common-law countries, the legitimacy of police work derives from the law and popular will. Police are to follow rules and regulations passed by elected representatives and the legality of their actions is bound to the protections granted by the Bill of Rights. Since the original English patrol system started by simply extending to police officers the right every English citizen had to arrest and/or charge suspects of criminal offenses before courts of law, identification with and approval of the citizenry became the moral foundations of police operations. In this tradition, the judgments of police officers must replicate to a large extent those of the policed because the exercise of police power is delegated and should be applied according to the criteria spelled out by the public. Unlike the Continental police, which were historically considered as servants of the imperial state, common law police forces were born primarily as servants of the law and the people. This Anglo-Saxon notion of representative policing presupposes a unanimous public opposed to violence and chaos, which would tolerate limits on citizens' freedom in exchange for a net increase of that freedom.

When the police were restructured to become a professional crime-fighting organization to replace the political patronage business after the Progressive reform era, a new kind of social control more disciplined than civil forces and more responsive than armed forces was thus instituted. Four innovative features distinguished American police forces ever since (Monkkonen, 1992). First, the adoption of a quasimilitary outlook led to the hierarchical organization of police work and personnel, with a vertical command and communication structure. While this model has facilitated efficiency and discipline, it also has promoted the notion that the police are apart from civilian life. The decivilization of law enforcement has made the consent of the policed a moving target that has to be negotiated and renegotiated in each community. This quasimilitary profession is based on a set of assumptions about the nature of social life and the worth of their mandate, which, when internalized, gives individual officers a moral justification for privilege and respect. Second, reform in municipal government gradually placed the police under the executive rather than the judicial branch. As a part of the mayor's executive office, the police have introduced an additional element of friction into the ideological tension that already existed between the courts, prosecuting attorneys, and the defense. The isolation from the civilian world and the daily involvement in intensely adversarial legal contests has further reinforced the "us versus them" siege mentality that shields the police from external input. As a result, police culture is to a great extent dominated by themes associated with suspiciousness and distrust of others.

The third characteristic of the modern, reformed police is the predilection for making their presence highly visible, first through uniforming its officers, and later through the deployment of marked patrol cars. Because of this high visibility, police officers have been the first and, for a long time the only, state officials easily seen by and accessible to the public. To many, the police are the incarnation of the Leviathan itself. All the emotions and sentiments that people harbor about their government are projected to the men in blue. Lastly, the police are conceived to bring regular and more active crime prevention to the community than the constables' passive and fee-based work. Consequently, street patrol aimed at detecting and scaring off would-be offenders established itself as the core of police work. All these features have survived to the present. Today, police forces remain paramilitarized, rank highest in terms of isolation and unionism among governmental bureaucracies, and still embrace a highly visible patrol as the preferred tactic of service.

Although police and the public have always interacted in an uneasy series of pulls and pushes, the rule of law and the police's independence from the judiciary have provided a crucial mechanism for preventing a lopsided balance of power. Perhaps the most frequent check on day-to-day police operations is the criminal courts, which see to it that police actions and reactions to the public conform to the Constitution. Despite the conflicting views of state authority that can be found in American society, the police will always have to abide by the supreme rule of policing by consent. In order to use force, to search and seize property, to make arrests or frisk intercepted civilians, police actions must be legitimized both formally and factually. On legal grounds, police act by the consent of the policed when they derive their authority from law and take an oath to support the Constitution. In doing so, police officers are obliged to acknowledge the law's moral force as well as the constraint of the collective will of the citizenry. On the pragmatic side, police must also be supported by a moral consent that permits the exercise of extended authority beyond specifically legislated mandates, such as the delivery of nonenforcement services. The moral consent of the policed depends on the actual approval and trust from the public accumulated over time. Therefore, we can say that the legal consent is deductively assumed and has a *de jure* existence backed by the legislative–judicial machinery. Moral consent of the policed has, on the contrary, an empirical basis, and its *de facto* strength is known by the quality of citizen support and satisfaction. Since the *de facto* consent is never perfect or absolute, unpredictability and volatility will always lay beneath police–community interactions. Police services generate public acceptance only as long as they are sensitive to community expectations, just in their delivery, and reasonably effective in controlling crime (Elliston & Feldberg, 1985; Skolnick & Fyfe, 1993).

The formal aspect and the factual aspect of police legitimacy are complementary, but do not always concur; this is particularly true in segmented societies in which elite groups control and manipulate the state apparatus to advance their own interests. The Rodney King beating and the subsequent riot in Los Angeles demonstrated how in disadvantaged and neglected areas popular consent is nothing more than passive acquiescence and has often been strained, sometimes in violent confrontation. When a group of Los Angeles Police Department officers decided to apply more force than was legally prescribed on a fleeing black motorist, institutional legitimacy was immediately torn down, which insidiously exacerbated the anger and distrust that had already been mounting upon the LAPD's fragile community relations. The riot of 1992 exposed not so much the collapse of consent, but rather the clear manifestation of a consent that had long since been withdrawn—if it had ever existed. Nevertheless, there were times when the breaking of the legal contract by the police was cheered by a significant portion of the policed. The participation of the police in suppressing civil rights movement activities in the South during the 1950s and 1960s received firm support from the dominant white population, thus police could have claimed the consent of the majority. This example reminds us how elusive and difficult it is to determine police legitimacy in a heterogeneous society.

A typical urban police department relates not to one but to many communities. Clusters of people banded by social background, ethnicity and race, age, and other common necessities or interest share the same right to be equally attended by public service institutions. What a police department views as good for one neighborhood may not necessarily be so in another; or it may be good only for that part of the community to whom the police are usually loyal. Instead of dealing with the citizenry as a whole, public agencies for the most part set up and maintain specialized neighborhood interest groups. Police rely on the creation of a friendly clientele (often led by business interests) and the cooperation of local leaders to garner support and legitimacy (see Buerger, 1994; Hunter, 1983).

Policing is a bidirectional enterprise: it includes police services to the public as well as citizen services to the police. A police force cannot be adequately and justly evaluated apart from the community it services because "a weak force enjoying public support is more effective than a powerful force without it" (Fielding, 1991, p. 132). See Figure 1.1.

POLICE RELATIONS TO THE PUBLIC

Citizens get in touch with the police primarily about conflicts and emergencies that arise within or near their households. A recent national study estimates that each year, one in five adults has face-to-face contact with a police officer (Greenfeld, Langan, & Smith, 1997). One-third of residents who have had contact with police have either asked for assistance from officers or provided it to them, whereas another one-third of those who have had contact with police have reported a crime, either as a victim or witness. In both situations, police officers are expected to employ their authority and skills to return troublesome or volatile situations into peace and tranquility, whereby the community order is pre-

Figure 1.1
The dependent variable: Police–citizen relations

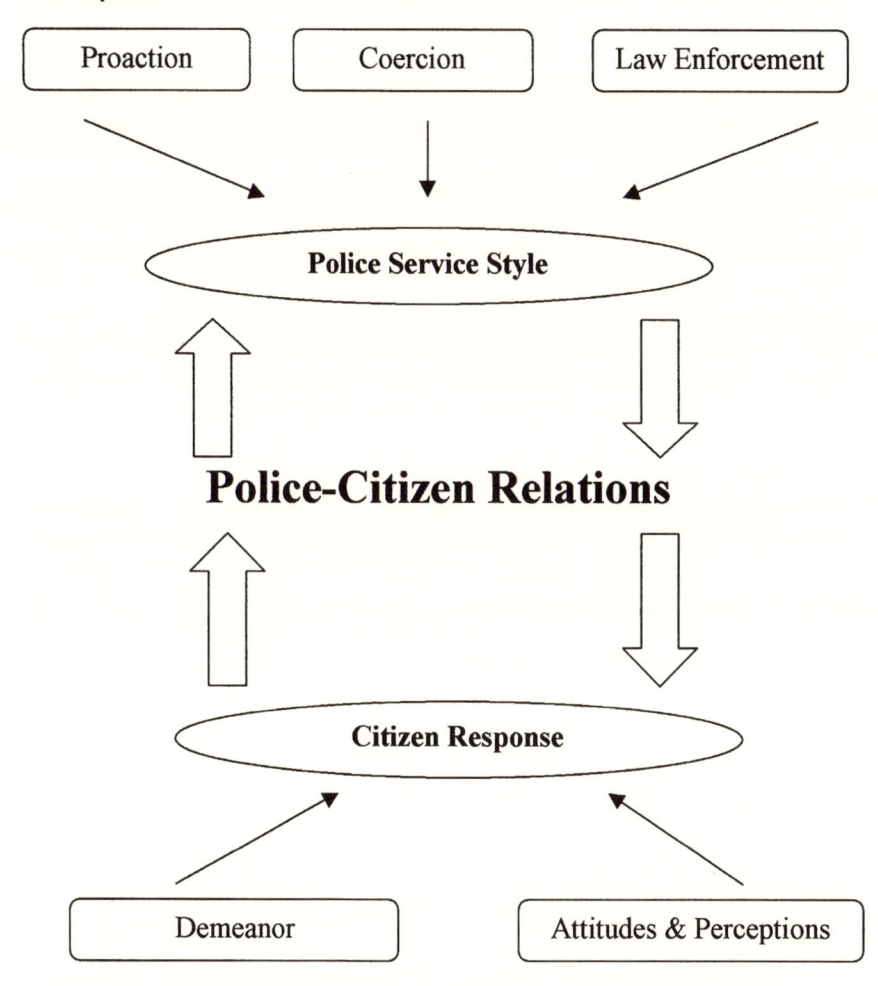

```
  Proaction        Coercion         Law Enforcement
       \              |                /
        \             v               /
         →   Police Service Style   ←
                    ⇅
           Police-Citizen Relations
                    ⇅
              Citizen Response
              /                \
         Demeanor         Attitudes & Perceptions
```

served. More importantly, they provide a fixed presence in the neighborhood by patrolling the streets with a suspicious eye for the wrong people in the wrong place at the wrong time, putting things in their right place and thus reproducing the existing efficient order and defending the status quo. The selective and patterned application of both enforcement and service rituals by the police dramatizes the loose boundaries between classes and groups and reifies urban order (Ericson, 1982; Manning, 1997).

Patrol officers evaluate who and what behaviors, if any, are out of order and then resort to the various tools at their disposal to rebuild order. Most of the time, police do not use the criminal law to restore calm; for instance, police rarely make arrests, although the threat of doing so always exists. This power to apply coercive and legal sanctions such as searches and arrests gives the police tremendous leverage in mediating disputes and make their interventions authoritative. Criminal law and procedures do not always guide or regulate officers' interventions; other factors gear the aggregate outcomes of police services. The ecology of police work is one of the most powerful determinants of police behavior. Police derive from the immediate social structure the strategies and tactics of coercion, manipulation, and negotiation to remind citizens where social boundaries are and what their places in the community are. Among dozens of tactical choices available to them, some are preferred over others under certain circumstances, which lead to fairly stable styles of policing. *Here, policing style refers to the aggregate quality and quantity of tactical decisions made by patrol officers in a delimited geographic area.* The delivery of police services can be conceptually categorized through three pairs of contrasting types: proactive versus reactive, coercive versus noncoercive, enforcement-oriented versus non-enforcement-oriented. It would be more useful to visualize these analytical categories as three independent, though not mutually exclusive, scales of comparison. Police tactical decisions during encounters vary in quality and in magnitude: some are more proactive than others, some are more coercive than others, and some are more enforcement-oriented than others. Although a policing style is not desirable or undesirable in itself, the summative arrangement of policing styles across a metropolitan region will not be ethically and politically neutral. There is good policing only when all the people are served effectively and justly.

Proactive Intervention versus Reactive Intervention

Police experts distinguish citizen-initiated reactive encounters from police-initiated proactive encounters. Police intervene in private affairs either by the explicit consent of the public or by their own official authority. Patrolmen are legally constrained from proactive observation of private places such as homes or apartments, unless they have the probable cause to believe that a felony has been or is about to be committed, and are voluntarily constrained from systematic proactive observation of semipublic places such as restaurants and malls. As a consequence, proactive observation is normally limited to public places such as parks and streets. Although it might appear that most of the time patrol officers take the initiative in reaching out to the public, it is much more accurate to conceive of police services as highly dependent upon citizen input. Historically there are more police–citizen encounters convened by requests from the citizenry than encounters resulting from patrol officers' spontaneous decisions to intervene. The U.S. Department of Justice's Police–Public Contact Survey found that nearly half of police–citizen encounters have been initiated by the public, while just under one-third of the contacts were initiated by the police (Greenfeld, Langan, & Smith, 1997).

Citizens participate in the policing of their own neighborhoods by either mobilizing or ignoring police resources to resolve conflicts or to render assistance with a problem. Their discretionary decisions to call or not to call the police influence the way in which the police approach the community. If a vast majority of contacts between officers and citizens come about as a result of people's requests for police presence, the police will basically be reacting to crises defined by the public and rely on citizens' preferences to decide what course of action to take. In "hot spots," where most service calls originate, patrol officers' decisions to process matters as criminal or noncriminal is largely based on citizen perceptions. The police not only depend on the public to report crime and disorder but also count on citizens for the identification of suspects. Since most crimes are already "cold" when officers arrive, success in solving crime depends on the victims or witnesses providing specific information that identifies likely suspects. Therefore, both patrol work and criminal investigation are reactive in nature.

Reactive policing involves the *a posteriori* intervention of the state aimed at restoring order. It is less complicated to establish the legitimate authority to intervene and assert authority in reactive encounters because the social support of the citizens (e.g., victims, witnesses, complainants, informants, etc.) who first mobilize the police can usually be assumed (Reiss, 1971). Citizen invitations are the major legitimizing avenue for the police to enter private places as well as to employ coercive or legal tactics to handle trouble. In reactive policing, state coercion is more restrained and defers to the citizen's right to be left alone. As such it has the potential to strengthen police–community relations by reducing charges of police harassment. Despite this virtue, the reactive nature of traditional policing has lately become the main target of criticism from advocates of community policing. Two of the criticisms are relevant to our discussion. First, a lot of crimes, especially acts of incivility and disorder, do not produce concrete victims and witnesses, while victims of some other offenses (e.g., fraud) may not even know they have been victimized. Reactive interventions are incapable of effectively detecting and controlling these victimless or lowly visible crimes. Coincidentally, drug dealing, prostitution, loitering, and public drinking have been identified as signs and causes of the breakdown of neighborhood moral order. Reactive policing and crime prevention are just incompatible. Second, in a paradoxical twist, a reactive approach to citizens' needs and expectations diminishes police contacts with the people who need them. When patrol officers stay in their cars and only talk to citizens when a problem or crisis has occurred, the sense of police presence in the community is weakened. This passive stance undermines any serious effort at crime prevention and impoverishes police knowledge of the community. "Taken together, this means that the police feel distant from a neighborhood's citizens: being distant, they seem both unreliable and uncontrollable. The price is that citizens, and particularly those who are afraid, do not call the police and, instead, absorb their losses and live with their fears" (Moore, 1992, p. 113).

Another complaint about the overwhelming reactive character of American policing focuses on its susceptibility to be tainted and manipulated by social inequalities and prejudices. Although reactive policing appears more democratic than proactive policing by giving all citizens an equal right to pick the target of police control, the absence of an equal willingness to exercise this right turns it anything but egalitarian (Sherman, 1992). In a society where group intolerance and animosity still exist, reactive delivery of services is extremely vulnerable to ethnic, class, religious, and sexual biases in citizen decisions to invoke police coercion against others. There are too many examples of this unholy collusion in history. For instance, capitalists successfully used police forces to break labor strikes, while Southern whites effectively enlisted officers to resist the pressure from the federal government to end racial segregation.

Proactive operations allow police to launch preemptive strikes against selected offenses, offenders, or areas before or during the actual occurrence of the criminal event. Modes of police-initiated interventions are multiple and differ in scope. Some are situationally prompted, while others are planned strategies instructed from downtown headquarters. The problem-oriented policing proposed by Herman Goldstein (1979) seeks to maximize the capabilities of police proaction and highlights certain general principles (e.g., problem scanning, causal analysis, response planning, and outcome assessment) for more effective crime control. Energetic displays of enforcement initiatives have a superb ability to attract media attention and to ignite public debate. Whenever an outcry for safer streets erupts, police managers can hardly resist the temptation of staging some kind of visible proactive activities both to prove their responsiveness to resident concerns and to instill a sense of police presence in the community.

Patrolmen see the streets of their assigned beats as their territories. When they are not reactively handling dispatched calls, patrol officers often engage in spontaneous searches for behaviors and people out of order. The proactive tactical choices most popular with individual officers are stopping and questioning citizens; frisking is reserved for a few suspicious persons. Many regard field interrogation as a legitimate and effective crime-reduction tactic and believe that stopping and questioning suspects in public places can produce arrests for wanted criminals and communicates a message of powerful police presence. Police proactive interference in people's private lives is also seen as a useful tool for instilling order and discipline in areas where poverty and disorganization have worn down traditional forms of authority and organization. Despite its apparent community-building function, the widespread use of proactive policing has caused a great deal of anger and constitutes the most controversial source of tension between the police and minority or lower-class communities in our days. People thirst for more protection but loathe being suspected or disrespected. The situation becomes especially problematic when most citizens stopped or frisked by the police show similar demographic characteristics: male, black, poor, and young. An analysis of 171 American cities found that aggressive traffic citation and frequent street stops disproportionately increased the volume of arrests among black residents (Sampson & Cohen, 1988). In New York City, citizen complaints of serious police violations of departmental procedures and criminal laws and the amount of money paid out in civil settlements have noticeably risen after patrol officers began proactively pursuing petty offenders under the guidelines of quality-of-life policing in the early 1990s (Harcourt, 1998; Human Rights Watch, 1998). A Hispanic police officer from the New York City Police Department reflected on this treacherous dilemma after the horrendous incident in which an Haitian immigrant was physically and sexually abused by a few policemen in Brooklyn:

For years the police department has allowed crime to concentrate and flourish in certain areas, and overnight that has changed. We now have aggressive enforcement without any understanding of neighborhoods or history. We have gone from a tolerance of crime in certain areas to zero tolerance without any concern for how the neighborhoods might react. As a result there are more serious incidents and an escalation of police aggressiveness that leads to what local areas see as harassment and escalates into brutality. ("A Beating," 1997, p. 38)

Concentrating overzealous policing in inner-city neighborhoods might be effective in the short run but never cost-effective if dire social consequences are taken into consideration. For example, in an attempt to fight firearm-related crime, the Kansas City Police Department implemented an aggressive gun detection program by subjecting a 10-by-8-block area occupied by poor minority residents to intense street stops and searches (Sherman & Rogan, 1995). During the experiment period of 29 weeks, the assigned special unit seized 29 guns and contributed to a 49 percent decline in gun crime. This success was attained by saturating the entire neighborhood with 1,434 traffic and pedestrian stops and 3,186 arrests and ended abruptly when the expensive deployment was terminated. Although no civilian complaint for police misconduct was filed during the experiment, evaluators sensed the danger of eroding police–community relations. For how long can an impoverished neighborhood tolerate thousands of arrests of their young male residents? In addition to threatening police legitimacy, tagging vast numbers of young males with arrest records may hamper their entry to the labor market and lead them to become angrier and more defiant. In big cities, aggressive police proaction is usually welcomed by tourists and working- and middle-class voters; but in the long run its negative effects may instead cause increases in crime in targeted areas.

Police officers are trained to be suspicious of citizens with certain characteristics and to develop criteria for deciding what is worthy of proactive activity. Imprinted with "visual shorthand" or "shared recipe" for suspects, police officers are disposed to stereotype and actively search for suspects based on these cognitive categories (Skolnick, 1967). The judgment is made upon the suspected individuals, their physical context, and the discordance between them. Patrol officers particularly develop and use cues concerning "individuals out of place" and "individuals in particular places" (Ericson, 1982, p. 88). In New York City, as in other major metropolitan regions, the racial, economic, and geographic distances that exist between police and the policed further degenerate this instrumental suspiciousness routinely displayed by the officers into a genuine expression of estrangement. Despite important progress made in the diversification of the organization, the highest managers of the NYPD are overwhelmingly white. Moreover, many officers have been raised and even more live in the suburbs. Estrangement breeds not only suspicion, but opposing views of justice. When a West African immigrant was wrongly killed with 41 shots by four white police officers in the Bronx in March 1999, most residents of the borough thought the officers should be prosecuted and punished for unwarranted brutality, whereas survey respondents from Long Island, where some of the perpetrators lived, had no problem in justifying the action of the police and believed they should be acquitted. Traditional use of aggressive tactics in Chicago's inner-city areas also undermined efforts to create partnerships between the police and the policed. Hispanic residents now fear the police that blacks have long feared (Body-Gendrot, 2000).

In contrast to the offender-centered nature of spontaneous police proaction, planned proactive campaigns usually target specific offenses (e.g., traffic, drug dealing) and sometimes specific geographic locations. The most widely adopted strategies for policing places and problems are crackdowns and market disruption (Bayley, 1994). Crackdowns seek to deter criminal activities such as drug sales, prostitution, and mugging through the saturation of hot spots with visible patrol and enforcement.

Market disruption is geared toward the removal of illegal transactions through the reduction in profitability of market-oriented crime by stationing uniformed officers and enforcing municipal ordinances in vice marketplaces. Outcome evaluations of these efforts suggest that while short-term campaigns can produce immediate residual results, deterrent effects are rarely sustained over time. The effectiveness of crackdowns and market disruption has also been challenged on the grounds that enforcement against situations or places merely shifts crime problems to other nearby addresses. Opposite this displacement argument is the benefits diffusion hypothesis, which maintains that the opportunity-blocking tactics reduce crime not only at the targeted place but also at nontargeted sites (Green, 1996). The most likely answer to this unsettled debate is that the same proactive operations conducted by different agencies in different contexts produce very different results.

In comparison to reactive patrol work and criminal investigation that enjoy public support, all kinds of proactive policing put police–community relations through a rigorous test. Since reactive encounters are sought out by victims, witnesses, and other law-abiding citizens in need of help, positive experiences are likely to result from these voluntary contacts because in them, police play a supportive role. In contrast, proactive encounters with citizens are likely to be involuntary contacts with an inquisitorial purpose. Such situations are adversarial and prone to confrontation, thus are very volatile. The hostility that could arise from proactive stops may far outweigh any gains in crime reduction. Although sweeping high-crime areas to fight crime and disorder can be welcome by local residents even at the cost of a heavier fiscal burden (Green, 1996; Trojanowicz & Smyth, 1984), many people who thought of themselves as law-abiding citizens might view the police as a new occupying army. In the cities of Houston and Newark, the roadblocks, speeding crackdowns, and foot patrols led to confrontational relationships with more people than before (Skogan, 1990). That all major modern urban riots erupted after allegations of police harassment or brutality reminds us why negative consequences of aggressive proactive practices cannot be taken lightly.[1]

Coercive Intervention versus Noncoercive Intervention

Bittner (1974, 1983) has described policing as a mechanism for the distribution of provisional, yet non-negotiable, coercive remedies upon emergent problems. Police represent the only agency authorized, under law, to invoke a wide spectrum of compulsive tactics to handle citizens' conflicts and deviance; their right to retaliate if the citizens fail to comply distinguishes them from other social service institutions. The ability to resolve the dilemma of achieving just ends with coercive means is a basic virtue a good policeman must develop (Muir, 1977). Coercive control influences the conduct of ordinary citizens through threats of harm and its credibility relies on the acknowledged record of the actual application of legal violence. Measures of legal pressure include the authority to issue commands, to deprive people of their liberty through arrest, to subdue resistance through the application of physical force, to induce quick compliance by drawing guns, or even to use deadly force to protect endangered lives.

Jerome Skolnick and James Fyfe (1993) have presented a graphic description of progressively coercive tactics routinely used by the police to request citizen cooperation. The spectrum of tactical options ranges from the mere presence of uniformed officers, persuasive and commanding verbalization, firm grips, and painful compliance to impact techniques. Police achieve the goal of controlling others through either the power of the word or the power of the sword. Physical maneuvers are in principle more forceful than verbal commands, and the levels of coercion varies within each of these two modes. The symbolic ostentation of authority (e.g. patrol cars, uniforms, and badges) represents the least degree of force available to officers and is employed to convey their authority to the public on a daily basis. When symbolic coercion fails to produce the desired tractability, police can start to speak in resolute tones to impart intimidation and threats to manage the situation. The next step up the scale from persuasion is the issuing of commanding orders. A cross-jurisdictional analysis of 7,500 adult arrests reveals that commanding, threatening, or cursing languages have been used in one-third of arrests, while in only 18 percent of all arrests have suspects challenged the authority of the police with antagonistic language (Garner & Maxwell, 1999). If the recalcitrant citizen refuses to obey, officers treat the encounter as a confrontation and are allowed to use physical force. They can first grip on parts of the citizen's body to immobilize the person without causing pain; if this step proves useless, police can apply a number of come-along holds to gain the subject's submission by inflicting pain without serious harm. Police officers are trained to administer highly forcible charges (kicks, baton blows, chemical sprays, and stunning electronic weapons) to overcome resistance. Despite the differences in the skill and preferences for one or another method of control, all officers contemplate the use of the most coercive tactics if the situation so requires.

Overall, patrol officers provide assistance far more often than they allot non-negotiable coercive solutions. Among all categories of tactical behaviors, "leaving the scene after listening to the parties without doing anything else" was found the most commonly made tactical choice by American patrol officers (Bayley, 1986). Next came "giving friendly advice," and "making an arrest" ranked third in the list of behavioral solutions. When force is used, it typically occurs when officers are making an arrest and the suspect is resisting, and involves grabbing, pushing, or shoving (Adams, 1999). Weapons are threatened, displayed, or used in only 5 percent of all arrests made (Garner & Maxwell, 1999). Not even situations involving violations of criminal law necessarily require the imposition of brute force. Officers have many more opportunities to assist the victim than they have to arrest the suspect because a majority of crime-related encounters deal with "cold" criminal incidents. The actual use of physical coercion and restraint is proportionately rare and most policemen are never put in the extreme position of having to use deadly force against someone. However, police use of force is still significant in absolute terms and could be problematic if it is biased against certain groups. National data estimated that less than 3 percent of those who have had face-to-face contact with police, or 1.2 million people a year, have been subjected to the use or threat of force, including handcuffing (Greenfeld, Langan, & Smith, 1997). Although police rarely make arrests or utilize physical force, the threat of doing so always exists. Ultimately, a mix of assistance and coercion is always present in every encounter.

Whether the assignment involves chauffeuring the mayor, enforcing a court order of protection, caring for injured motorists, helping to rescue a child, abating a loud nuisance, or settling heated disputes, police officers are expected to overcome any resistance or obstacle in the completion of the task. Urban citizens know that state intervention is at their disposal, and that "calling the cops" is one of the most dissuasive tools for solving problems. However, ordinary people only occasionally resort to this tool; and when the police are called into a dispute, they do not necessarily impose the most drastic measures available to coerce a solution. Nevertheless, the capacity to use it lends thematic unity to all police–citizen encounters. The police officer is symbolic of the law, the ultimate rational basis of collective organization in modern societies. In this secular age, the police typify the civilized totem whose presence is deeply longed for and whose authority is intensely feared. If a citizen refuses deference to or openly resists the officer's authority, he may be suspected of publicly announcing his secession from the community, and become the target of various punitive sanctions.

The use and misuse of discretionary coercion hinge on the most delicate juncture of police–citizen relations. The exercise of coercive power is treacherous and has ensnared more than one urban police department into public disdain and fury. Most patrol officers are aware of the principle that the nastier one's reputation, the less nasty one has to be (Muir, 1977). The dissuasive effects of coercive interventions determine that the stronger the police's reputation for being resolute, tough, and aggressive, the less ironhanded they actually have to be. Patrol officers are frequently performing before an audience, who either through direct observation or media accounts learn to respect and accommodate police toughness. But to perform the tough-cop show is a risky business. Intrusive tactics of high coerciveness such as traffic stops and arrests have considerable potential for officer rudeness and nastiness. Empirical evidence has shown that extreme cases of brutality are much more frequent in police cultures associated with proactive and coercive practices (Sherman, 1992). The cardinal risk of too much reliance on coercion is that of treating the exaction of citizen compliance as the chief goal of policing. In fact, most arrests are made with no intention to prosecute; arrests are instead often made to show who is in control or to teach the person a lesson.

Coercive repression of disorders in disadvantaged neighborhoods could be highly successful in reversing decline and disorder, but is also likely to alienate local residents. A March 10, 1991, *Los Angeles Times* poll reported that most Los Angeles residents believed in the LAPD's crime control capacities but distrusted the police (cited in Skolnick & Fyfe, 1993). In the wake of the gross abuse of police authority in Brooklyn's 70th Precinct, reputed police specialist Joseph McNamara questioned the propriety of relying almost exclusively on the vigorous action against quality-of-life violations to fight crime ("A Veteran Chief," 1997). He maintained that the outrageous incident of police abuse was caused by supervisors' acceptance of extra-legal tactics common to quality-of-life policing. Patrol officers often forget that manipulating coercive practices such as searching people unable to provide photo ID and penalizing persons riding bicycles on the sidewalk could elicit bitter criticism from the public and their officials. In an antagonized environment, highly coercive contacts first arouse emotional reactions from citizens, which elevates the required doses of force to keep the situation under control. Policemen who depend on coercive force to make their jurisdiction a less threatening place make it a more dangerous place for themselves and for others (Muir, 1977). Effectiveness in subduing people's bodies does not guarantee winning people's hearts.

Law Enforcing Intervention versus Non-law Enforcing Intervention

Law enforcement is a dimension of police work conceptually distinct from proaction and coercion and centers on whether or not a problematic situation is resolved through formal legal procedures. Thus, an outcome is judged as enforcement when formal legal actions, such as giving a citation or a written warning, arresting, reporting, booking, or pressing charges, are taken. An encounter results in nonenforcement when informal or extralegal measures, such as referring, counseling, advising, mediating, or rebuking the parties, are invoked to settle a dispute. Curiously, law violation does not automatically instigate police enforcement of law, for in many other occasions, officers use harassment and manipulative techniques to confront law violators. The defining factor is not whether a law has been broken, but whether the formal governmental control is brought into citizens' lives through the formal activation of the criminal process.

When a felony suspect, credible witnesses, and strong evidence are all present in an encounter, the number of discretionary options available to the patrol officers becomes appreciably more limited. Almost without exception, the alleged felon has to be, and is, arrested. In most encounters, however, felony suspects are not in sight. Police officers work primarily with victims, complainants, and parties in dispute, situations in which the decision making becomes more complex, since there are only a few inflexible rules guiding police action. Therefore, criminal law is only used as a residual resource when other methods of resolving a situation are unavailable, inappropriate, and unsuccessful. When the decision is made to take formal legal steps to process the case in the field, the central issue is first whether or not an official report of the incident will be written, then if the suspect is also at the scene, the possibility of arrest will also be contemplated. Filing incident reports and making arrests, the two gatekeepers of the formal legal process, are both legally prescribed and socially produced (Black, 1970, 1971).

Writing a report, a tedious and unrewarding task for an officer, represents the official recognition of an incident as legally deviant as well as formally "detected." A decision to record or not to record an incident can be one of the most critical decisions within the criminal justice system because it provides the first official account on which later decisions may be based. On top of legally relevant factors (e.g., offense seriousness), variables such as preference of the complainant, the relational distance between the victim and alleged offender, and the demeanor and social status of the complainant affect whether or not a report is written (Black, 1970). The complainant plays a dominant role in this first stage of the criminal process, although the impact of community characteristics on police enforcement of law is no less relevant. For example, police are much less likely to file incidents involving black victims in racially homogeneous neighborhoods but do not make such distinctions in heterogeneous neighborhoods (Smith, 1986). Official reports are also more likely to be filed in residentially unstable and high-crime areas. Overall, criminal law is more visible and more widely experienced in disadvantaged neighborhoods.

Compared with report writing, arrest has attracted more intense empirical scrutiny. Since arrest infringes on the individual liberty of the citizen, any systematic bias in this specific field practice will seriously undermine the integrity of police work. According to Black's (1971) data, complainants again constrain police actions through their expression of dispositional preferences and their relational distance to the alleged offender, while the demeanor of the violator is also an appreciable determinant of routine police arrest decisions. Key legal factors such as evidentiary strength and seriousness of the offense are always important in inducing formal legal responses from the police. Quantitative research from the past 30 years agreed on the consistently significant importance of the suspect's social status in provoking police arrest: lower-class suspects are consistently more likely to be arrested than higher-class suspects (Riksheim & Chermak, 1993; Sherman, 1980). Suspects' demeanor and complainants' preferences are equally strong predictors: probability of arrest increases substantially when suspects are uncooperative, abusive, and antagonistic as well as when the complainant or the victim requests an arrest.

Another issue that has been of great concern is the quality of arrest. A good arrest withstands the due process test and leads to successful prosecution and sentencing of the offender. Certain citizen groups often angrily complain that their members are at a higher risk of being arrested and that these arrests are made on a less stringent, if not capricious, basis. When arrests are made for the purpose of dispensing summary punishment rather than with the intention of initiating a criminal prosecution, they are beyond the law. Research found that a considerably greater proportion of black arrests were later declined for prosecution than arrests of whites (Free, 1995; Hepburn, 1978). The suspicion that black arrestees are more likely to have their charges dismissed by either the police or prosecutor is also corroborated by a RAND study, which found that 51 percent of all black arrests resulted in dismissal or acquittal, compared with 40 percent for whites and 44 percent for Hispanics (Petersilia, 1983). Although these findings could be interpreted as black suspects receiving more lenient treatment at the prosecutorial stage of the criminal process, police scholars are inclined to view the evidence as suggesting that blacks are arrested at higher rates and on the basis of less rigorous legal criteria. While procedural rules authorize the police to make arrests on probable cause, prosecutors are required to prove beyond reasonable doubt the guilt of the defendants. This higher evidentiary standard forces prosecutors to correct the bias practices of the police through dismissing a large volume of weak cases. Among the costs of making arrests that are not subsequently prosecuted or prosecutable is the enormous potential for arbitrariness and abuse.

With the advent of problem-oriented policing, recent developments in formal processing tactics centers on the enforcement of civil law (Green, 1996; Kelling & Coles, 1996). The reliance on civil remedies are specifically intended to increase surveillance for property owners who allow their properties to have crime problems or risks for parents who allow their children to violate truancy or curfew regulations. Also known as third-party policing, this strategy focuses on the coercion of nonoffending persons (e.g., parents, landlords, business owners) to take actions that are outside the scope of police routine activities and are designed to discourage disorder through manipulation of the offenders' immediate environment. In order to boost the legitimacy of these unconventional practices, police usually seek to team up with other city agencies to carry out the task.

Black (1976) distinguishes four modes of official social control: penal, compensatory, therapeutic, and conciliatory. Each mode adopts a particular perspective to define deviance and responds to this definition accordingly. The enforcement of criminal law corresponds to the penal control in which the justice system acts against the alleged law-breaker in the name of common good and seeks to prove his guilt. Yet more often than not, police officers simply encounter people in need of assistance unrelated to any violation of law and recurrently employ compensatory, therapeutic, and conciliatory techniques to ameliorate bad situations construed as obligations to be fulfilled, interpersonal damage to be repaired, and disputes to be resolved.

CITIZENS' RELATIONS WITH POLICE

Police–citizen encounters represent routines for the police but crises for the public, as such police–public contacts define police as professionals and the public as their clients. In this civic and professional enterprise, police departments try to bring about community trust and support to achieve their goals of crime control and prevention. Without such support, public dissatisfaction will ultimately rub down the overall effectiveness of the police. Thus to be competent and efficient, both quality services and positive public image must be maintained. Public image is important for two reasons. First, when citizens are not personally receiving police assistance or control, they relate to the police through their perceptions, beliefs, and values held as members of the community. In this sense, police public image *is* police–citizen relations. Second, public image is vital because it influences the way citizens respond to the police, the political support they provide, the actual cooperation they lend to the police, and their willingness to participate in police programs.

The ultimate authority of the law is the coercive power of the state. But law is almost powerless if it is not supported by public sentiment. Effective policing, therefore, depends upon opinion and sentiment even more than upon the powers of badge or weapon. British philosopher Bertrand Russell (1969) called the power not based on assent or consent the "naked power." The naked power wins submission from its subjects only through fear, not willing agreement. Its "nakedness" varies proportionately with the lack of acquiescence on part of the subject. Police power may be naked in relation to some hostile citizens but not in relation to other, more sympathetic groups. The relative amount of attitudes and demeanors in favor of police role and services is one of the most important indicators of police legitimacy in a community.

Unlike any other governmental agency, public relations are essential to effective police work. Key components of police routines are based primarily on citizen input. Citizens are the eyes and ears that detect criminal offenses; a large number of crimes would never receive police attention without public involvement. Most crime suspects are identified and arrested based on the information provided by victims and bystanders; without civilian participation in criminal investigation only a handful of crimes would be solved by detectives alone. The overwhelmingly reactive nature of American policing underscores this public attitude–police effectiveness linkage. Citizens who believe that the police are capable of "doing something" are most likely to report victimization than those lacking such a confidence (Block, 1974), and people who perceive less unfairness in police practices are more likely to cooperate with the police when the situation requires (Hahn, 1971). Policing is, after all, a profession in which inducing good rapport from the clients forms a critical component of police job expertise. Therefore, to gain the approval of most of the people most of the time represents the stepping stone for successful police work.

Police–citizen interactions involve direct human relations as well as indirect human relations (Cox & Fitzgerald, 1996). Direct human relations are established during face-to-face situations where citizens and police officers encounter each other. In this context, verbal and nonverbal behaviors become the principal means of communication and reciprocal definitions. Positive contacts consist of those information exchanges that facilitate police work and emotions that express mutual respect. Negative encounters are those contacts filled with tension and hostility, in which rough language is used and threats of physical confrontation loom. Indirect human relations are inferences about and impressions concerning potential in-person encounters that arise from personal witnessing or secondhand accounts of encounters between police and other citizens. Thus the public image of the police supplies the cognitive and affective elements for a citizen to forge a mental image of what can be expected from the police in a face-to-face situation. It corresponds to the judgments citizens hold toward the police. For instance, the belief that police forces are nothing but occupation armies to control and harass minority citizens is only one of the many impressions that predispose a police–citizen encounter toward a dangerous confrontation. Police departments thirst for supportive impressions from the community because their legitimacy has to be permanently nourished not only by the power of the state, but also by citizens' deference to it (Manning, 1997). Numerous benefits can be expected from robust indirect human relations: greater personal safety and job satisfaction for the officers, increased citizen involvement during investigation and adjudication, more credibility in addressing local problems, and a stronger moral buttress from the community they serve.

Citizen Demeanor in Face-to-Face Contacts

The debate over the impact of what citizens do and say during individual encounters on police decision making is alive and fruitful (see Klinger, 1994, 1996; Lundman, 1994; Worden & Shepard 1996). Deference and respect from the complainants are rewarded with police filing incident reports and making arrests on their behalf (Black, 1970, 1971), whereas a hostile demeanor from a crime suspect is likely to be retaliated with the police decision to arrest. Although the influence of citizens' demeanor on police behavior has been fairly established, its causes are less clear. What factors determine citizens' behavior in a situation? Undoubtedly some situational characteristics of the encounter influence people's willingness to help police. Citizens are less likely to cooperate with patrol officers in field interrogations when no reason is provided, but when the reason is courteously given, they reciprocate with willing assistance (Wiley & Hudik, 1974). People also demonstrate more cooperation with police investigations when crimes against persons are involved. The seriousness of violent crimes urges citizens to ally with the police despite the social or ideological differences that separate them. However, the exchange of rewards between police and citizens will never be equally reciprocal.

Although police–citizen encounters involve the exchange of deference and maintenance of proper demeanor, relations between officers and citizens are governed by an asymmetrical status norm in a typical encounter (Sykes & Clark, 1975). The amount of deference displayed by the uniformed representatives of law will always be less than that displayed by the policed civilian. The seriousness of the offense involved and the demographic status of the citizen encountered determine the levels of respect and obedience owed to the officers. The greater the violation, the more the citizen must defer in order to prove that they do not intend to subvert the hierarchical arrangement of authority. Greater conformity and cooperation are also expected from the poor, minorities, and youth. This requirement of extra deference from the less powerful to the police is simply a symptom of the rank concession syndrome: when members of a subordinate social group accept their status as socially inferior, this subordination is first internalized and then acted out. The obligation to defer to police authority is differentially scattered across social groups.

What citizens do in a crime-related encounter, and how they do it, can decide the outcome of the criminal investigation, which basically means talking to people (Bayley, 1994). Officers ask questions and listen to victims and witnesses, and then make quick judgments about whether the incident is serious enough to warrant formal handling, whether credible witnesses have been fairly identified, and whether there is sufficient evidence to arrest and successfully prosecute suspects. The identification of suspects makes up the heart of the criminal investigation; in most cases it leads to the gathering of pertinent physical evidence. In the best-case scenario, citizens volunteer information to the police with accuracy and swiftness, accelerating the formulation of a hypothesis about who committed the crime and where to collect the physical evidence to support arrest and prosecution. In other, rougher situations, a variety of persuasion techniques have to be tried to coax intelligence out of the citizens, who may reluctantly offer a reserved account of the incident or simply refuse to cooperate. The image of an effective crime-fighting force is difficult to maintain when citizen collaboration is lacking. If perpetrators cannot be identified on the scene, police are not likely to find the criminals on their own. In the worst case scenario, intentional acts of sabotage by key witnesses can nullify any investigation effort. Citizen demeanor matters.

Citizen Attitudes Toward Police Services

The very institutional role of the police in society complicates the formation of a monolithically positive public opinion about law enforcement. Ambivalence permeates the public view of police. Citizens and the police treat each other as friends as well as enemies, maintaining contacts that are usually peaceful and friendly on the surface, but with an undercurrent of mutual distrust and suspicion (Flanagan & Vaughn, 1996). With specific reference to the law enforcement side of policing, the relationship between the police and the policed is to a great extent adversarial in nature. Officers deal with their clientele as antagonists in that they issue summons, conduct interrogations, stop cars, and or make arrests. All these activities can potentially stimulate a vast spectrum of negative attitudes, ranging from apathy and indifference to militant antagonism. The creation of a professional, and trustworthy public image will remain a monumental task in a fragmented society because a lower level of social integration and normative unity in a community undermines the moral authority of the police, hence encouraging public view of police officers as adversaries (Banton, 1963).

Positive attitudes toward police encompass beliefs and evaluations that affirm the effectiveness, fairness, and integrity of police services. They strive in places where people believe the police are achieving the objectives for which they are created and treating citizens properly, morally, and justly. In contrast, negative attitudes abrade police–community relations by hollowing the factual basis of police legitimacy. Perceived inadequate protection and discriminatory practices from the police expose an ill-functioning state authority, while feelings of governmental unresponsiveness severely damage the moral underpinnings of a liberal state because democratic procedures are of value only if they establish some sort of accountability of public officials to ordinary citizens.

Shocked by the civil disorders of the 1960s, government officials have become increasingly concerned with the question of community perception of police and funded many studies of attitudes toward the police in years immediately after the urban riots. Some correlates of attitudes toward the police are well established and the consistency of findings accumulated over the past 30 years allows us to discern trends in public perceptions of police services. Overall, people have more positive attitudes concerning local officials (i.e., police) and more negative attitudes toward more general and distant political institutions (i.e., the justice system) because distance and exclusion create a sense of powerlessness (Lipset & Schneider, 1983). In fact, citizens are relatively satisfied with the performance of police who are more immediate to citizens' daily lives and thus enjoy wider approval than many other state bureaucrats. Yet not everybody equally benefits from the physical immediacy of police; those who have the most negative feelings toward the police have felt more powerless and alienated toward the larger political system than others (Albrecht & Green, 1977). After all, specific evaluations of police officers are firmly nested in global beliefs about the police as a political institution. Citizens assess the quality of police performance in individual encounters based on their general satisfaction or dissatisfaction with the police's role and image in society (Brandl, Frank, Worden, & Bynum, 1994). The flip side of the truism that most people approve of the police most of the time reads "Some people disapprove of the police all the time, whereas sometimes most people disapprove of the police." That some segments consistently feel unprotected or harassed by the police violates the democratic promise that all citizens, including those less privileged, have some perceptible stake in the system. A just state cannot claim to be the impartial manager of society as a whole, unless it emphatically identifies exclusion as a moral problem and responds to it vigorously as a political challenge.

There have been two major criticisms against the array of past research on citizen perceptions and evaluations of the police. First, "almost without exception these studies have assessed attitudes toward the police in a social vacuum," and only at the individual level (Alpert & Dunham, 1988, p. 93). Individual experiences and values will never be sufficient causes for the formation and propagation of collective beliefs about political institutions because rather than a product of individual psychology, the public image of the police is socially constructed. The second critique concerns the lack of a theoretical framework to guide the empirical exploration (Homant, Kennedy, & Fleming, 1984). Neither the selection of predictors nor the presentation of findings has been grounded on a broader conceptual paradigm; and most studies are characterized by small and unrepresentative samples from which generalizations can hardly be made. Like police behavior research, the study of citizen demeanor and attitudes toward police has been caged in exploratory individualism.

Symbolic interactionism has traditionally provided the main analytical assumptions (not framework) for the examination of police–citizen relations, seeking to explain human behavior as the outcome of the meanings attached to persons and events. Police and the public act toward each other on the basis of meanings that they attribute to each other (e.g., dangerous, repressive, protective, respectable) and their actions. Perceptions, attitudes, and behaviors are causally linked in a closed loop. It is often thought that by encouraging police–citizen cooperation and by changing negative cognitive dispositions (e.g., prejudices, unrealistic expectations) police–public relations can be prodigiously improved. Many specialized programs such as Neighborhood Watch, elderly and juvenile services, Community Officer assignment, and media campaigns have been inspired by these visions of behavioral engineering. Despite its merits, symbolic interactionism has been criticized for its exclusive attention on microsocial processes and subinstitutional phenomena (Habermas, 1981). It fails to acknowledge the weight of macrosocial structures and historical factors, especially economic forces and institutionalized political power.

SUMMARY

Patterns of behavioral and attitudinal exchanges between the police and the public mold police–citizen relations. Police service the public with tactical decisions that in the aggregate can be more or less proactive, more or less coercive, and more or less enforcement-oriented. Citizens, in turn, reach out to the police through their demeanors in face-to-face encounters and more stable attitudes toward police. Citizen demeanors can be either friendly or hostile, cooperative or indifferent, whereas public perceptions of police can be supportive or disapproving. There exists a causal linkage as well as a moral connection between public support and police effectiveness that neither police nor the public can afford to ignore. On the one hand, statistics have shown that police detect crimes and catch criminals mainly with the help of input from ordinary citizens; on the other hand, the ideal of democratic governance requires that the coercive weight of state power be equally beneficial and responsive to all segments of society.

The study of police–citizen relations has always been dissected into a nonintegrated analysis of police behavior and public attitudes and has been guided by beliefs derived from symbolic interactionism. By focusing exclusively on the interactions between police officers and individual citizens, it overlooks the structural aspects of the neighborhood environment that substantially enhance or reduce the availability of feasible options for closer police–community cooperation. Within this analytical paradigm, both police and the public are abstracted from the concrete world of economic inequality and residential segregation.

NOTE

1. Yet the relationship between police proaction and public satisfaction is not as simple as we might assume. A methodical assessment of San Diego's field interrogation program found that most citizens subjected to proactive stops and questioning felt that the contact was justified and properly conducted (Boydstun, 1975). After analyzing data gathered in 60 neighborhoods, Whitaker and colleagues concluded that for most citizens, aggressive police patrol had almost no negative effects on public evaluation of police services or crime-reporting behavior (Whitaker, Phillips, & Worden, 1983). The absence of negative side effects on police–community relations in these studies can be explained by the fact that the surveyed residents of high crime areas were the direct beneficiaries of effective preventive policing.

CHAPTER 2

The Residential Organization of American Metropolises

Policing is an urban affair *par excellence.* Although some 18,000 state and local law enforcement agencies police cities and their suburban rings in the United States (Eck & Maguire, 2000), only local police departments maintain a permanent and visible presence in neighborhood streets. They are the "cops" people see when they call 911 and refer to as "our cops," for good or bad. Whereas federal and state police forces are mostly empowered by specific mandates, the mandates of criminal law enforcement and order maintenance for municipal police forces are "open-ended, comprehensive, and ill-defined" (Bittner, 1983, p. 1135). Municipal police settle disputes, provide assistance, and invoke criminal laws amid the inequality and heterogeneity that characterize American society.

Patrol officers are a unique denizen of the city streets. They develop an intimate knowledge of the places they work not matched by many of the residents who live there. They know it better than their own neighborhoods, but they often are not "at home" there. Even though uniformed officers do not know most of the citizens they see or are called to assist, everyone in the neighborhood knows they are "the cops." Meaningful cultural themes and adaptive behavioral patterns are articulated from the everyday interactions of the police with the public on the street, in vehicular stops, or at private premises (Crank, 1998). The peculiar territorial clustering of the public provides the work environments for the police that are replicated in similar fashion across municipal districts. Residential location connects people to a range of political institutions, including their police, in a fateful way.

AXES OF METROPOLITAN RESIDENTIAL SEGREGATION

The policed world is composed of human settlements highly ordered by their physical design and land uses in which many distinctive regions (such as ethnic enclaves, vice areas, and industrial districts) develop and change in relation to one another. The concentric zone model of city structure advanced by the School of Chicago in the first quarter of the 20th century is the oldest explanation of urban population change and neighborhood formation and states that the various land uses in industrial cities have formed a series of concentric rings (Burgess, 1925). At the center of the city is the central business district that spills into a zone of factories. Beyond this commercial center are rings of residential areas that become more expensive with greater distance from the noise and pollution of the city's center. Although the concentric zone model has been expanded and revised, its two main arguments are still widely accepted: (1) Urban populations spread into distinctive residential areas according to their socioeconomic conditions, and (2) the geographical allocation of human settlements maximizes efficiency for the metropolitan region as a whole. Three demographic characteristics have invariably been found as organizing factors of residential neighborhoods: *social standing* based on wealth and prestige; *race and ethnicity*, and *household life-cycle characteristics* as reflected by the family size and marital status of its members (Johnston, 1976; Shevsky & Bell, 1955; Short, 1996). These dimensions of social life represent the main propellers of housing demand.

On the surface, demands created by class, ethnicity, and age factors explain a great deal about how Americans are dispersed into distinctive neighborhoods. Demographics-based demands influence people's choices and match different groups to different types of housing in different parts of the metropolitan region. In reality, a fierce urban struggle evolves behind the serene facade of residential selection. Place entrepreneurs strive, through collective actions and often in alliance with other business elites, to create conditions that increase the exchange values of determined areas (Logan & Molotch, 1987). They take a keen interest in the ordering of urban life because place is a market commodity that can produce wealth and influence for its owners and traders. Through property investing and real-estate financing, these powerful entities develop the best places to maximize their potential to attract and accumulate capital. Place entrepreneurs speculate on land use trends and attempt to influence the larger arena of decision making with the sole purpose of creating differential land prices. Urban growth disproportionately inflates land prices in strategic neighborhoods, exacerbating inequalities and spatial segregation between rich and poor, black and white. From the perspective of the growth machine, the metropolitan region is a system that ranks places according to the ease with which they can attract capital—a reality that then alters the life chances of local residents and their institutions.

People look for safety, comfort, and stability in their communities. The very concept of neighborhood often instills a nostalgic sense of solidarity and the romantic ideal of self-governance in a seemingly indifferent and anomic universe. It is the people themselves that either make or break a residential area (Bratt, 1983). In describing neighborhood strengths, terms like "close-knit community," "friendly people," and "good neighbors" are employed again and again to describe the goodness of a neighborhood. Behind the manifest desire to have good neighbors rests the quest for homogeneity. Given that heterogeneity is frequently associated with uncertainty and fear, ordinary people prefer cultural uniformity rather than diversity, and have systematically made their decisions about where to live on this basis. For homeowners and mortgage lenders, social homogeneity guarantees the territorial integrity and impermeability of their places, and thus best protects their own interests (Banerjee & Baer, 1984).

Police forces are keepers of the metropolitan order composed of interrelated, graded communities. Spatial territory is more than a geographic assignment to the police but a prize freighted with human values and meaning that they not only have to patrol but also control (Crank, 1998). Today's police are not, and cannot afford to become, monoliths that are impervious to the neighborhoods they serve. Although a common residue of moral values associated with traditional small towns and symbolic of mainstream America is in all police forces, there is a myriad of diverse neighborhoods that each police department has to service. Policing in metropolitan regions requires adjustment to the intensification of between-neighborhood differentiation and within-neighborhood homogenization, which perpetuates the organization of American neighborhoods after a few core demographic factors: socioeconomic status, race and ethnicity, and age composition (Jargowsky, 1997; Myers, 1983; White, 1987).

Socioeconomic Status

Since housing is allocated primarily on the basis of ability to pay and the best housing goes to those who can afford it, housing markets in a capitalist economy are a show of courtship between place entrepreneurs and middle- and upper-class households. Class differentiation in residential neighborhoods accelerated with the massive housing construction in suburban areas encouraged by the federal government following the end of World War II. Urban white-collar residents took advantage of the availability of thousands of inexpensive, look-alike houses and flocked to the suburbs in unprecedented numbers so that by 1970 more Americans lived in the suburbs than in the central cities (Edmonston & Guterbock, 1984).

The rapid growth of suburbs not only created wealthy neighborhoods, but also deeply weakened the economic balance of the older central cities. The flight of relatively affluent people, who paid more taxes, has forced the urban taxpayer to finance increasingly expensive social programs for the poorer people who have remained behind. The gradual reduction in tax revenue was only a sign of the general decay in human and social resources. The dilapidated inner city became synonymous with low-quality housing, crime, unemployment, and female-headed households (Logan & Schneider, 1984; Stahura, 1986).

The most representative government response to the economic decline of the central cities was urban renewal, which usually involved substantial funding from the federal government and investment from the private sector to rebuild deteriorated neighborhoods. Many of these renovation projects successfully revitalized declining neighborhoods through large-scale renovation, but lamentably without preventing the displacement of original residents (Weiler, 1983). For whom were the neighborhoods restored? Inflating land value and rentals evicted low- and moderate-income families from rehabilitated neighborhoods, leaving behind modern apartment buildings and office spaces that would generate more and more profits for place entrepreneurs. Victims of the growth machine were often deposited in public housing units in economically and politically deprived ghettos.

Despite urban planners' efforts to sustain socioeconomically diverse but integrated neighborhoods, America is still a country as segregated in terms of income, education, status, and jobs as 30 years ago. Every city has its very rich areas, where big houses pose in manicured gardens and luxurious cars sit in expansive driveways, and also its very unattractive districts, where low-income families live in poor-quality, high-density housing close to the defunct sunset industries. There are a wide variety of middle-income districts in between these two extremes. A major structural impediment for the achievement of residential integration is the difficulty, if not the impossibility, of stabilizing an economically mixed neighborhood. Ethnic diversity and a mixed economy do not raise the exchange value of a place. For most households, status attainment translates fairly directly into housing purchases in selected neighborhoods. Accordingly, census data demonstrate that expenditure on housing as indicated by rental level and home value exhibits levels of segregation equivalent to that of other status measures (Jargowsky, 1997; White, 1987). Professionals and managers are the most secluded from other occupational groups; they use place status to amass privileges for their locations often at the expense of lesser locales. With the help of "community organizations" and municipal authorities, they manipulate transportation routes, control education boards, secure desired zoning, and keep out unwanted groups. In comparison, rather than actively participating in the housing market, lower-class households live in the least desirable areas with no real alternatives offered to them. They are decision-takers rather than decision-makers. Under the logic of growth machine politics, the spatial concentration of educated and white-collar households helps raise the land prices of their territory. The same distancing of the advantaged expresses a strong need to view vulnerable groups as different, as lesser, and as outsiders.

Functionally, those most active players in and the main beneficiaries of the market economy related to those disfranchised in a symbiotic dependence. The former groups consume the products and services that the lower status groups help to produce. However, geographically, the better-off segments do not need to live in close proximity to those of lesser wealth because the life world of the better-off is larger than their living neighborhood for which the space-based solidarity is much less important. The much more concrete and space-bound life world of the less influential is in contrast more dependent on the services that the police provide.

Race and Ethnicity

Households vary in their ethnic identity, which can influence where they want to live and where they can live. Where there are significant differences between a majority culture and a minority subculture, this distinction is frequently expressed in spatial separation. The social mobility of nonblack immigrants has traditionally propelled the processes of residential succession and spatial assimilation (Massey, 1985). The spatial differentiation of the urban economy (e.g., low-cost housing ringing city industrial centers, proximity to low-skill jobs and fewer limitations on public transport) facilitates the spatial concentration of ethnic groups. Recent immigrants usually occupy the lowest echelons of the social ladder and settle in aged housing vacated by fleeing middle classes. When a neighborhood achieves a critical mass of immigrants, ethnic stores spring up, specialized service establishments are formed, churches are founded, and social clubs are organized, giving rise to a clearly identifiable enclave of ethnic institutions. But as members of ethnic enclaves prosper economically and become culturally assimilated, the movement of dispersion is set in motion. The accumulation of wealth through hard work and savings as well as the acquisition of the language and other skills push upwardly mobile migrants to seek out better neighborhoods where more established ethnic groups are a majority. Ethnic segregation declines monotonically as socioeconomic status rises, with the exception of black segregation.

Blacks are nevertheless a tragic exception to the principle of spatial assimilation and have remained the most segregated of any racial or ethnic group. They are as highly segregated from whites as from other racial groups. Even newly arrived, foreign-born immigrants show a level of segregation less than half that of the black population, who meet serious difficulties in climbing the social ladder and translating economic advancement into residential relocation (White, 1987). The rigid segregation of black citizens stems more from prejudices and discrimination in the housing market than from other socioeconomic processes (Massey, 1985; Wilson, 1987). Opinion polls show that although white Americans cherish expressions of cultural differences and religious plurality in their neighborhoods, when it comes to racial issues, 9 out of 10 white respondents prefer neighbors of their own skin color (Harris & Associates, 1978). White residents often fear that if a few blacks move into their neighborhood, the entire area will be invaded, property values will be lowered, crime rates in the neighborhood will soar, and they will be victimized (Jaynes & Williams, 1989).

Prejudices and housing discrimination based on half-truths and half-lies have sealed a large number of low-income blacks known as the "truly disadvantaged" or the "urban underclass" in inner-city ghettos. These communities suffer rampant problems of poverty, family disruption, and crime as a direct consequence of recent transformations in the global and local political economy (e.g., the shift from good-producing to service-producing industries, the increasing polarization of labor market into low-wage and high-wage sectors, and the relocation of manufacturing industries out of central cities).

Life-cycle

Age is central to the analysis of residential movement for the life events of migration, fertility, and mortality, and pushes and pulls households from one neighborhood to another (Myers, 1983). Many social roles, from schoolchild to newlywed to retiree, are largely restricted to particular age groups. The age structure of a community is often as important as any other structural or cultural traits of the community population. The space requirements of a family change as its members progress through different stages of life. Although age segregation is not as strong as race and socioeconomic segregation, crude measures of life course evolution, such as the proportion of elderly population and household size, consistently evidence their influence in neighborhood formation (White, 1987).

Many of the better-off central city enclaves continue to serve as "staging areas" or areas of first residence for young adults before they move to the suburbs to raise their children. In fact, the largest group of household heads in families that move into gentrifying central city areas tends to range from the mid-20s to the mid-30s, and resettlers in the mid-30s to mid-40s age range represent the next largest group (Gale, 1983). An acceptable housing price, the investment potential of the property, accessibility to place of employment, and the architectural attraction of the house draw a great deal of middle-income younger singles and childless couples to historic urban neighborhoods.

A very different "age" story is told, nevertheless, in other inner-city neighborhoods where new immigrants and minorities dominate. The flow of these socioeconomically disadvantaged groups also affects the age structure of their own communities. "The black migration to urban centers—the continual replenishment of urban black populations by poor new comers—predictably skewed the age profile of the urban black community and kept it relatively young" (Wilson, 1987, p. 36). When racial transition is massive, instead of shifting to older ages, as is the tendency over time, the age composition shifts to younger ages at an alarming rate. This age unbalance places enormous strain both on public services like public schools and also on space use such as playground activities and sidewalk recreation. A demographic truism has that the higher the median age of a neighborhood, the greater its representation in higher income categories and professional positions. Not surprisingly, residents of black and Hispanic neighborhoods are on average younger than residents of other areas, and consequently experience higher unemployment and crime rates. Much of what has gone awry in the more deteriorated urban areas is due in part to the sheer increase in the number of young people, especially unskilled and unsupervised youths.

Persons over age 35, mostly couples with children, are the most likely to start as owners, usually in suburbs, offering larger apartments or single-family houses and good local schools. Dramatic increases in homeownership for this age group far exceeds that for any other group of movers. As a result of this family-settlement process, the 30-to-39 age range shows the heaviest migration out of urban areas of all the adult years (Myers, 1983). The in-migration pattern in suburban areas is nearly a mirror image of the neighboring central city: the largest net adult in-migration to suburbs is found in the 30-to-39 age range. Although recent cohorts of young adults have been maturing more slowly in terms of their family formation than their parents, as time goes by, small children will inexorably grow older. When young people leave their parents' homes, the household size is reduced again. The booming school enrollment and the strength of property values depend on whether empty-nest households decide to stay or to move. If they opt to stay, new public safety concerns will surface. It has been found that the older the residents of a neighborhood, the less common activities they engage in (Fischer, 1982). The isolation from each other and the thinning of social capital make these especially vulnerable to the fear of crime, thus posing a special challenge to law enforcement authorities.

THE POWER STRATIFICATION OF NEIGHBORHOODS

The geographic stratification of residential settlements concentrates valuable social resources in some neighborhoods and deprives others of the resources necessary for a prosperous community life. Enclaves of social power and powerlessness are thus born. There is no social power without allocation of social resources; and furthermore, social power predicates the ability to mobilize these resources to achieve prized goals. Among the less-advantaged areas, some are relatively depleted of wealth in relation to other better-off communities, while others are absolutely poor in that the survival of their residents is threatened. In contrast, privileged residents of a few exclusive neighborhoods enjoy the highest levels of material well-being, have the most direct access to the process of political decision making, and engage in the creation and consumption of the finest commodities of high culture. Class structure and residential segregation ensure that social power, manifested in the capacity to influence law enactment and policymaking as well as the ability to muster wealth and privileges through legal means, be spatially scattered in an uneven fashion. The greatest achievements (including material comfort, participatory democracy, and social progress in general) of this country are still foreign to many citizens secluded in urban ghettos. As a rule of thumb, the more lower-class, nonwhite, and young residents live in a neighborhood, the more marginal is the standing of such a neighborhood in the social power scale. By the same token, the more upper- and middle-class,[1] white, and adult citizens are found in a community, the closer is such a community to the core of social power.

The incomparable growth in strength and affluence of America sadly mirrors, to some degree, the jobless, ruthless, voiceless, and futureless development of many third world countries. The overall enrichment does not expand opportunities for employment among the poor. The fruits of massive economic transactions benefit some, but leave hundreds of inner-city neighborhoods struggling in despair. Powerful political institutions fail to tear down the deep sense of alienation and hopelessness shielding those disadvantageous areas. Even when welfare remedies are pumped into them, no brighter prospects are left for future generations. In fact, in this prosperous country, third-world-like communities abound in big urban conglomerates. Typical traits of underdevelopment infest these neighborhoods: higher fertility and lower literacy rates, more violence, higher unemployment rates, shorter life expectancy, and the list of calamities goes on. Even the most basic asset—domestic property—is owned by people and institutions located outside the neighborhood. What we observe is a deepening marginalization of communities inhabited by minorities, immigrants, and the poor, with many of their basic needs met by the public welfare system and many of their activities closely monitored by the justice apparatus. Their inability to exchange commodities and influence with external social actors roots them to one place as it also inhibits their capacity to exercise control on economic and political institutions; this isolation from social and cultural life of the larger society testifies to their peripheral position. Market mechanisms fall short of creating opportunities in communities dissociated from the market, and political activism rarely leads to prosperity in these places.

The majority of the middle-range neighborhoods have a fair stake in the current system of social reward; most of them are able to secure their shares in the competitive markets of housing, employment, health care, education, and political participation. The developmental paths of both middle-class neighborhood residents and middle-class residential neighborhoods evolve around different stages of the family cycle. Maintaining an intact family requires sustained involvement in conventional activities (e.g., keeping a decent job, planning ahead, sending children to school, conforming to mores and norms regulating sexuality, and preferring social stability over change), and only culturally conditioned and logistically endowed families are able to embark on the journey. Households that actively engage in the elaboration and accumulation of cultural and social capital are rewarded with a place in the center of the social stage. It is from this pool that the main bodies of consumers, skilled laborers, and active voters are drawn. Social institutions are structured in such a way that citizens residing in middle-class neighborhoods are equipped to create values for other people and to engage in free, peaceful, mutually beneficial, and multifaceted exchanges. In fact, the most important thing these people do in metropolitan regions is to exchange things—goods, services, and money, but also ideas, knowledge, and influence—with each other. The values and interests of middle-class families are vehemently defended in the political arena, shaping the ideological outlook of mainstream society. By all counts, the middle class has become the icon of the United States, and its growth and decline have been an important gauge of the strength and vitality of the whole country (Short, 1996). When socially powerful segments are linked by geography, their affluence allows them to build a sphere of influence with people and institutions located elsewhere. Although neighborhoods that house these white and middle-class families often expand geographically toward the outer peripheries of cities, they firmly take hold of the center of the social power structure.

Being officially backed by traditional political institutions that are both framed by power elites and bolstered up by white and middle-class constituencies, policing cannot be other than a semblance of those interests that define their very *de jure* legitimacy. The interests and values nourishing vast white and/or middle-class families form the glasses through which police see things and people and think of themselves as representatives of a higher morality embodied in a blend of American traditionalism, patriotism, and religion (Crank, 1998; Wilson, 1968). Police identify with these segments of the population to the degree that citizens who uphold the virtues of middle-class respectability are taken to symbolize the community interests police officers see themselves as standing for (Ericson, 1982). Policing is, after all, conducted according to the feelings and interests of the dominant majority. In order to survive nobly in an ever civilizing society that is setting stricter and stricter standards of justification for state use of coercive force against its citizens, police openly identify with "the conventional symbols of order" and vigorously invoke "the law, the absolutistic morality, and the myth of neutrality of the state" (Bittner, 1970; Manning, 1997, p. 95). To the police, the "public" means essentially white middle-class adults and their offspring (Mayhall, Barker, & Hunter, 1995). Despite their overall blue-collar background, the police have views quite congruent with middle-class and white neighborhoods and quite incongruent with lower-income and minority communities (Alpert & Dunham, 1988). Not surprisingly, outcome evaluations of community policing programs conclude that although highly praised by residents of white and middle-class neighborhoods, police innovations rarely meet expectations in areas where the community is fragmented by race, class, and lifestyle because, like old-fashioned policing, they favor the tastes of the dominant groups, letting whites and homeowners enjoy most of their benefits, while renters and minority groups perceive they are excluded (Skogan, 1990; Skogan & Hartnett, 1997). In core jurisdictions, the public welcomes the reinventing of law enforcement and greets police experiments with excited applause, while in peripheral enclaves, the initial tepidity of the residents always cools down quickly as time goes by.

The demographic composition of a neighborhood determines, to a great extent, whether worldview consonance or incongruity will permeate the relationship between police and the policed. As such, it will impact upon both the attitudinal and behavioral outcomes of this relationship. Groups who share with the police the same vision of orderly community become their significant others. Police address their performance to this specific audience, and from this audience, police expect approval and rewards. In socially powerful areas, police offer their protection to the reference population and act in accordance with their general moral and social position. These neighborhoods are the true constituencies that have an active role in the formation of criminal justice policy, with whom police share their concerns and show their responsiveness and only they have "the right language and the necessary confidence to demand better policing" (Short, 1996, p. 69). In neighborhoods where the ideological congruence between the police and the community is absent, vain efforts at negotiating common priorities and mutual collaboration become sour sources of profound frustration. Rather than defending them from common enemies, police just maintain a minimum tolerable level of (dis)order by keeping them from annoying each other in public spaces. Here the police try to co-opt the support of the community when urged to do so, but their approach is consistently criminal-repression oriented. Strictly speaking, these less endowed communities do not represent police constituencies but only passive consumers of police services because they rarely engage in defining the processes of their own governance and regulation (Duffee, Fluellen, & Roscoe, 1999).

THE DEMOGRAPHIC ECOLOGY OF DEVIANCE

Policing, that is, the sum of individual officers' skills and inclinations, is expected to create an atmosphere that makes it possible for people to carry out their daily activities with the confidence that they will not encounter criminal attacks. These high expectations for the police ignore the fact that market forces and public policy may inevitably affect quality of life. The flow of capital from one neighborhood to another alters the distribution of life chances, whereas government actions are often supportive of, if not themselves geared by, these powerful business interests. Just as the distribution of valued resources across different neighborhoods is unequal, many of the correlates of crime and disrepute—poverty, idle youth, family disruption or discrimination—are unevenly scattered along the lines of residential segregation. The core/periphery dispersion of social power across neighborhoods prescribes the spatial concentration of social stigma and perceived criminal threat in certain areas. The varying experiences of deviance provide the basic materials with which the police and the public construct and live their realities in such a way that social status and the moral standing of a neighborhood exercise independent, although mutually reinforcing, effects on police–community relations.

The Ecology of Crime

Residential segregation concentrates on the main structural determinants of high criminality and not on others; as a result, some neighborhoods experience more serious problems of crime than others.[2] Class, ethnicity, and age have consistently been among the historical correlates of crime. For example, despite the dramatic decreases in violence and crime across the United States during the 1990s, the three most vulnerable groups for violent crime remain men, African Americans, households of extremely low income, and those under 19 years of age (Bureau of Justice Statistics, 2000).

Socioeconomic Status

The proposition that neighborhood poverty, and not individual deficiency, produces crime is one of the earliest and most significant contributions of American criminology to the explanation of crime and delinquency (Shaw & McKay, 1942). A number of studies have assessed this hypothesis and most often yielded supportive findings, although not all of them agree on the strength of the relationship between low economic status and crime rates—some show a direct and important link between poverty and official crime (Block, 1979; Curry & Spergel, 1988), whereas others reveal a weak or trivial independent relationship (Messner & Tardiff, 1985; Sampson, 1985, 1986a). The criminogenic effects of poverty are somewhat conditional upon neighborhood context of residential mobility. Crime and delinquency are particularly serious in poor communities experiencing rapid population turnover (Smith & Jarjoura, 1988). The availability of social and human capital serves as a buffer against the strain of weakening social cohesion and control set off by uncontrolled residential mobility. Education, jobs, and intact families turn neighborhoods into worthy and defensible territories.

Chronic joblessness deprives residents in impoverished areas of concrete goals, while the inability to support their families gives rise to feelings of futility and incompetence. Worse, the exclusion from the legal labor market makes them vulnerable to the temptations of making their ends meet through organized or disorganized illegal activities. Burglaries, the dealing of stolen goods, and welfare fraud provide needed income, whereas vice industries such as drug dealing and prostitution become the only available forms of recapitalization (Hagan, 1994). Jobs and capital lost to the relocation of manufacturing industries are partly channeled back and redistributed through these criminal activities.

A neighborhood's socioeconomic status colors police perceptions of criminality. In areas with a disproportionate amount of crime, police may correspondingly increase their patrol assignments, and in some cases, respond to citizen demands that the police clean up their streets (Black, 1970; Hagan, Gillis, & Chan, 1978).

Race and Ethnicity

Empirical studies have always found higher rates of crime, delinquency, and violence in minority and ethnic neighborhoods (Block, 1979;

Messner & Tardiff, 1985; Roncek, 1981; Sampson, 1985; Shaw & McKay, 1942; Smith & Jarjoura, 1988). But researchers have not agreed on the causes of this urban phenomenon. Some studies report a sharply attenuated effect of neighborhood racial composition on rates of violence once family structure and socioeconomic factors are accounted for (Block, 1979; Messner & Tardiff, 1985; Sampson, 1985), while others highlight the mediating effects of community disorder (Skogan, 1990). Since these ethnic or racial neighborhoods experience the highest rates of family disorganization, male unemployment, and incivilities (Skogan, 1990; Wilson, 1987), their members are condemned to put up with a staggering amount of criminal victimization, which is both cause and consequence of all the social problems listed above.

Minority and ethnic neighborhoods are extremely isolated from other communities, which hampers the development of manpower and financial support needed to bond with institutions and resources that would allow them to organize and prosper. The ensuing crime and violence turn residents away from each other, and remove conditions for normative agreement and enforcement of standards of acceptable behavior. Structurally disorganized minority neighborhoods are conducive to the emergence of cultural value systems and features that legitimate, or at least provide a basis of tolerance for, crime and deviance (Sampson & Wilson, 1995). The criminal disruption of impoverished ethnic communities is ultimately deeply tied into discriminatory forces of the housing market, which rely on segregation to enhance the exchange values of certain areas as well as a political-economic arrangement that fiercely resists trickling down crumbs of ever-growing wealth to these groups.

Life-cycle

Teenagers and young adults are overrepresented among law-breakers known to the police (Steffensmeier & Allan, 1995). Biological and social factors seem to intersect to bring about the delinquent tendencies of youth. These young citizens may commit illegal acts for exploratory and excitement-seeking purposes during a period of high energy discharge in which physical strength, psychological drive, and the reinforcement effects of adrenaline peak. But as their psychobiological energy declines with age, the intensity of their criminal behavior dwindles as well (Gove, 1985). In addition to this developmental factor, the economic and status subordination to which young people are subjected also contributes to their higher involvement in crime and delinquency. Youths form a powerless class of their own because they are excluded from gainful adult employment and depend on their parents or guardians for material and emotional support, a condition that creates an imbalance between their aspirations and their resources. Age constitutes a potent mediator of inequality in the illegitimate world as it does in the legitimate opportunity structures of society. Just as the low-wage, dead-end jobs of the legitimate economy are disproportionately held by the young, so too are high-risk, low-yield crimes committed by the young (Steffensmeier & Allan, 1995). Age fragmentation in the current labor market instigates the breakdown of public safety in some neighborhoods.

In the inner cities of this nation, where the labor market for young adults is dominated by marginal jobs with low hours, low pay, high turnover, and limited benefits and opportunities for advancement, the other goals of conventional life—marriage, family, community involvement—are more difficult to attain, and the proportion of the population still attracted to illegitimate alternatives will be greater. (Steffensmeier & Allan, 1995, p. 103)

Lorraine Green (1996) noted in her evaluation of Oakland's problem-oriented policing program that the predominant age group of people living in a place shaped the social routines and control mechanisms to be developed in that area. This observation corroborated an earlier finding that the teen–adult ratio was one of the major determinants of crime, fear of crime, and community instability (Newman & Franck, 1980). These findings indicate that the higher density of adolescents and young adults lays extra pressures on neighborhood order and can potentially steer the deployment and tactical behavior of the police.

The socioeconomic status, ethnic composition, and age structure of a neighborhood determine the types and volume of criminal events that the police have to handle. Criminal justice scholars have repeatedly expressed their concern with the detrimental consequences of a convergence of minority status, poverty, and youths in the dilapidated sections of a big metropolis (Bursik & Grasmick, 1993; Wilson, 1987), which increases the complexity of police–citizen relationships. "Macrosocial patterns of residential inequality give rise to the social isolation and concentration of the truly disadvantaged, engendering cultural adaptations that undermine social organization" (Sampson & Wilson, 1995, p. 53). Criminal motivations and illegitimate opportunities are indisputably examples of such adaptive innovations. Among other "cultural adaptations" generated by patterns of residential segregation, a widely shared fear of crime stands out as one of the most insidious saboteurs of community order.

The Ecology of Incivility

Disorder and fear of crime play such a pivotal role in building neighborhood solidarity that their reduction has become both a goal of community policing and a direct measure of police performance (Bayley, 1994; Skogan 1990). The influence of public fear in shaping governmental policy is particularly evident when police managers resort to creating a safety crisis to rally citizen support. Many police officers truly believe they can alleviate citizens' fears (Guyot, 1991), and there exists evidence that under favorable circumstances, well-designed police strategies effectively enhance people's sense of safety (Police Foundation, 1981; Trojanowicz, 1983). The susceptibility of perceived risk to police intervention renders a heightened fear of crime both a threat to and also an opportunity for the strengthening of police–public cooperation.

Physical outlook, cultural artifacts, and resident characteristics give meaning to judgments about neighborhoods. Dilapidated buildings, graffiti, and uncollected garbage are the strongest signals that convey the message that no one really cares about the neighborhood and that the solidarity among residents has completely broken down (Wilson & Kelling, 1982). Since the neighborhood represents one of the most intimate and familiar contexts that provides a basis for distinguishing between "us," and "people different from us," fear of crime may reflect, in large part, a fear of people whose actions may be unpredictable or of strangers over whom one has little control (DuBow, McKabe, & Kaplan, 1979).

Lawrence Cohen and Marcus Felson (1979) argue that crime occurs when routine activities (i.e., life sustenance activities) of a motivated offender and a suitable victim meet in a particular location in the absence of a guardian capable of preventing the victimization. If motivated offenders assess the risk of being apprehended based on the information about the availability of vulnerable victims and the presence of capable guardians before committing a crime, it is also valid to infer that ordinary citizens make use of the same information in judging their own risk of being victimized. This thesis can easily be turned into a neighborhood theory of fear of crime. Neighborhoods whose residents perceive a high concentration of motivated offenders and vulnerable victims among them are more likely to have a serious problem with fear. Prevailing cultural stereotypes, with or without factual support, associate both proneness to deviance and vulnerability to criminal attacks to certain demographic characteristics. The patterns of residential segregation by social standing, ethnicity, and age may therefore predispose certain neighborhoods to experience higher degrees of fear because of demographic cues. Fear of crime signals presence of strangers, strangers defined in terms of people with different race and class characteristics.

Fear of crime is also fear of disorder and decay. People express deep concern over "threatening and fear-provoking conditions, rather than on discrete and legally defined incidents" (Skogan & Hartnett, 1997). Incivilities such as broken windows, uncollected trash, public drinking, and prostitution are both causes and consequences of weakening community solidarity in neighborhoods where residents are not able to effectively attend to their maintenance (Wilson & Kelling, 1982). The amalgam of decay, incivilities, and signs of disorder incite not just fear, but crime itself, for potential criminals recognize such deterioration and assume that no one cares or no one is in charge. Residents are believed to be so indifferent and helpless to what goes on in their surroundings that they will not confront strangers or intervene in an emergency. A public safety crisis does not begin with serious or violent felonies, but with violations of norms about public behavior. Social disorder, appearing as a series of primarily episodic events, is a matter of visible behavior or behavior with visible consequences. The most common forms of social incivilities include public drinking, panhandling, youth loitering, drug use, and commercial sex, all of them raising public complaints about official inaction as well as spuring controversies when authorities decide to sweep these activities (Kelling & Coles, 1996). They produce psychological havoc and discord in the community by raising fears, diminishing trust, inhibiting social interactions and the use of public spaces, and pitting some citizens against others.

Policing disorder is nowadays considered a core task that leads to effective crime prevention, although many individual officers still see it as a diversion from "real police work." Community-oriented policing demands that police be alert and sensitive to citizen perceptions of what local problems are. In fact, drunkenness, disorderly conduct, vagrancy, and vice activities have never ceased to cause people worry and continue to dominate the daily routines of police. The so-called quality-of-life policing that claimed success in reducing crime in New York City has now been adopted by other urban police departments. It focuses on public disorders that destabilize communities and seek out any available means, including pressuring for interagency cooperation (Kelling & Coles, 1996) and resorting to civil actions against noncriminal citizens (Green, 1996), to aggressively enforce the standards of acceptable conduct set by local residents. Embracing the belief that individual liberties are not absolute but must be balanced against the need to maintain basic levels of order, the assertive policing of community disorder has produced both a number of success stories and an equally large number of lawsuits against municipal police and authorities. The debate over the legitimacy and effectiveness of disorder control is not settled yet, and more research attention should be directed at its consequences on police–citizen relations.

Socioeconomic Status

Residents of poverty-stricken areas are deeply suspicious of one another, hold only a weak sense of community, and feel that it is their neighbors, not outsiders, whom they must watch with care (Garofalo & McLeod, 1986, Greenberg, 1983). Distrust and fear are so high in disadvantaged neighborhoods that communal cooperation reaches its lowest point in these areas. In contrast, middle-class families residing in economically stable and culturally homogeneous communities intervene when they see problems, confer more respect to their neighbors, and feel personally responsible for as well as in control of conditions in their neighborhoods (Skogan, 1990). The number of motivated predators increases in impoverished areas where legitimate means of obtaining economic and material rewards are depleted, which spreads the fear of crime to epidemic levels. In comparison, the general well-being in middle-class neighborhoods diminishes the incentives for engaging in illegal activities. Good schools, thriving megachurches, and other community organizations reinforce the network of informal controls, multiply the density of capable guardians in public spaces, and thus harden potential targets against criminal attacks.

Public health crises (e.g., high infant mortality, short life expectancy) and economic decline (e.g., closed stores, vacant parking lots) that characterize most low socioeconomic areas can jeopardize feelings of community safety among people through the process of ecological contamination. Data from a national survey reveals that good health reduces the perceived risk of victimization and enhances a sense of security (Ferraro, 1995). That people in better health feel less vulnerable to victimization hints to the possibility that anxiety about injuries and diseases resulting from unsafe work and environmental conditions could spill over to other realms, for instance, increasing fear of crime. Viewed from this perspective, fear of crime becomes part of the subculture of helplessness in inner-city neighborhoods.

Critics of quality-of-life policing have charged that the definition of social and physical disorder as community problems to be policed is applying, in reality, middle-class standards of behavior on populations that do not consider targeted activities especially troublesome (Bursik & Grasmick, 1993). Notwithstanding, supporters firmly believe that incivilities, as failures to self-impose restraint and obligation, violate universally accepted norms of conduct, about which a broad consensus exists, despite social, ethnic, and class differences (Kelling & Coles, 1996). Empirical evidence does not support this "class-bias" hypothesis that only middle-class homeowners, with the value of their property at stake, are offended by violations of civility. The ratings of perceived disorder by owners and renters are generally not significantly different; they provide similar assessment of what their neighborhoods are like in terms of local problems (Skogan, 1990). Nevertheless, the dismissal of class bias in the definition of disorder and incivility is accompanied by the confirmation that class bias exists in the actual experience of community decay. Neighborhood poverty (an indexed score on unemployment, income, and education) determines who will have to live with incivilities. Households in low-income, high-unemployment, low-education neighborhoods report more serious problems of disorder in their streets, regardless of other contextual characteristics of the neighborhood. The collusion between better-off neighborhoods and official authorities further aggravates and reinforces the disorganization in disadvantaged neighborhoods. Many undesired public programs traditionally associated with incivility and disorder have been imposed upon these economically poor and politically powerless neighborhoods. Residents of Harlem and other areas of New York City, for example, had voiced their anger over the intentional diversion of housing and shelter programs for the homeless, the mentally ill, and drug abusers into their neighborhoods while other sections of the city have very few or none of these programs (Chira, 1989). While the privatization of space intensifies in better-off areas, social marginalization increases in inner-city neighborhoods through discipline, surveillance, and welfare systems that seek to keep peace for the state and its constituents, rather than to empower the have-nots. Political powerlessness effectively transforms economic poverty into chaos in the streets.

Race and Ethnicity

Many Americans still associate minority status with criminal threat and are ready to respond to such a threat with spontaneous or concerted actions. The growth of the minority population in a city is frequently a powerful catalyst of public fear and change in criminal justice behavior. Municipal police expand as the danger represented by minority residents grows. But as the minority population becomes a majority large enough to achieve political power and authority, the size of police manpower levels off (Jackson & Carroll, 1981). Interestingly, the segregation of minority citizens also decreases police size (Liska, Lawrence, & Benson, 1981). The concentration of minority populations in isolated ghettos functions as a mechanism of group control by reducing the occurrence of interracial victimizations and thereby lessening the need for more overt forms of police surveillance.

These patterns of official perception of threat only confirm the enduring belief that crime is primarily committed by members of minority groups, by residents of undesirable neighborhoods. Collective fear of crime becomes a "symbolic response to neighborhood heterogeneity" (Bursik & Grasmick, 1993, p. 104), while crime control develops into "watching for people of particular races and aggressively monitoring the circumstances under which different races come into contact" (Skogan, 1990, p. 105). The criminal threat posed by a large concentration of minorities, however, is not only felt by white citizens *exclusively*. National studies suggest that even when levels of official crime and incivility are controlled, minority respondents living in neighborhoods dominated by minority peers judge their risk of crime to be higher and are more afraid (Ferraro, 1995). Most Americans, regardless of their own ethnic ascription, share the archetype of "normal predator" so firmly embedded in the collective psyche.

In Skogan's study of community decline, the race of a person has no influence on his or her perception of incivility. Black and white respondents are not more or less tolerant of incivility than each other, and when living in the same neighborhood, they largely agree on the extent of disorder. Nevertheless, the absence of statistical connection is only found at the individual level (Skogan, 1990). There is a strong relationship between levels of disorder and the concentration of racial and ethnic minorities. Regardless of race or ethnicity, respondents living in minority neighborhoods report higher levels of disorder near their residences. Overall, measures of neighborhood context are more powerful in predicting disorder than indicators of personal traits. Environmental variables accounted for 95 percent of the explained variance, compared to 5 percent for individual factors. Almost all that is explained is accounted for by between-neighborhood differences, including differences in race.

Life-cycle

The age structure of a community can promote or impair trust among residents. Fear of crime increases either by perceived growth in the number of potential predators as reflected by a large number of idle youth in the neighborhood or by a large concentration of seniors who tend to perceive themselves as vulnerable targets. Crime statistics, media portrayal, and public beliefs all agree that adolescents and young adults are likely to engage in deviant behavior, from bad-taste pranks to vicious predatory activities. Controlling and supervising the behavior of local youth then become the easiest test of community control. Willingness to monitor spontaneous play groups and to intervene to prevent truancy and street-corner loitering by teenage peer groups are effective informal mechanisms by which residents themselves take care of a delinquent threat (Sampson, Raudebush, & Earls, 1997). Research has found that neighborhoods in which more respondents feel that neighbors would call the police if kids were spray-painting a building have significantly lower levels of fear (Covington & Taylor, 1991).

Paradoxically, youths themselves perceive a higher risk of being victimized. People aged 18 to 24 exhibit the highest level of fear (Ferraro, 1995). Their preoccupation is not unfounded: National statistics indicate that the risk of victimization by violent crimes peaks at ages 16 to 19 for both sexes and declines with age thereafter (Greenwood, 1995). Mirroring their disproportional involvement in committing violent offenses, juveniles are also disproportionately represented as victims; they heighten levels of fear in their communities as well as experience deeper concerns for their own physical safety.

However, the younger age group is not the only victim of criminal fear. Most studies plotted a U-shape curvilinear relationship between age and fear (Ferraro, 1995). Fear of crime is highest among the younger population, declines steadily in adulthood until advanced age, and rises again for elderly residents. Older people, whose lifestyle is distinguished by reduced participation in community life and a decline in health, tend to perceive themselves as particularly vulnerable to crime in that they are more open to attack, powerless to resist assaults, and less resistant to physical and emotional traumas (Skogan & Maxfield, 1981). Yet, unlike the threat perceived by the younger group, older people are the least likely to become victims of both property and violent crimes (Bachman, 1992). This apparent "irrationality" has led some researchers to think that for older citizens, fear of crime is more of a problem than crime itself (Clemente & Kleiman, 1976). The strategic implications that police managers can, and should, derive from these findings cannot be overemphasized. Not only do the levels of fear have significance in shaping police-citizen relations, but also the different "age" sources of fear require different interventions.

Youths contribute to community nuisance and disorder in various ways. Public drinking frequently involves groups of teenagers loitering in and around public spaces. Corner gangs can take the form of bored and restless youngsters blocking sidewalks, talking loud, and fist fighting. They also find excitement in harassing women and the elderly through verbal innuendo and intimidation. Bands of idle youths can also be involved in vandalism and graffiti and claim impersonal spaces and public transportation as their turfs through these disruptive behaviors. As a result, it is expected that stable neighborhoods mostly inhabited by mature households will be less disturbed by problems of disorder. "Areas with older, long-term residents . . . were more successful at maintaining acceptable standards of public conduct and housing conditions" (Skogan, 1990, p. 58).

THE MORAL HIERARCHY OF NEIGHBORHOODS

Police–citizen relations rest upon a moral reality structured by the same market and political forces that formed segregated and unequal neighborhoods in the first place. The power stratification of neighborhoods produces a parallel moral hierarchy of neighborhoods defined by the social stigma and threats associated with varying levels of crime and disorder. This moral scale includes an upper tail composed of the very safe and fortified neighborhoods and a lower tail of underclass neighborhoods, where a disproportionate number of potential criminals and vulnerable victims is confined. It also has a broad middle area for most middle-class neighborhoods with a relatively low level of deviance.

Unlike marginal areas that are predated by criminal acts and demoralized by a general sense of unworthiness, neighborhoods inhabited by active voters and stable-income professionals experience less fear and disorder, which strengthens their moral standing in relation to other communities. Upper- and middle-class families spatially position themselves out of reach of criminal deviants, make use of both technology and hired manpower to secure their vast private space, and strictly abide by the shared code of civility and order when interacting with each other. They all understand that the best way to clean up the streets from unwanted disturbances and to prevent the decline in property values is to physically and culturally preserve the class and race homogeneity of their communities.

High rates of crime, fear, and incivility are a social stigma because places of residence not only reflect the status of their inhabitants, but also confer status upon them. Strangers draw favorable inferences about someone who claims to reside in a quiet suburban community where the grass is mown and most single-family houses are owned by college-educated professionals. But they will be leery of those who admit to living in a neighborhood dilapidated as a result of density, transience, poverty, and inferior public services. Physical disorder and social incivility of a community discredit its residents as incapable and irresponsible citizens who maintain a parasitic subsistence in the society. Beginning with aging and decay, stigmatized neighborhoods progress through a series of collateral penalties (including decreasing land value, banks' refusal to invest and lend, and deficient public services), to further normative breakdown, then more criminal sanctions and official neglect, and eventually an acceptance by the residents of a morally deviant status. Living in a no-go area where rape and assault are common, where drug dealers do business on street corners with impunity, where prostitutes stroll the sidewalks waving to passing cars, and where people sell used electronic products out of the trunks of their cars decreases one's respectability in the eyes of others.

Rodney Stark (1987) identifies a number of harmful effects of social stigma that disgrace powerless communities and spark a series of damaging migratory movements. First, stigmatized neighborhoods reduce residents' stake in conformity because investing in traditionally valued activities such as schooling and working only yields negligible returns in the absence of opportunities. People living in slums see themselves as having less to risk by being detected in acts of deviance; moreover, the risks of being caught also are actually lower in these areas. Although police often harass residents of minority ghettos, prostitution, public drinking, gambling, and even simple assaults are often tolerated and dismissed as "typically black," which drives businesses and intact middle-class and working families out of inner cities (Meares & Kahan, 1999). As more successful and conventional people flee or resist moving into discredited areas where nothing very much matters and just about anything goes, the best role models are pulled out of defamed neighborhoods and the more negative role models affiliated with the underworld of drug and vice business immigrate. Finally, stigmatized neighborhoods become overpopulated by the most demoralized kinds of people following the out-migration of more respectable residents. Even if residents of stigmatized neighborhoods do not themselves violate the laws, they become discouraged about the social control of others. The most extreme form of demoralized human settlement is *skid row* (a natural habitat of delinquents, the mentally ill, and winos, who are incapable of functioning with reasonably appropriate manners, or others who have retreated from conventional social life), which poses a unique challenge to legitimate and effective policing (Bittner, 1967).

Police view themselves as moral agents whose responsibility it is to rout out troublemakers through the selective application of law and summary coercive sanctions. The moral dimension of police services is the heart of police identity. It prescribes a presentation of police work as waging a just war against ruthless enemies and also justifies all that they do to control their turf, including the "righteous abuse of suspects." The category of "suspects" encompasses a great variety of "assholes" (Van Maanen, 1978), from known criminals to whoever fails to unequivocally support the police. Morality, as an occupational sentiment, transforms officers' territories into dominions. Crime, fear, and incivility defy police sovereignty. In morally defective neighborhoods, police pursue their sacred high purpose more vehemently: confrontation with human evil occurs everywhere. Here, true police work concentrates and morality is correspondingly acted out through tough words and powerful acts. "The expectation that the police will control crime at the societal level is enacted at the individual level as the ability of the police officer to control his or her beat. The beat of an officer is thus transformed into a moral responsibility, the officer's dominion. The notion of beat control is an imperative with a powerful moral thrust" (Crank, 1998, pp. 154–155).

If stigma arouses scorn and pity toward the stigmatized, threat stirs up fear and hostility toward the perceived sources of danger. In large metropolitan regions where the suburban stability and social homogeneity of middle- and upper-class neighborhoods are insulated from the miseries of inner-city communities, the geographical proximity of stigmatized ghettos to sensitive elite symbols (central business districts, prestige medical centers, and universities) enables the poor, minorities, and recent immigrants to threaten the stability of the surrounding urban system (Logan & Molotch, 1987). The establishment's inability either to fix the political and economic structures that have given birth to the incorrigible problems of inequality or to completely conceal and isolate the dreadful reality of concentrated poverty has created a paradoxical configuration of social threat. Disruptive ghettos and their fearful residents maintain an extreme *social* distance from the centers of power but at the same time, keep close *geographical* proximity to the same vital locales. Although crime, fear, and incivility affect primarily residents of marginal communities, they destabilize the complacent tranquility of the mainstream society by subverting the dearly held values and codes of conduct of middle-class constituencies. This spatial organization of socially valued assets and potential criminal insurrections occasions the instability that must be controlled by the state apparatus.

In order to legitimately control unconventional groups and to police peripheral areas with effective punitiveness, the behavior of the powerless must be constructed and coded in terms of serious threats to both the physical and moral integrity of society at large. Social threat refers to the behaviors of individuals or groups that jeopardize the continuity of the existing social order and the preservation of dominant values (Tittle, 1994). However, when marginal groups are stripped of basic social power and left without a significant role in the arena of political and economic competition, securing shares of material and social rewards through illegal means becomes a viable option. Class and racial subordinate groups subjected to overbearing deprivation in a relatively well-off society are less committed to the status quo and thus are more likely to behave in unpredictable and unconventional ways (Liska, 1992). Criminal threats thus grow. Laws are promulgated and the police are commissioned to suppress this particular kind of social threat through diverse combinations of aggressive and coercive strategies.

Police actions in public spaces and in private places reify moral labels and dramatize the moral hierarchy of neighborhoods. Police "services" reduce the cultural capital of the less powerful communities. Sanction-oriented interventions diminish the cultural and social resources of the peripheral neighborhoods, while service-oriented policing valorizes the moral superiority of the better-off core neighborhoods. Police enforcement activities such as stops, searches, questioning, and arrests serve fundamental symbolic functions. These "black marks" are carefully recorded and reproduced at various critical points of capital accumulation (e.g., in courts, at job interviews, in subsequent encounters with the police, and in applications for education) and solidify the subordinate status of minority and lower-class citizens and their places (Manning, 1997). Psychologically, the existence of social stigma makes the intrusion of police coercion in high-crime, high-fear, and high-disorder neighborhoods less problematic. Politically, the presence of criminal threat provides rational justification to the application of heavy-handed preventive tactics in those dangerous areas. The moral attributes of neighborhood are achieved or ruined through political action, rather than through the qualities inherent in the area. Places are morally defined through social relationships of power.

SUMMARY

Policing in American metropolises has historically responded to the population shifts and the social strains that these changes bring into being. Municipal police carry the responsibility of establishing public order from chaos through their daily interactions with common citizens whose life stories are framed to a large extent by powerful social forces. The operation of these economic and political forces, reflected partly in the supply and demand for housing, allocates different households to different areas of the city and surrounding districts. The city and its land uses are both the prize and the outcome of the struggle for social power among different interests, which result in the inflexible segregation of neighborhoods based on class status, ethnic composition, and life-cycle characteristics. This particular residential organization generates profits for land entrepreneurs, provides safety and satisfaction to middle classes, and protects the status quo.

Neighborhoods that make up metropolitan regions are stratified along two continuums, which are, in turn, closely related. First, in terms of material affluence and political influence, residential districts can be located in the core/periphery continuum of social power. Neighborhoods primarily inhabited by white, middle-class, and mature households are more actively involved in the productive and administrative affairs of society, while areas populated mainly by minority, lower-class households with a relatively larger number of young children endure a passive existence, maintaining a subordinate position in relation to other communities. Residents living in core areas have a higher stake in the status quo and thus tend to see the police as cherished allies, a role police uncritically, and in a way inevitably, assume. In contrast, exclusion from the market and the government denies the less powerful neighborhoods the capacity to voice publicly their concerns and the ability to promote their interests and values. Alienated from the mainstream, these citizens and their places become police properties to be controlled rather than constituents to be consulted. The social distance from the core of the social power is translated into ideological discrepancies, that is, incongruency in values and expectations, between police forces and the peripheral neighborhoods. Policing without empathetic identification with the policed predisposes police–community interactions to gear toward potential difficulties.

The same demographic factors that pattern the stratification of neighborhoods by social power also produce structural conditions that define a hierarchy of places according to their respectability. Wealth and ethnic homogeneity turn core communities into organized and peaceful territories, whereas peripheral neighborhoods witness an unacceptable growth of motivated offenders and vulnerable victims within them. When community safety grants a respectable reputation to the neighborhood, higher levels of deviance cause stigma and jeopardize residents' lives. Both social stigma and criminal threat, as imputed attributes and internalized identities, reduce the number of alternatives for police and citizens to route their exchanges. Police–public relations will vary following the power stratification and moral hierarchy of neighborhoods.

NOTES

1. Social classes refer to, in this treatise, strata made up of similar individuals or households with shared characteristics, interests, and stakes in the system. Class status is understood as primarily determined by employment prestige, income, and political influence. The tri-level (upper, middle, and lower classes) language used throughout the present work rejects the notion that a single ruling minority dominates all aspects of social life. Rather, in a liberal capitalist society, a plurality of elites (the upper classes) maintain among themselves, and with the rest of the society, cooperative as well as conflictual relationships.

2. What remains unsettled is the appropriateness of inferring causal links among macro-level variables. Robert J. Sampson (1995) pointed out that the unit of analysis does not define the level of causal explanation because the information contained in aggregate data is not necessarily generated by macrosociological processes. The difference in crime and delinquency rates among neighborhoods may be due to the variation in the distribution of people who have individual characteristics (e.g., sex, age, race, etc.) connected to a high likelihood of criminal behavior, rather than to any processes operating at the neighborhood level. This criminological debate offers no interference to our inquiry into the influence of the aggregate amount of crime on police–citizen relationships. After all, the uncertainty about the causal mechanisms of crime production does not challenge the fact that different neighborhoods experience different crime rates. In addition, the relationship between this differential distribution of criminal threat and the variation in police–citizen relations constitutes the focus of our inquiry.

CHAPTER 3

The Ecology of Police–Community Relations: Hypotheses

People call the police and request their presence to handle a variety of matters besides criminal ones. Officers serve the public and expect from them respect and cooperation in an often tedious, dangerous, and hostile work environment. Since modern metropolises have developed into various communities with peculiar human characteristics and routine round patterns, residential fragmentation interacts with the consequent spatial distribution of power and stigma to produce unique modes of police–citizen relations across neighborhoods. In this chapter, I will conceptually link the two major structural dimensions of residential neighborhoods (social power stratification and moral hierarchy) to variations in the two constitutive aspects of police–community relations (police service styles and citizen response). Drawing insights from extant literature and research, I formulate four general causal hypotheses associating demographic traits and public safety with changes in police behavior and citizen attitudes.[1] Figure 3.1 summarizes this ecological model of police–community relations.

THE ECOLOGY OF POLICE BEHAVIOR

Demographic Patterns of Residential Segregation as Determinants of Police Behavior

Given that police work is built around encounters with citizens, the way police respond to mobilizations from citizens or intervene in the

Figure 3.1
The basic conceptual components of an ecological model of police–citizen relations

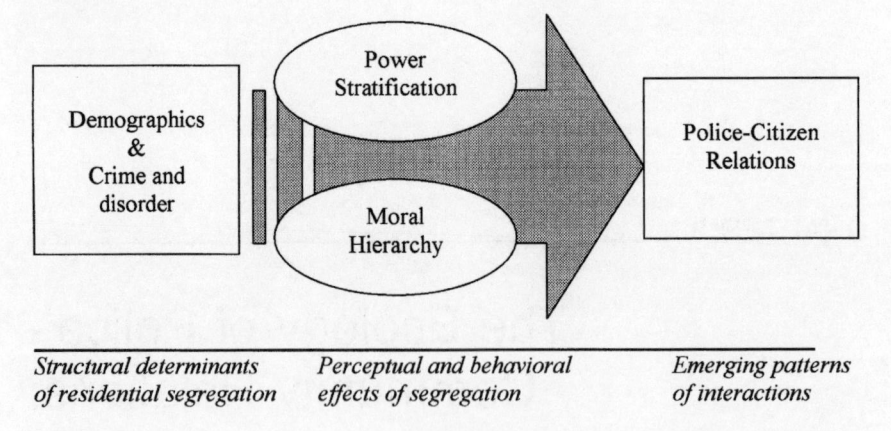

```
┌─────────────┐        Power                    ┌─────────────┐
│ Demographics│     Stratification              │             │
│      &      │ ══════════════════════════════▶ │Police-Citizen│
│  Crime and  │      Moral                      │  Relations  │
│   disorder  │    Hierarchy                    │             │
└─────────────┘                                 └─────────────┘
```

| *Structural determinants* | *Perceptual and behavioral* | *Emerging patterns* |
| *of residential segregation* | *effects of segregation* | *of interactions* |

lives of people on their own initiative are largely determined by the influence and needs of the policed community. The spatial arrangement of political leverage and the geographic distribution of emergencies confine how police and citizens exercise discretion in their transactions, and particularly, how and why they reproduce and renegotiate the extant social order. The clustering of households by ethnic identity, class status, and life-cycle stage ranks urban and suburban neighborhoods along the core/periphery spectrum, depending on the amount of social influence each one of them manages to hold. Based on shared consciousness and common lifestyles, residential neighborhoods evolve into distinct hierarchical collectivities, each of which possesses a corresponding mode of relating to the political decision-making process.

John Short (1996) developed a tri-tier model of urban politics, which provides a very didactic and incisive description of the sociopolitical context in which municipal police are inserted. He distinguishes three different types of communities, each of which maintains a unique kind of relation to the political decision-making apparatus. These modes of power sharing are political partnership, political communion, and political exclusion, and can be meaningfully applied to the analysis of community–police relations.

The wealthy households encompass the rich and the very rich, all of whom, although sharing much of the popular culture, are exiled in remote areas. The most influential and affluent minority usually keeps a low profile, which is often expressed in where they live and how they live. With some exceptions, the wealthy move away from conspicuous to inconspicuous consumption and reside in secluded housing, hidden from public view. These beneficiaries of structured inequality are in the process of seceding from the larger society, insulating themselves in protected, luxurious, and private communities, if located in downtown, combined with corporate offices and exclusive recreational facilities.[2] The type of relationship this privileged group maintains with the state apparatus of control is best described as *political partnership*. Political partnership occurs because the wealthy share the same interests as the political elite (sometimes they themselves are the political elite) and can therefore adopt an overwhelmingly conciliatory approach toward the police. Despite this political interdependence between wealthy groups and police institutional interests, individual police officers can still feel alienated from the residents of these exclusive places. Many patrolmen believe that they are often treated like inferior parties and not welcome because the presence of on-duty officers in upscale restaurants or stores is bad for establishments' reputations and discourages customers. Patrol officers and residents of advantaged neighborhoods rarely interact at the street level. Their interactions mainly occur in social meetings and political rallies attended by higher-ranking police officers and representatives of the privileged groups. As a New York City officer serving an exclusive section of Manhattan observed, "the boss [the precinct commanding officer] here has to spend most of his time massaging the important people in the community. He has to be a real diplomat because they sure know how to use their phones and who to call to get action" (Reuss-Ianni, 1983, p. 41).

The next category is represented by the professionals and the white-collar workers, who make up the middle classes. They are capable of paying market prices for their dwellings and display a lifestyle symbolically condensed in the automobile and the suburb. They enjoy a *political communion* with the police, who willingly acknowledge the rightfulness of the demands from the middle class for a tranquil environment, free of crime and unnecessary government intrusion. The survival of the police in a post-capitalist democracy rests on its alliance with high-consumption households. Criminal justice debates are centered on meeting the safety and retributive justice needs of the middle classes; police executives strive to capture the hearts and minds of these same constituents. It is not an exaggeration to say that the history of the recent politics of law and order (e.g., the Crime Bill of 1994), in which the police have been a major player, is essentially one of the struggle for the middle classes.

Low-skilled workers and the underclass occupy the lowest step of the ladder and are stocked in the city as a reserve force for menial work. The gap between these groups and the middle classes is somewhat offset by the public sector: welfare payments provide them with additional means to survive. But if there is a significant cutback in welfare allocations, the inequalities among and the segregation of different income groups are likely to increase. The relationship of the least powerful to the police is one of *political exclusion*. Their interests are rarely given much attention and their grievances seldom articulated or formulated. Even when some of these concerns cross over class lines and become a criminal justice issue, subsequent decisions may consistently go against them. The main reason is because, to the rest of society, the very existence of marginal neighborhoods is a prime public safety problem; to the police in particular, residents of these areas are seen as a source of social disruption. The official abandonment of these impoverished and dangerous areas is so thorough that certain patrol beats or precincts in major metropolises are often used as "training fields" for the youngest and least experienced officers (Marshal, 1997) or as "dumping grounds" for incompetent and undisciplined officers, many of whom have been found to take pride in their reputation for being brutal and corrupt, and believe that supervisors and internal affairs investigators will not venture into their territory (Mollen Commission, 1994).

The construction of urban space is a constitutive process. The social relations of dominance and dependency set limits and exert pressure for certain kinds of spatial organization, which is indeed a part of the internally structured whole of a metropolitan system of social power. The capacity of the police to maintain legitimacy in their contacts with citizens of different districts depends, to an important degree, upon their service styles in each one of these communities. The exercise of discretion and selective response is inevitable because material resources and manpower are limited. The police will never be able to enforce every law with equal force in every neighborhood; they have to adjust to the geography of social influence and tailor their work to the relational distance between their assigned geographic districts and the economic and political decision-making apparatus. The role of the police in preserving private property, clearing up streets, and suppressing social deviance makes political neutrality no more than rhetorical imagination. Priorities have to be set, and that is, of course, a question of politics. Being an institution of coercive control, the police force is itself a prize eagerly sought by all participants of the power contest; no group can ever claim to be a power broker in urban politics without securing the support of the police. "Police constituencies can be identified narrowly by observing only those persons or groups who take a direct and visible interest in police behavior or more broadly by designating those that have an interest in shaping the quality of life in urban systems, for which the police provide a primary function. [. . .] those who shape the city shape the police" (Duffee, Fluellen, & Roscoe, 1999, p. 5).

The demographic context of policing predicts and explains how it varies across communities. Consider first the core/periphery standing of a neighborhood in the geographic organization of social power.

The police are more likely to be found in places where certain people live or congregate than in other parts of the city. Though this pattern of manpower allocation is ordinarily justified by references to experientially established needs for police service, it inevitably entails the consequence that some persons will receive the dubious benefit of extensive police scrutiny merely on account of their membership in those groupings which invidious social comparisons locate at the bottom of the heap. Accordingly, it is not a paranoid distortion to say that police activity is as much directed to who a person is as to what he does. (Bittner, 1970, p. 98)

Police activity is also directed at where a person *lives*. There is compelling reason to believe that not only the manpower but also the level of authoritative intervention of police varies with the marginality of an area. The weight of social control has long been known to flow from the core to the periphery (Black, 1976). Strictly speaking, authoritativeness increases with marginality. In other words, *police authoritative intervention is a negative function of the relative power status of a neighborhood*. Recall that the three modes of authoritative policing can be differentiated: proactive, coercive, and enforcement oriented.

Proaction

Proactive policing is in nature nearer to the ideal of crime prevention. Proactive tactics such as field questioning or street sweeps promise to disrupt crimes in progress and to deter would-be criminals; their success depends on reliable intelligence and cues about current or imminent evolution of criminal activities. The preferred targets for proactive policing are almost always located in territorial units where ethnic minorities and unschooled and unemployed youth are overrepresented. Both the human and physical factors of marginal areas lure the police to initiate contacts with citizens aimed at establishing a symbolic presence of law.

First, insofar as disadvantaged groups are more likely than others to engage in conduct objectionable to white middle-class values, their concentration in an area will require a higher degree of surveillance and deterrence. To start with, more intense and visible patrol routines are carried out in areas with more realistic criminal threats. The lower intensity of police patrol in upper- and middle-class neighborhoods reflects the fact that the behaviors of the citizens of these areas are of little concern to the police. Their lives are scarcely touched by patrol work. In contrast, a powerful police presence is maintained in marginal neighborhoods where ethnic codes of self-presentation (including ways of dressing, talking, and acting in public spaces) signal uncertainty and unpredictability. Signs of unfamiliarity and offensiveness can quickly arouse suspicion among the guardians of moral order. Police indeed behave more proactively by initiating more contacts with citizens in racially heterogeneous neighborhoods (Smith, 1986). Youths attract police attention too. For the police, the juvenile problem exists when groups of adolescents are found in places or at times they are not supposed to be. Long before it takes the shape of an incident, any juvenile gathering is already a nuisance to be controlled. As far as patrol officers are concerned, adolescents do not so much cause trouble, they are trouble; and in order to thwart this threat to public order, police engage in preventive intervention.

Second, the physical design and conditions of peripheral communities are very suitable for the transactions of illegal goods and services. Lots owned by no one and places shielded from view characterize many housing projects and provide secrecy and isolation. The gigantic size and lack of use of public spaces interferes with opportunities for social cohesion and natural surveillance in high-rise buildings (Murray, 1995). Poorly lighted streets and run-down neighborhoods fall quickly into the hands of vice criminals. Prostitutes service their clients inside cars parked in vacant lots and drug-dealers turn abandoned apartment units into crack houses. Situational crime prevention doctrines urge police to intervene before citizens call in areas with severe physical deterioration (Clarke, 1995). Signs of poverty and official neglect have often become the targets of police preemptive strikes. In drug-enforcement programs, for instance, officers visit and issue summons to less valuable properties or run-down buildings with "blight, abandoned cars, rodents, . . . but no drug problems" (Green, 1996, p. 37)! Although communities in decline can gain some protection from proactive prevention activities, proactive policing is likely to result in an imposed alien peace rather than renewing community cohesion and empowerment.

Since police see their "real role" as society's strike force against dreadful street predators and embrace dealing with felonious offenses, which may require physical force, as "true cop work" (Bittner, 1982), places located at the bottom of the social heap become their favorite beats where their bravura and toughness can be tested. They do not wait for crime to be reported, but aggressively search for suspects. Unlike white-collar crime, which is mostly committed by respectable people with respectable occupations in respectable settings and controlled by special enforcement agencies, crime by the poor is more likely to be committed in public spaces. Plainclothes and uniformed officers inundate dangerous places to actively look for dangerous people to comply with the official mandate of street crime control as well as to fulfill the occupational imagery of street crime fighter. As such, I hypothesize that *all else equal, the relative volume of police proactive encounters with citizens increases with the proportion of minority, poor, and young residents.*

Coercion

The greatest strain in police–community relations is the failure of citizens to pay due deference to representatives of law and order, who from a position of authority seek to keep peace based on a consensus-coercion balance (Turk, 1969). To the extent that a strong consensual relationship is established, as it is in white and well-to-do neighborhoods, citizens will offer no resistance and become conditioned to act out the prescribed roles of authorities and subjects. Patrol officers operate in these places under strong popular mandate surrounded by public respect. When this consensus breaks down, citizens feel provoked and oppressed and are likely to resist police authorities and be retaliated against with coercive force in field encounters (Lanza-Kaduce & Greenleaf, 1994). Street-level resistance to police authority can be measured by verbal incivility, by displays of anger, by threats, or by violence directed toward patrol officers. In socially and ethnically peripheral areas, discrepancies in values and expectations between police and the policed seriously weaken the factual foundation of police legitimacy. The grudging acceptance of police authority could be withdrawn instantly in the context of face-to-face confrontation and shift the consensus–coercion balance to an excessively coercive power relationship. In areas where the approval of police legitimacy is only tentative or conditional, the higher degree of distrust obligates the police to rely more on verbal and physical coercion to instill respect and affirm order.

An additional inducement for coercive control is set off when a disproportionate number of adolescents live in and move around places with a short supply of public recreational spaces. Youths who grew up in anonymous areas with no reference point derive meaning from their confrontations with the police, which dramatize rites of entry to adulthood (Body-Gendrot, 2000). People expect a normal level of coercion from police in confronting teenage youths—mocking and yelling at them, pushing or grabbing them. In order to efficiently keep juveniles under control, police officers minimize their involvement with the youths by "resorting to strongly coercive measures without first assaying the feasibility of alternatives, except in cases where violence or arrest might produce protests from politically powerful parents" (Bittner, 1976, p. 81). Youth's vulnerability to police coercion rests, ultimately, in their legal and social subordination to adult authority and discipline. Yet despite their secured superiority and control of the situation, police officers avoid assignments involving young people and are not skilled in the handling of juvenile problems because of the low status of juvenile work in the traditional hierarchy of police values. No credits are gained by careful consideration of juvenile problems and thorny consequences might result from entangling parental grievances. Policing juveniles is not rewarding at all.

The power differentiation of neighborhoods creates a social psychological condition that further reinforces the current geographic distribution of coercive power. Behaviors of noncompliance and disrepute are dangerous not only because they subvert the established order, but also because they threaten the personal safety of individual officers, who must assert their control of the situation, forcefully if needed. To the patrol officer, the authority of the state is also his personal authority. Challenges to police authority are felt as violations of self-esteem. To deny or raise doubt about an officer's legitimacy is to shake the very ground upon which his self-image stands (Van Maanen, 1978). Therefore, neighborhoods predominantly populated by minority, youth, and the poor receive more coercive treatment because they grant less deference and friendliness to the police. Peripheral neighborhoods are the wild frontiers; it is here where most of the assaults and murder of and by the police occur. The cognitive isolation and emotional detachment of the police from some segments of the population precipitates violence (Skolnick, 1967) and provides "a ready rationalization for violence directed toward an ungrateful, hostile, and quasi-human public" (Manning, 1997, p. 113). Data show that the use or threat of force against encountered suspects is more likely in primarily black or racially mixed neighborhoods (Smith, 1986). Studies on fatal shootings by police also concluded that neighborhood racial composition had been consistently found as a powerful predictor of police use of deadly force (Riksheim & Charmack, 1993). An analysis of 170 American cities reveals that police use of deadly force increases in cities with large black populations (Jacobs & O'Brien, 1998). Cities with more blacks and a recent growth in the black population had higher rates of police killing blacks, but the presence of a black mayor reduced these killings. Thus, *all else equal, the relative volume of police coercive encounters with citizens increases with the proportion of minority, poor, and young residents.*

Law Enforcement

Research has found that the lack of distance and impersonal separation between law enforcement agents and the community in rural and small-town areas strongly discourages the police or sheriffs to formally enforce criminal law: it always upsets some part of the community (Weisheit, Falcone, & Wells, 1999). In addition, rural policing is more personalized and less legalistic than municipal policing because nearly all sheriffs in the counties require deputies to reside in their legal jurisdictions, whereas less than 50 percent of municipal departments have such a requirement (Bureau of Justice Statistics, 1991). Being members of different social groups and living in suburban communities turn many municipal police officers into outsiders within their patrol beats. Formalism and legalism ensue. Consequently, large municipal police departments are more concerned with enforcing criminal law and controlling crime through arrests than smaller agencies (Meagher, 1985).

Black (1989) proposes that the greater the social elevation of the mediator above the adversaries, the more authoritatively and punitively is the mediator likely to behave. This hypothesis resonates Bayley's observation that "if policemen are close to a community, they are less likely to act as enforcers, even though the proportion of enforcement requests is higher" (1985, p. 133). If both Black and Bayley are correct, then the identification of the municipal police force with mainstream expectations and interests will have an important impact on police discretion. As officers look at residents of marginal areas through middle-class eyeballs, they see themselves as further away from the world of the poor and minority; and this relational distance increases their likelihood of imposing legalistic and punitive solutions. In neighborhoods overridingly inhabited by white, middle-class, and two-parent families, the social contiguity between police and the public encourages informality and more empathetic considerations. Officers understand that legal intrusion such as arresting or even simply handcuffing a middle-class citizen in his or her own neighborhood can detrimentally tarnish the person's reputation, needless to say that a criminal conviction can ruin his life and family. "It is commonly understood that the law is not to be invoked against citizens with unblemished records who are suspected of technical or relatively trivial breaches of the law" (Bittner, 1982, p. 274). The market-oriented style of policing is generally designed to meet demands arising in "homogeneous middle-class communities" and seldom invokes law to control situations (Wilson, 1968). Reasoning and persuasion are preferred over arrests. In contrast, lower-class citizens are often believed to be immune to police–induced disgrace because they are already stigmatized as losers in life. Indeed the record-blemishing effects of formal legal proceedings mirror the wider distribution of esteem and credit in the society at large.

The breakdown of self-regulatory capability reflected in the failure of family, school, and church to provide nurturing and guidance to their members also invites more aggressive police law enforcement. Police are not indifferent to this state of normlessness.

Life in the city has many conditions, circumstances, and troubled people, and when troubled people are left to themselves, they are likely to cause, or get into, great calamities of various sorts. The officers worked on the assumptions that ex-cons without jobs are likely to commit crimes again; intergroup tension may lead to violent confrontations; children without recreational facilities tend to get into mischief, and so on. According to this assumption, when such potential is not checked, it leads to consequences that will sooner or later have to be handled by detectives, riot squads, or juvenile officers, depending on a specific situation. (Bittner, 1975, pp. 298–299)

Sooner or later, the normative vacuum impels police officers to address situations in which people are simply unable to regulate their own lives adequately. The task is straightforward: to maintain a minimum level of order through coercion and law. In concrete operational terms this means that more incidents will be recorded as troubles and more people will be labeled as troublemakers in politically marginal and economically disadvantaged neighborhoods.

Legal observer Jeffrey Rosen (2000) has recently pointed out the fallacy of applying "zero-tolerance" policing in segregated cities such as New York City. Championed by William Bratton, the former commissioner of the NYPD, "zero-tolerance" policing seeks to increase police discretion to catch felonious criminals by enforcing laws for offenses that lower the quality of life. Yet the goal of zero tolerance is itself illusory. Given limited resources, the police cannot arrest and book all minor offenders with equal force. Like the enforcement of laws against more serious crimes, zero tolerance is necessarily selective in practice. Since residents of minority and poor neighborhoods live in crowded housing with little private space, they spend more time on the street, and thus become easy targets for aggressive policing. As a result, according to Rosen, pot smokers in the Bronx, Brooklyn, and Harlem are arrested under zero tolerance, while Wall Street brokers who live in expensive penthouses in Manhattan are factually permitted to light up pot cigarettes without fear of police harassment.

Among all enforcement behaviors, arrest and official report filing have been most closely studied; their relations to neighborhood characteristics rest on a wealth of empirical evidence. Political and racial heterogeneity variables were significant predictors of police arrest behavior in many studies, although they usually interact with other community-level factors such as style of city government (Slovak, 1986), urbanism of the neighborhood (Crank, 1990), and official crime rates (Liska & Chamlin, 1984). The only structural factor that consistently exercises direct influence on arrest decisions is neighborhood poverty or low capital income, which is positively related to higher rates of arrest (Crank, 1990; Liska & Chamlin, 1984; Smith, 1987). In all cases, police are more likely to arrest in low-income neighborhoods. While arrest is most likely in lower-class settings, other forms of social control—therapy, restitution, or education—are used among middle and upper classes in analogous situations (Manning, 1997). It should not surprise us that suspects encountered by police in lower-status neighborhoods ran three times the risk of arrest compared with offenders encountered in higher-status neighborhoods, independent of type of crime, race of offender, offender demeanor, and victim preferences for criminal arrest (Smith, 1986). Higher percentages of foreign-born and rapid population turnover encourage police to record incidents as crimes (Warner, 1997), and just as higher residential instability increases police filing of incident reports (Smith, 1986). In culturally heterogeneous communities, police may find it increasingly important to deal with problems formally to protect the hegemony of the dominant values and beliefs. Insofar as blacks and immigrants are disproportionately represented among the poor, this bias has the potential to produce a disproportionate rate of black and foreign-born arrests. In other words, collateral racial discrimination could result from pervasive economic discrimination in police arrest practices.

The police, when applying formal social control or refusing to do so, enact the core/periphery neighborhood hierarchy. There is no enforcement of law without power differentials. As Black points out, discrimination in the administration of law is an "aspect of the natural behavior of law, as natural as the flying of the birds or the swimming of the fish" (1989, p. 22). Owing to the institutional design under which police are mandated to enforce criminal law that focuses on crimes by poor people and need not be concerned with specialized crimes committed by the rich and powerful, policing is apt to include elements of class and racial bias. In sum, *all things equal, formal law enforcement by the police increases with the proportion of minority, poor, and young residents.*

Safety Consequences of Residential Segregation as Determinants of Police Behavior

As police professionalism entrenches deeply into the rhetoric of the war on crime, crime statistics become the measure of police effectiveness. Police budgets, manpower, administration, strategy, and tactics are repeatedly cited to explain and predict variations in the crime rate, and are also expected to substantially reduce it. Lamentably, crime better predicts police behavior than police behavior predicts crime. Yet strangely, there is still no *crime theory* of police behavior. No empirical attempt has been made to investigate the impact of community disorganization and moral anarchy on the interactions between police and citizens. Contentment with current explanations of crime and disorder has precluded further inquiry into the influence of crime on other important aspects of community affairs. In the macro-system of urban life, crime and delinquency are not only consequences of community decline and social inequality but also causes of social relations developed within the system.

The crime-fighting mandate requires police to restrain the crime-prone population and to react to higher levels of violence and disorder with the tools they are familiar with: situationally justified force and selectively enforced law. If reactions to illegal and predatory activities account for police authoritativeness, we can expect more proactive, coercive, and enforcement-oriented contacts between police and citizens in the neighborhoods with the most crime, fear, and incivility.

Crime is a two-way mirror in police–citizen relations. On the one hand, delinquency and disorder are the lenses through which the public judges the effectiveness and integrity of the police (Alpert & Dunham, 1988). People, guided by the media and their sense of general well-being, surround their police with praise or grievances according to the perceived safety of their neighborhoods. On the other hand, the amount of deviance is taken by the police as the ruler by which to gauge the moral worth of residents living in their jurisdictions (Muir, 1977). As criminality in a district worsens, police perceive offenders as social scum and victims as equally undeserving, in part because victims and offenders are often the same people or at least share similar lifestyle characteristics (Stark, 1987; Warner, 1997). Morally discredited people deserve what they get, and eventually "become ashamed to give their address as they know it will penalize them in the eyes of the police" (Body-Gendrot, 2000, p. 8). The police and the public understand and misunderstand and treat and mistreat each other in a territorial context knitted by the social relations of power, friendship, solidarity, and animosity they did not bring into being but are forced to reproduce day after day. Macro studies have examined the influence of threatening acts such as crime and riots (Jackson & Carroll, 1981), threatening people such as nonwhites and poor (Jackson, 1986; Jackson & Carroll, 1981; Jacobs, 1979), and threatening distributions of racial segregation and income inequality (Jackson & Carroll, 1981; Jackson, 1986) on police size and crime control activities. The evidence reveals the pervasiveness of differential sanctioning in which individuals whose particular lifestyles, histories, or group memberships signal a greater threat to society at large are more severely sanctioned, independent of the current charges.

When a social system is stratified, fear felt by the upper strata can quickly mutate into social processes that would eventually become an important ingredient in public policymaking and delivery (Tittle, 1994). Officials in charge of enacting and enforcing the law tend to implement the feelings of those they believe are most important and relevant. In the long run, these emotions will be expressed as deep-seated cultural themes, major institutions, and institutional processes. "Tough on crime" and "war on drugs" are just a couple of examples. Official rhetoric and public policy are exercised in a way consistent with these accepted social threats. Policing is not an exception. The identification with middle-class respectability makes many police officers react negatively to any groups whom they cannot place within it (Ericson, 1982), and proceed to elaborate recipe knowledge and organizational beliefs in accordance to their generally "sexist middle-class morality" in order to set acceptable responses (Manning, 1997).

Fear of crime, viewed from a macro-perspective, is a political phenomenon linked more to demographic heterogeneity and economic inequality than to crime itself. Stigmatized places where threatening people live are restricted from participating in the distributive exchanges of social commodities and relegated to become the main targets of retributive monitoring and sanctioning. Hence fear of crime is seen as a collective *symbolic response* to neighborhood heterogeneity and disorder (Bursik & Grasmick, 1993), and *symbolic assurance* becomes the most adequate strategic option to affect public belief about crime (Ferraro, 1995; Hening & Maxfield, 1978). If community residents feel intimidated by the strangeness, unfamiliarity, and indifference of their neighbors, then, this thesis argues, police can increase their visibility and accessibility to scare off violators of accepted conventions, to eventually re-create the desired uniformity and familiarity.

Police are a symbol of social stability and should be considered an essential aspect of the social structure. Emotionally and politically conservative, they rarely openly question the rationality of the body of laws they are to enforce. Conservatism, as an emotional predisposition, colors police occupational subculture with rigidity, proneness to categorize people and behaviors in clear-cut stereotypes, intolerance of unconventional innovations, and a penchant for the punishment of wrongdoers. As a political persuasion, conservatism stresses an individualistic, moralist view of social problems. Inadequate moral character rather than structural disjunction is attributed as the principal cause of poverty and crime. Just as poor and deviant individuals are less respectable than law-abiding middle-class citizens, socially marginal and morally disrupted communities are seen as in need of treatment. Events and conditions in the neighborhood environment not only indicate the probability of deviant disorder but also reveal the appropriate levels of proaction, coercion, and law to be applied.

Stigma and threat legitimize force and punishment. The continued occupation, or at least preoccupation, of the police with potential violence compels the development of a perceptual shorthand to identify certain kinds of people as symbolic assailants (Skolnick, 1994). The existence of symbolic assailants, in pursuit of law and order, with its hidden prejudices against groups of people as bad guys, justifies overaggressive tactics and provides the police with retrospective rationalization for seemingly excessive repression (Crank, 1998). The morally borderline neighborhoods are always viewed by the police as mysterious and unfathomable places marked by "the architecture of fear"—churches with no windows, restaurant counters protected by bulletproof glass and libraries with sealed windows and razor ribbon placed atop their roofs (Hearn, 1997). The stigma and perceived threat attached to areas with higher volumes of crime, fear, and incivility emphasize persistent poverty and imminent danger personified in the residents, especially the lower-class young black men who walk the street. Police maintain a fundamental aggressiveness or even hostility toward young blacks. In their worldview, the poor, the unemployed, the residentially unstable (many of whom are young blacks moving around urban ghettos) should not be out of work and indebted to society. Going to jail for a few days may be a reasonable way for them to repair their obligations and an efficient administration of summary justice without trial. "The master status assigned to black males undermines their ability to be taken for granted as law-abiding and civil participants in public places; young black males, particularly those who don the urban uniform (sneakers, athletic suits, gold chains, "gangster caps," sunglasses, and large portable radios or "boom boxes"), may be taken as the embodiment of the predator" (Anderson, 1990, p. 167).

Crime and policing result from the same ecological circumstances. Social control as the acting body of informal customs and formal laws defines what is correct conduct and prescribes the appropriate response to deviant behavior. Police control increases in neighborhoods where conformity to the mainstream standard of conventionality and respectability decrease. Thus, crime, fear of crime, and incivilities stimulate police control, which through aggressive coercion and enforcement of law reaffirms and strengthens the collective values and bourgeois identity that sustain the current social order. The intensity of police behavior flows then from areas with few public safety problems to places with deep social stigma and serious criminal threat. *Police authoritativeness is then also an inverse linear function of the moral standing of a neighborhood.* For the officers, it is easier to act more empathetically and informally toward someone they do not know very well if that person is found in a place hospitable to norms of civility. It is less difficult to refrain from imposing coercive or legal sanctions against a citizen if that person's trustworthiness is vouched for by stereotypes of respectability. Thus, *higher levels of incivility, fear of crime, and crime will generate a more proactive, coercive, and enforcement-oriented style of policing.*

The anticipated consequence is that to a degree all persons residing in high-crime areas need not in fact be criminals, but need merely to conform to the stereotype to become symbolic assailants. Since police forces are homogeneous in values and attitudes, and because their work routines put them in regular contact with ethnic and class groups different from themselves or their ideological patrons', the symbolic assailant may take on the characteristics of economically and ethnically marginal groups in their jurisdictions. If an honest citizen lives in a neighborhood heavily populated by criminals, just as the chances are high that he might be a criminal, so too are the chances high that he might be mistaken for one. The fewer the honest citizens in such an area, the more the police will be perceived by them as brutal, offensive, and unreasonable; and justifiably so, because the chances are greater that the police will treat honest citizens as criminals. For these law-abiding citizens, the inevitable message is the futility of honesty. Whether the proactive, coercive, and enforcement activities of the police are or are not truly appropriate depends on who is judging it: the police working in a high-crime area or the honest citizen living in such an area. Entire neighborhoods are then converted into potential threats.

THE ECOLOGY OF COMMUNITY RESPONSE

Demographic Patterns of Residential Segregation as Determinants of Community Response

Citizen Demeanor during Encounters

The first aspect of citizen support of police work is the observable behavior of citizens evidenced in concrete situations. What do citizens say and do to and for the police when they meet in face-to-face encounters? Acts of willing compliance and active collaboration enhance the effectiveness of police work and heighten police morale. Likewise, verbal and behavioral languages that refuse cooperation or deny respect to the officers invalidate police claims to status and cut them off from a vital source of information. How are these sequences of police–citizen interactions structured across neighborhoods in the metropolitan mosaic?

The relative position of a residential area in the core/periphery scale determines whether cooperation or conflict prevails in police–community interaction. *Citizen support is thus a direct function of the relative power status of a neighborhood.* Cooperation sprouts in places where there are ideological congruence and affective identification between police and the policed. Values establish what is regarded as desirable, fear decides who are the dangerous, and expectations dictate how the problems should be ironed out. Agreement on these issues is easier to reach in core communities characterized by ethnic homogeneity and family integrity, where effective control is maintained in part by residents themselves. Affluent areas are more likely to maintain community organizations that achieve unity and become effective and to have residents that participate more in local politics.[3] In their treatise on urban political economy, Logan and Molotch (1987) argue that the interrelated advantages of wealthy neighborhoods, not personal attributes of race, class, and profession memberships, contribute to the successful mobilization of financial and political resources, residential stability, and an array of organizations long in place. As a governmental institution, the police must take into consideration the opinion of the political community at large, which serves as the primary reference group of the police. Sensitive to the punitive power of public opinion, major police departments assign personnel specifically to the task of improving relations with such political superiors as mayors, city managers, and city councils, most of whom are drawn from upper and middle classes. Policing white and middle-class neighborhoods is made easier because of the shared primary culture that accords the general framework within which police and the public make sense of themselves, each other, their roles, and the social situation. Community trust and cooperation arise out of the view that police function as the "thin blue line" standing between order and chaos.

Peripheral communities of lower economic status with plentiful stocks of unemployed minority or immigrant youth develop cognitive and affective categories quite different from the mainstream approval of police role and functions. Subcultures form within specific age and ethnic groups, as well as within social classes, occupations, and lifestyles and provide the means for establishing group and neighborhood identity, and are discernible largely through stylistic expression, particular language, and demeanor. The relationship of a subculture to the so-called dominant culture is one of subordination and relative powerlessness. Subcultures that grow out of adversity and oppression are as likely to be predatory as subversive. Power relations are therefore an important dimension of the sociology of police–public relations. The urban police must interact with a number of different subcultures scattered across the city. The youth subculture and the minority and ethnic subcultures are of special significance to the police, whose own occupational subculture gravitates toward a strong in-group loyalty, political and moral conservatism, an emphasis on physical prowess and machismo, rugged individualism, and a sense of alienation from the citizens. The conflict between police occupational subculture and diverse urban subcultures underlies confrontational police–citizen contacts.

Youth, of whatever ethnic and class affiliation, are the pariah and, often, victims of discrimination in some respects. When processed by the criminal justice system, for example, their due process right is frequently denied. During their transition from childhood to adulthood, adolescents' attitudes toward authority and their proclivity toward delinquency often undermine police–youth interactions. One theme that accompanies the emergence of adolescence is the conflict between authority and freedom and conformity and independence. Concrete authority figures (such as the president and the police officer) represent the abstract construct of government in grade-school children's minds and are perceived as powerful, trustworthy, or even infallible (see Radalet &

Carter, 1994). There is a wealth of positive feeling for the government that extends to include law and police in the earlier stages of life. But this image gradually becomes strained as a child goes through the transformation of adolescence. The discovery that the police have the duty not only to capture bad people but also to punish them leads to mixed feelings and conflict between the new punitive and oppressive image and the old affective impression of benevolence and dependability. The change in attitudes toward authority introduces new tension into youth's relationship to the police; and juvenile–police encounters become more and more subject to the volatile status contest. Adventures that violate rules set by parents or societal authorities present an attractive opportunity to test their maturity, while the risk of getting caught after a rule violation and the thrill of getting away with it offer a chance to demonstrate to oneself and one's peers the attained independence and freedom. The rejection of much of what adolescents associate with family values, religious beliefs, and standards of dress and conduct helps them to establish an identity clearly distinguishable from that conferred by family membership.

Both sporadic delinquent escapades and more stable gang involvement provoke police-suppressing activities, often of proactive character. Even seemingly nondelinquent behaviors have the potential to increase the number of contacts between juveniles and the police. Hanging out on a street corner or cruising in cars produces complaints over the improper use of public spaces; public drinking and playing loud music clash with other people's expectations of public order and therefore prompt police control. Statistics reveal that youths between the ages of 11 and 18, more than any other age group, confront and are confronted by the police; over half of the arrests made by the police are of people under the age of 18 (Mayhall, Barker, & Hunter, 1995). A recent national survey also finds that teenagers are most likely to experience a police-initiated contact, whereas persons age 60 or older are the least likely (Greenfeld, Langan, & Smith, 1997). While the police routinely apply proactive coercion to manage juveniles, it is applied to those groups most distrusted and less deferential. Partly as a result of frequent bruises, teenagers feel more harassed by and demonstrate less deference to police officers and are tempted to give police a hard time because they would not be left alone (Bittner, 1976; Cox & Fitzgerald, 1996). The resentment at being hassled is often bitter enough to produce more serious reactions and ugly flare-ups and to cause many young people to grow up accepting hostility between police officers and kids as a natural fact of life. It is important to emphasize that not all adolescents are members of the youth subculture of rebellion; race- and class-disadvantaged youngsters are more likely to engage in belligerent, disrespectful, and remorseless exchanges with the police. The demeanor of juveniles living in more affluent areas is perceived as reasonably polite, respectful, honest about their involvement, remorseful, and willing to offer something in the way of restitution.

Minorities have traditionally figured most visibly in confrontations with the police in many urban localities (Greene, 2000; Lundman, 1996). Where there is not a high degree of consensus between police and the public, contacts between them are usually contentious (Walker, Spohn, & De Leon, 1996). For many black and immigrant residents of the inner city, the white world of prosperity and power are still remote and inaccessible. Although part of the criticism against the police by minorities is actually intended for the larger power structure that withholds economic, political, and cultural assets from them, collective memories of civil rights struggles, urban riots, and the intermittent flow of harrowing incidents of police brutality and misconduct keep reminding them of the complicity of the police apparatus in perpetuating their subjugation. The cognitive components of this subculture of discontent do not need to have a high degree of logical consistency or sophistication to achieve efficacy. Anger over discriminatory police harassment, impotence and restlessness resulting from perceived inadequate police protection, or bitterness over the constant use of belittling language by the police are sufficient to coin virulent feelings and behaviors during encounters with the police. The most devastating consequences of nurturing memories of oppression and vicarious experiences of police misconduct among members of poor minority neighborhoods is their permanent hostility toward police. The probability of open confrontation and passive resistance is likely to increase, as residents are more likely to question the inevitability of their plight in the current arrangement of power and wealth and challenge the legitimacy of police authority.

The more marginal a residential area is in relation to other districts, the more rancorous are police–citizen contacts and less cooperative are residents. A friendly demeanor and supportive actions toward police prevail in areas inhabited by white, middle-class families where the protection of property rights and the enforcement of dominant morality are consonant to their ideological identity and central to the preservation of a good life. Police views of social problems echo harmoniously with their perspectives and beliefs about the supreme goodness of an orderly society. The peace and tranquility of core neighborhoods reaffirm the image that residents are good neighbors capable of self-control and are interpreted as evidence of effective policing. Mainstream neighborhoods police themselves thus become friendly beats under control, in which the probability that police commands will be obeyed is higher. Unlike the rough confrontations with the police and the unique consciousness of subjugation that compose the score by which members of the social periphery sing, mutual respect and collaborative efforts at coproducing the desired order resound out of the harmonious duet.

Attitudes toward and Perception of the Police

Other than citizen performance in actual encounters, *attitudes and beliefs* toward the police role and services presents another set of indicators of community relations to police and policing. Although not readily accessible as is citizen conduct during encounters, attitudinal contour exerts profound influences on individual and group acceptance of police legitimacy not promptly amenable to planned change or interventions. Complex interactions between individual- and structural-level variables determine attitudes toward the police and ultimately the cooperation of citizens with the police.

At the individual level, the characteristics of citizens have consistently demonstrated their importance in shaping the public image of the police. Among them, race has been the demographic factor that has received the greatest scrutiny. Black citizens perceive that police provide their communities with inferior and inadequate services, fail their expectations, and respond slower to their calls (Arthur & Case, 1994; Furstenberg & Wellford, 1973; Hahn, 1971; Jacob, 1971; Webb & Marshall, 1992). When compared with whites, blacks are usually less satisfied with and more critical of the police (Decker, 1981; Reisig & Parks, 2000; Weitzer & Tuch, 1999). Ethnic and racial minorities historically have viewed themselves as the prime victims of police brutality and the police as oppressors of individual rights and freedoms (Flanagan & Vaughn, 1996). Unfortunately, their perception may not be too exaggerated. Let us take a look at the example of Los Angeles. Four thousand four hundred misconduct complaints were filed against the LAPD between 1987 and 1990; 41 percent of these were filed by blacks, who make up only 13 percent of the population (Skolnick & Fyfe, 1993). The ethnic composition of the neighborhood has been of particular importance in the formulation of attitudes toward the police (Schuman & Gruenberg, 1972; Weitzer, 1999). A large within-race variation in satisfaction and dissatisfaction was observed and this within-group difference was primarily explained by neighborhood residence. The specific neighborhood culture and the physical context of involuntary contacts with the police have also been cited as predictors of variations in the public image of the police (Jacob, 1971; Walker et al., 1972; Weitzer, 1999). Perceptions of injustice are strongest among residents of the least affluent black neighborhoods (Weitzer, 1999). Some researchers even conclude that public attitudes toward the police are less regulated by a person's race per se but rather by the neighborhood context in which that person is situated (Cao, Frank, & Cullen, 1996). As new immigrants are flooding into major cities, packing already disorganized neighborhoods, and the number of new minority groups is growing in this country we can expect that other socially and politically disadvantaged people, particularly the Hispanics, are likely to report similar experiences (e.g., Davis, 2000).

Experts in urban demography and culture have noticed more conflict between white, mainstream, and black ghetto cultural identities that arise from residential segregation (Massey & Denton, 1993). On the one hand, middle- and upper-class values idealize self-reliance, education, hard work, and postponement of gratification as a means to achieve respectability and success as reflected in material rewards and economic advancement in society. In pursuit of these goals, men seek employment and financial security before marrying and women believe that men will support the children they father. On the other hand, ghetto blacks grow up in isolated neighborhoods where joblessness is endemic, schools are poor, and violence (from both their peers and the police) is common (Wilson, 1997). Under these life conditions, education does not lead to economic emancipation and the prospect of finding a meaningful job to support a family is dim. A subculture of segregation thus emerges among dwellers of inner-city communities that provides them with defined identities and makes their lives more bearable. Values that are in opposition to the ideals of America's middle and upper classes evolve into an alternative worldview that makes sense of their perceptions and experiences of neglect and oppression by the status quo (Anderson, 1990; Massey & Denton, 1993). One enduring theme of this subculture of segregation is the war of resistance against the police. For more than a decade, young rappers have vividly depicted their own neighborhoods as war zones and the police as a repressive army in songs that carry dreadful names such as "The Killing Fields," "Anti-Nigga Machine," "Who Will Protect Me from You," "Endangered Species," and others (Kelly, 1994).

The second most unwavering correlate of negative attitudes toward police is young age. Young people, the "normal" troublemakers going through the crime-prone stages of their lives, generally report less favorable views of police officers who closely monitor their activities. Youngsters give police the lowest ratings for performance competence and impartiality of all age groups and rate the quality of police service poorer than others (Boggs & Galliher, 1975; Hurst & Frank, 2000; Walker et al., 1972). Overseas studies also agree on this point and dig somewhat deeper into the problem. Youth from southern England display a polarized view of the police: depending on their conceptualizations of how police power is used, they perceive the police as either "guardians" or "bullies" (Waddington & Braddock, 1991). Young blacks, unlike their white and Asian counterparts, have virtually no conception of police as "guardians." A Portuguese study of college students reveals that the political ideology young people adhered to is important in determining their view of police coercion. Radical students feel less tolerant and more antagonist toward police use of force (Vala, Monteiro, & Leyens, 1988). Both in America and in Europe, relations between teenagers and the police are often strained because youth frequently feel harassed and may not demonstrate the deference to which officers feel entitled during encounters. Police officers may treat rude conduct as indicators of improper socialization and harbingers of delinquent misconduct. A British home secretary has even described their youths as "dangerous brutes with an aimless lust for violence who are one of the main factors undermining the peace of British society" (Fielding, 1991, p. 111). However, not all ages are this feared by the authorities. When there is trouble between the police and the youth, it is more likely to involve older adolescents who are going through a period of turmoil and change (Cox & Fitzgerald, 1996). Encounters with these older juveniles constitute a significant portion of police contact with citizens, hence the improvement of police–juvenile relations is an integral part of broader police community relations. Moreover, the image that adults forge of the police is partly influenced by the relationship they believe to exist between their children and the police. Thus, as a rule of thumb, the public image of the police improves whenever and wherever the supply of youngsters diminishes significantly.

The impact of socioeconomic status on people's perceptions and evaluations of police is also very important, albeit somewhat more equivocal. Although some earlier pieces of research suggest that respondents with absolute low income were either more dissatisfied with their specific encounters with police, tended to give the lowest evaluations of police performance, or both (Jacob, 1971; Schuman & Gruenberg, 1972; Walker et al., 1972), a few other individual-level replications indicate that the social status of the respondent was not necessarily related to attitudes (Boggs & Galliher, 1975; Worrall, 1999). But a more recognizable picture emerged when data were collapsed and comparisons among different groups were made. The urban minority poor had had the least favorable attitudes toward the police compared to rural, semi-rural, and urban nonpoor (Albrecht & Green, 1977). Moreover, when the territorial clustering of social classes is taken into account, an even clearer pattern surfaced. The statistically powerful influence of contextual factors such as "area income score" and "neighborhood culture" in these studies led to the conclusions that a strong influence of personal wealth was not evident and that the importance of neighborhood-level variables should be emphasized over that of individual-level measurement of social class (Decker, 1981; Weitzer, 1999, 2000). Residents of neighborhoods characterized by concentrated disadvantage express significantly less satisfaction with the police (Reisig & Parks, 2000). For poor black communities, it is double jeopardy, as both race and class characteristics place them in an extremely powerless position. In fact, more benign style of policing in the middle-class black neighborhoods led to better perceptions of police treatment in these areas than in the lower-class black communities (Weitzer, 2000). When differences in attitudes toward social deviance, the police, and the law were studied in 343 urban neighborhoods in Chicago, it was found that neighborhood class status further affected perceptions of crime and justice among residents of minority communities (Sampson & Bartusch, 1999). Blacks were much more cynical toward law and its enforcement mainly because they were more likely to live in disadvantaged neighborhoods. Recent evaluations of community policing also found that citizen expectations are least favorable in the poorest jurisdictions, and that police–citizen meetings tend to take on an adversarial style in the same disadvantaged districts (Skogan & Hartnett, 1997).

Overall, positive attitudes toward and higher evaluations of police are an inverse function of the relative marginality of a neighborhood. The more peripheral a neighborhood is, the less likely are its residents to have a positive view of police. Citizens living in homogeneous middle-class communities perceive the police as people's servants accomplishing, with dedication and sacrifice, the difficult and valuable task of preventing the outbreak of the Hobbesian war of all against all. Contrarily, people left behind in peripheral neighborhoods do not see themselves as residual population and experience police as merely the coercive arm of a disinterested and unresponsive executive government to strengthen the legality of current arrangement of domination and subordination. The discrepancy in perceptions of the police between the core and the periphery suggests how each party's collective view may be only a partial and distorted impression of the reality. Although only an impression, its political repercussion can far exceed the realm of public safety and impact on the stability of the system.

Safety Consequences of Residential Segregation as Determinants of Community Response

Both the police and the policed often forget to acknowledge that crime, fear of crime, and incivility mediating between them are embedded in structural contexts and a wider political economy that stratifies places of residence. Take the case of violent crime. Research has consistently shown that the community can insulate or protect people from violence or, conversely, can create or enhance risk. As the gap grows between neighborhoods in terms of the quality of life and life chances, the likelihood of violence increases dangerously in the most disadvantaged areas (Blau & Blau, 1982; Sampson, Raudenbush, & Earls, 1997). Societal neglect engenders violence and invariably damages police–community relations. Wilson (1968) noted that the citizen and the patrolman form an unfavorable impression of each other in high-crime areas where violence is common. A Chicago study also found that minority citizens appear more dissatisfied with police services largely because they are disproportionately concentrated in impoverished and dangerous neighborhoods (Sampson & Bartusch, 1999). However, even in neighborhoods where the rate of violence is high, attitudes toward the police are similar among groups, suggesting that residents' estrangement from the police is better explained by unsafe neighborhood conditions than individual characteristics of citizens. Police are obligated to shoulder the anger and hostility emanated from the unequal distribution of victimization risks and the public thinks that their precarious residential conditions are contrived by police negligence or incompetence. But when the patrol area is a middle-class neighborhood where crime is relatively rare and has mostly to do with stolen property, both the police and the public are less likely to be and act suspicious. In this context, safety against crime and freedom from fear of victimization are promises kept only for the better-off in respectable neighborhoods, but prove to be empty slogans for the powerless struggling in stigmatized areas.

There is an experiential component in the evaluation of police behavior. Prior personal contacts with the police can influence the nature of subsequent judgments of law enforcement. For example, victims of residential burglary reported more negative attitudes than their nonvictim counterparts, primarily due to a lower image of police (Homant, Kennedy, & Fleming, 1984). Victimization experiences erode people's confidence in the ability of the police to fulfill their crime control mandate of providing effective protection. Victimization need not be actual or personal to be influential in people's assessment of police services; vicarious experiences through the process of social network contagion can be equally consequential. In New York City, individuals with a family member who had been previously arrested provided lower evaluations of the NYPD (Davis, 1990). The aggregation of victimization experiences in high crime and high disorder neighborhoods is certainly counterproductive to public satisfaction with police services. There is also a direct influence of ecological factors in the formation of public perceptions. Perceptions of a "clean neighborhood and nice people" and a "lack of crime and drugs" greatly improved residents' assessment of New York police services. For poor attitudes toward police, the two most frequent reasons given were "too much crime" and "too much drugs," whereas for fair attitudes, the most frequent reasons given were "low crime," "low drugs," and "the right neighbors." Demographics, crime, support for police, and place of residence are causally intertwined.

Inner-city areas, where the concentration of poverty underpins the linkage between weak labor force attachment and crime, have witnessed the legitimacy of police actions being replaced by illegal services provided by criminal organizations or local gangs (Hagan, 1994). In these communities, the withdrawal of economic and social resources has forced a process of recapitalization that involves the rapid expansion of deviant service industries so often targeted by police crackdowns and market disruption operations. Ghetto-based gangs and criminal organizations can successfully transform into active sponsors of community welfare and order. Sudhir A. Venkatesh (1997) argues that residents receive street drug dollars and gang mediation/protection services in impoverished communities because of official neglect. The evisceration of public institutions caused by cutbacks in federal and state funding paves the way for the increasing acceptance of street gang resources by residents; the erosion of police authority is gradually replaced by the growing legitimacy of street gangs, drug dealers, and pimps who give back to the community by providing economic opportunities and protective services. A neighbor in one such neighborhood reported: "Yeah, right, [Saints] make our lives miserable, but if we piss them off, police ain't gonna come 'round here and help us out. And, shit, I gotta tell you, that most of the time is nice, 'cause they make sure I don't get robbed up in here, they walk through the buildings like ... police never did that!" (Venkatesh, 1997, p. 103).

As the moral reliability of the neighborhood declines residents believe there are fewer trustworthy people among them, and fewer people who can be relied upon to uphold common values. When the swarms of vice providers and consumers reach an accommodation with beleaguered communities, police begin to have a weakened sense of identification with the neighborhood and become contemptuous and dismissive of its worthless residents. Community decay deepens as cooperative activities dwindle and the responsibility for monitoring young people and strangers falls upon the patrol officers. Residents are dissatisfied with poor police protection and low-quality services and long for the same policing service as any other community, but are instead perceived by the police as indifferent toward crime problems and unwilling to work with law enforcement to deal with disorder and deviance. As long as the police keep on selling the image of crime fighters to the public, but are not able to reduce the amount of crime, the lack of public support in disorderly communities will persist. The anger of poor and minority residents can be seen as a sign that they have been completely turned against their insincere public administrators.

It is not a mere coincidence that when grassroots movements or collective actions are initiated by neighborhood residents, police are usually approached as a target of protest rather than an external ally for empowerment (Duffee, Fluellen, & Roscoe, 1999). The absence of political articulation and empathic connection between police rhetoric and grassroots expectations engender deep cynicism and learned pessimism in the neighborhoods that are most in need of greater and more effective police protection. Therefore, I hypothesize that *citizen support is a direct function of the neighborhood's moral standing.*

SUMMARY

The goal of this ecological model is to theorize on the interactions between policing styles and citizen response in light of the political economy of places and the resulting residential differentiation of American society. The convergence of specific needs, values, and types of political influence in an area brings forth a specific neighborhood culture and a particular community climate that encourages and determines the mode of police–citizen relations.

The demographic composition of a neighborhood defines its own relational distance to the nucleus of social power. The official mandate and the formal legitimacy granted to the police by the sociopolitical establishment has led the police to identify ideologically, affectively, and behaviorally with the interests and worldviews of the ethnic majority and socioeconomic mainstream. Communities enjoying political partnership and communion with the police see law enforcement forces as friendly armies of protection, while politically excluded districts become prime candidates for heavy-handed police control characterized by proaction, coercion, and enforcement of law. The selective application of proaction, coercion, and law enforcement by the police is backed by a nesting of reserve sources of legitimizing power set up in such a way that police authority can always overcome opposition and contest from the periphery. The chief significance of the legitimacy of differential policing for the metropolitan system is that it makes the flow of state coercion predictable and beneficial to the enfranchised constituents of the police. Therefore, the first hypothesis concerning police behavior postulates that:

Police authoritativeness is positively correlated with the social power status of a neighborhood. The ecology of police work is not only defined by the ethnic, class, and age structure of the community but also by the degree of moral chaos that can be found in the area. The rhetoric of a war on crime chisels the self-definition of police, who market themselves as soldiers of law and order to the public. No matter how unsubstantial law enforcement is in the police's daily workload, preventing crimes and catching criminals will always be its formal *raison d'être*. Demands for police action to impart symbolic justice are generated by the crime, fear, and disorder experienced by the community. Therefore, police services respond to the social stigma and criminal threats that a neighborhood displays and allocates proaction, coercion, and enforcement of law accordingly. Thus, I hypothesize:

Police authoritativeness is positively correlated with the moral standing of a neighborhood. Face-to-face interactions generate perceptual habits, which can, in time, condition the way police and citizens respond to each other in subsequent encounters. Shared images and expectations of the police are indicative of the community's stake in the social order. The quality of public support depends essentially upon the extent to which the ideological predilections and material interests of the police and the community tend to converge. Residents of marginalized districts are excluded from the political debate and are less likely to join community organizations or to participate in civic activities; their demands are rarely given attention just as their problems can hardly evoke empathetic understanding from citizens of higher social positions. Backing for the enforcers of law and order comes mainly from the authors of such law and beneficiaries of such order; but for people left out in the social peripheries, police services represent another form of malign neglect by the apathetic authorities. Thus, I hypothesize:

Positive citizen demeanor and attitudes are directly correlated with the social power status of a neighborhood. Not only do the police use the level of deviance to gauge the moral respectability of the policed, but also citizens rely on the amount of crime and disorder to evaluate police effectiveness. Police responsiveness and efficacy are equated with lower levels of crime and fear, which in turn influence people's attitudes toward police, during and outside police–citizen encounters. Therefore, the fourth hypothesis states:

Positive citizen demeanor and attitudes are directly correlated with the moral standing of a neighborhood. Power standing and moral status are not attributes of a neighborhood; it denotes a position in the metropolitan system of relations. The meaning of policing, like all aspects of urban politics, depends on the overarching political economy of places. In the police–community milieu, core communities are privileged because their occupants infuse the beliefs and concerns that nurture the political machine, and their lifestyles inspire respect. Peripheral neighborhoods have the opposite set of assets: subcultures dissociated from the mainstream, demands in conflict with the interests of the elite or the values of the middle classes, and, above all, alternative lifestyles that cause social stigma and perceptions of threat. These people are directly affected by proactive, coercive, and legalistic police practices but do not participate in the process of order maintenance. Here, police deliver "street justice" by meting out punishment with words, handcuffs, or nightsticks without bothering about charges or proving guilt or innocence. When police decide to improve the quality of life with formal enforcement, arrests and court actions cause repercussions that go beyond the punishment of a guilty party. Male citizens are taken away for incarceration and families of gang members or drug sellers are evicted by housing authorities or landlords because of their criminal relatives. Instead of enforcing peace, the delivery of "street justice" and the formal application of law by the police exacerbate resentment and hostility with equal force. For those trapped in their own neighborhoods, geography becomes their destiny.

Residential segregation produces and requires a fragmented system of policing, anywhere, anytime. The more social groups are spatially isolated from each other, the more unequal are the nature and quality of police–citizen relations among different neighborhoods.

NOTES

1. In order to keep the theory a structural view of social control, only demographic characteristics of residential segregation and the resulting patterns of crime and disrepute are considered as the exogenous determinants of police–community relations. It does not deny, however, that at the individual encounter level, police behavior and citizen demeanor interact in a reciprocally reinforcing way. A great deal of research has documented that patrol officers and citizens cause the actions and reactions in each other. Nevertheless, an ecological theory would assert that such causal interactions occur in, and are strongly shaped by, a particular structural context that cannot be easily altered by deliberate, unilateral efforts. In the aggregate, certain types of police–citizen street interactions dominate in neighborhoods with determined characteristics; these aggregate trends, again, are more causally related to macro forces than to micro events.

2. Private policing is becoming a popular commodity that is cherished by the American overclass. The control of major economic and political decision-making processes allows the rich to separate from the larger society, standing above the class structure and in isolation from public institutions such as municipal police. An explanation of the behavior of private police in these exclusive jurisdictions should be set apart and deserves an examination of its own.

3. Sidney Verba and Norman H. Nie (1972) did an elaborate statistical analysis of the way in which people participate in politics and came up with six forms of participation that are characteristic of six different kinds of citizens. About one-fifth (22%) of the population is completely inactive: they rarely vote, they do not get involved in organizations, and they probably do not even talk about politics very much. These inactives typically have little education and low incomes, are relatively young, and many of them are black. At the opposite extreme are the complete activists, constituting about one-tenth of the population (11%), who are highly educated, have high incomes, and tend to be middle-aged. They work in political campaigns, join civic organizations, contribute money to candidates, write letters to members of Congress, and even talk politics with friends and neighbors often.

CHAPTER 4

Data, Variables, and Analytical Strategy

I have articulated the basic concepts and causal relationships that would structure an ecological theory of police–citizen relations in previous chapters. I now focus on the crucial bridging of this theory to the real world. The process of linking abstract concepts to empirical indicators involves an explicit, organized plan for classifying the data in accordance with the formulated propositions. Multiple empirical evaluations, with a large number of specifications and assumptions in the empirical model, are essential to the evaluation of a formal theory. Recognizing that a single empirical study will never make conclusive statements about the value of a theoretical model, the empirical testing of this ecological theory has a very limited yet important goal, which is to assess the empirical viability of the hypotheses formulated. Relationship predictions that forecast how police–citizen interactions will change in relation to neighborhood context become empirically viable when corroborated by data. If a few unanticipated findings emerge, auxiliary hypotheses will have to be formulated to incorporate and account for existing anomalies. In order to develop into an established model capable of explaining historical facts, interpreting present situations, and predicting future trends, this ecological theory will have to withstand a large number of evaluative challenges using both natural and experimental data, multiple methodologies, and controls for alternative explanations.

The PSS data were originally collected to examine the delivery of police services in selected neighborhoods of Rochester, St. Louis, and Tampa–St. Petersburg. Information came from three sources: (1) observational data of general police shifts, (2) police officers' encounters observed during selected shifts, and (3) telephone interviews conducted with citizens who were involved in police–citizen encounters or who had requested police services during observed shifts. In this chapter, I will describe the operational transformations used to produce variables and the analytical procedures to be used in testing the empirical viability of the main argument of an ecological theory, which forecasts that policing fragments in discernible patterns following the structural segregation of residential neighborhoods in American metropolises.

MEASURES OF MAJOR CONCEPTS

Several major concepts underlie the ecological model of police–community relations. The key dimensions of police authoritativeness are proaction, enforcement, and coercion; likewise, citizen response to police services entails both observable demeanors during encounters and stable beliefs and attitudes toward police. Demographic structure and behavioral culture intersect and produce the social context in which police and citizens interact with each other. On the one hand, socioeconomic status, ethnic identity, and life-cycle characteristics determine the residential segregation and core/periphery stratification of neighborhoods; on the other hand, the amounts of crime and incivility make up the moral respectability of the neighborhood. Measures of demographic and crime characteristics provide proxy indicators of power stratification and moral hierarchy. There were three different units of observation in the original data: the shift, the encounter, and the citizen involved in the encounter. These individual-level measures were aggregated to form neighborhood-level averages, percentages, and rates. The blending of self-report information (citizen surveys) with observational data (encounters and patrol shifts) produces a comprehensive statistical description of the theoretical constructs and might minimize the random errors associated with each one of the data sources.

A total of 22 empirical indicators have been selected, 12 of them measure the six key dimensions of neighborhood structure, while the remaining 10 reflect different aspects of police–citizen interactions. Table 4.1 provides a summary of the descriptive statistics for the collection of empirical indicators.

Neighborhood Socioeconomic Status

Three aggregate measures (household income, education, and home ownership) are included to reflect a neighborhood's standing within the metropolitan system of social power.

Data, Variables, and Analytical Strategy

Table 4.1
Description of Variables

Name	Mean	Std. Dev.	Description
SES			
FAMINCOM	2.75	.86	Average family income indexed score.
EDUCATE	12.08	1.42	Average # of years of schooling.
HOMEOWN	49.21	16.73	% households that own their residence
Race & Ethnicity			
NONWHITE	29.30	34.89	% respondents self-identified as blacks or Hispanics.
Life-Cycle			
JUVENILE	44.02	10.30	% households with teenage youths.
AVERAGE	35.90	5.74	Average age of all members of household.
Crime			
CRIMERUN	245.45	109.75	# of radio-dispatched runs involving crime in progress per 100 8-hour shifts.
PRPCRIME	56.59	9.35	% respondents reported being victims of theft, larceny, burglary or car-theft.
VIOCRIME	8.78	9.66	% respondents reported being victims of robbery, assault or rape.
Incivility			
DISRDRUN	107.76	68.26	# radio-dispatched runs involving incidents of disorder per 100 8-hour shifts.
INCIVILTY	495.02	388.07	# enc. involving drinking, nuisance, loitering, vagrancy, & peddling x 100 shifts.
Police Proaction			
SECCHECK	48.24	81.69	# encounters in which police conducted residential checks per 100 shifts.
OVSTOPPD	160.65	78.09	# encounters in which police made on-view stops of citizens per 100 shifts.
Police Enforcement			
ARSTRATE	23.48	16.48	# encounters in which officers made non-warrant arrests per 100 shifts.
REPTRATE	170.61	70.06	# encounters in which officers wrote incident reports per 100 shifts.
Police Coercion			
VERBRATE	14.53	15.85	# encounters in which officers shouted or threatened force per 100 shifts.
PHYSRATE	26.04	19.10	# encounters in which officers used force or handcuffs per 100 shifts.
Citizen Demeanor			
CURSFITE	27.24	17.72	# encounters in which citizens cursed or fought officers per 100 shifts.
GAVEHELP	390.54	80.27	# encounters in which citizens volunteered information or gave description.
Citizen Attitudes			
MISTRUST	5.07	3.38	% respondents who knew of someone mistreated by the police.
RATEPOL	2.69	.39	Average rating of police delivering what people wanted.

Household Income

There is a stable split between the incomes and life chances of those in and those out of employment, between those in low-income employment and those in middle- and upper-income employment. Access, or lack of it, to gainful employment produces and sustains inequalities. In this study, the mean indexed family income score from responding households is calculated for each neighborhood (mean = 2.75, standard deviation = .86).

Education

Educational attainment is partly a function of income and schooling but also, and especially in the early years, a function of teaching inside the family home. Possessors of cultural capital use it to occupy preferred job positions and to secure their political influence through the command of language, symbols, and artifacts of the dominant culture. The average number of years of schooling completed by survey respondents is estimated for each neighborhood (mean = 12.08, standard deviation = 1.42). This operational choice is based on the fact that success in the educational system is largely dictated by the extent to which neighborhood residents have absorbed and been assimilated into the dominant culture.

Home Ownership

A dwelling is likely to be most households' single biggest investment. While renting is usually viewed as the tenure of last resort for the poor, an owner-occupied home is more than a dwelling: it is property, a source of future income, and a means of wealth creation. Homeownership is thus both a sign of economic emancipation and a reason for increased interest in politics, much of which is a way of maintaining or inflating property values and fighting against things or people that depress local property values. The percentage of owner-occupied dwellings in the neighborhood (mean = 49.21, standard deviation = 16.73) has been obtained from the citizen survey to provide an additional indicator of the neighborhood SES.

Race and Ethnicity

The racial and ethnic composition of a neighborhood is associated with specific roles and attitudes toward police. One measure of neighborhood racial composition is incorporated: the nonwhite population.

Nonwhite Population

Black and Hispanic residents are grouped under this rubric. A large part of the police clientele (both as victims and offenders), black and Hispanic citizens are numerically inferior and are in a weaker political position compared with national averages. In addition to their quantitative and political disadvantages, blacks and Hispanics have lower mean incomes and suffer higher unemployment rates. These economic and social hardships increase in neighborhoods with higher concentrations of minority residents. I use the percentage of survey respondents self-identified as black or Hispanic in each neighborhood (mean = 29.30, standard deviation = 34.89) as a key demographic variable to predict variations in police–community relations.

Life-cycle

Some biographical stages strain relations with authorities while others favor respect toward and dependence on police services. Biographical events of different significance are unevenly distributed across neighborhoods.

Teenage Population

Youths represent a major age segment of specialized police services. They require extra surveillance from law enforcement authorities, and at the same time, are more vulnerable to more types of abuse than any other age segments. The exclusion from both active economic production and political participation underscore their subordinate status. The percentage of households with teenage youths (mean = 58.41, standard deviation = 19.56) provides an important proxy for the level of social power a neighborhood surrenders through the size of its youth population.

Average Household Age

The average age of all household members (mean = 35.90, standard deviation = 5.74) is included as an additional empirical indicator of the life-cycle characteristic of a neighborhood.

Neighborhood Crime

Three variables are constructed to operationalize the conceptual construct of "crime." Although each one of these crime measures may contain specific bias, utilizing three different sources allows a more accurate picture than would have been possible with only one source.

Crime Known to the Police

Offenses reported to the authorities constitute one of the most widely used crime data sources. Crime counts are heavily based on those crimes made known to the police, missing incidents ignored or judged as not worthy of reporting by citizens. Despite its weakness, crime known to the police is more likely to have a direct influence on police behavior than the dark figures. The number of radio-dispatched runs involving actual or potential crimes in progress or other crimes reported per 100 8-hour shifts (mean = 245.45, standard deviation = 109.75) is an adequate choice.

Property Victimization

Since many crimes go unreported, asking about citizens' experiences as victims of crime becomes a reasonable alternative. The PSS victimization survey includes both reported as well as unreported crime. The percentage of respondents self-reporting having been victims of burglary, theft, larceny, and auto theft at home, on their blocks, or in their neighborhoods during the year before (mean = 56.59, standard deviation = 9.35) is calculated to represent victimization.

Violent Crime

Violent offenses are a particular kind of crime that pose an inherent danger in police work. A high rate of violence not only makes police work more hazardous, but also predisposes officers to become more ready to resort to violence to defend themselves or to exact compliance. The violent crime rate is based on the percentage of survey respondents who had been victims of robbery, assault, rape, or burglary (committed or attempted) during the year prior to the interview (mean = 8.78, standard deviation = 9.66).

Incivility and Disorder

Social incivility and disorder encompass those social behaviors that convey the erosion of conventionally accepted norms and values. Two indicators of incivility and disorder are constructed from two different sources, one from the general shift dataset, and another from observational encounter data.

Incivility Known to the Police

The first indicator is a measure of the amount of incivility and disorder that was reported to the authorities and was considered by the dispatcher as accurate and serious enough to warrant police intervention. The raw number of incidents are aggregated and standardized to obtain the number of radio-dispatched runs dealing with disorderly conduct or other disturbances per 100 eight-hour shifts (mean = 107.76, standard deviation = 68.26) for each neighborhood.

Incivility Dealt by the Police

Next, the number of encounters involving public nuisance, drunks, disorderly conduct, vagrancy, loitering, noise disturbance, or peddling per 100 shifts is calculated (mean = 495.02, standard deviation = 388.07) as an alternative measure.

Police Proaction

The legitimate capacity to intervene in citizens' private disputes without invitation defines the ultimate authority of the police to establish law and order in people's lives. Two variables are constructed to reflect police discretion to initiate uninvited activities toward citizens or their property: residential security checks and on-view nontraffic stops.

Residential Security Checks

Patrol officers are constrained from conducting intrusive monitoring of private premises unless they have reason to believe that crime has been or is about to be committed. Ecological hypotheses anticipate that both suspicion of crime and eagerness to protect private properties are unevenly distributed across space. The number of officer-initiated residential security checks per 100 eight-hour shifts (mean = 48.24, standard deviation = 81.69) is estimated to reflect police tendency to initiate actions.

On-view Nontraffic Stops

Although conducting traffic stops is a prototype of police proaction, it does not trigger the stigmatization and disruption of life routines that an enforcement of penal law produces. In order to better describe police proactive use of penal sanction, it is necessary to eliminate traffic activities and focus on those stops aimed at the discovery of potential criminal offenses or offenders. Thus, the number of encounters in which police made on-view stops of citizens per 100 shifts (mean = 160.65, standard deviation = 78.09) is included.

Police Enforcement of Law

Police discretion has been one of the most decisive factors in determining whether the formal criminal process will be initiated. A police decision in a given situation typically raises difficult questions: Was a conscious decision made to take the action that has been taken? By what standard? And subject to what review? The aggregation of these individual decisions forms the prevalent style of police service delivery. Arrest and official report writing are used to operationalize this aspect of police work.

Arrests

An arrest is the most representative exercise of police authority. The number of police encounters resulting in nonwarrant arrests is used to gauge police arrest behavior per 100 shifts (mean = 23.48, standard deviation = 16.48).

Report Writing

The filing of incident reports leaves a permanent record of offenses and often results in offenders entering the criminal justice system, which may prompt other follow-up actions. The decision not to write a report and the related decision to "mark" an incident or citizen can eventually influence other agencies in the system whose actions are in turn strongly influenced by police reports. The number of reactive encounters in which officers made official written reports per 100 eight-hour shifts is estimated (mean = 170.61, standard deviation = 70.06).

Police Coercion

There are literally dozens of verbal and physical tactics police are trained to employ to maintain control and preserve authority. The use of hostile language and handcuffs against citizens is included as empirical indicators.

Use of Commanding Language

The verbalization of requests for compliance by the police is generally deemed more coercive than symbolic displays of badges, batons, and marked patrol cars. Intonation, vocal quality, and vocabulary selection reveal the level of subordination encountered citizens are thought to hold. Verbal coercion is operationalized as the number of encounters in which officers intimidated citizens by shouting at or bellowing at them, or threatening to use force against them per 100 shifts (mean = 14.53, standard deviation = 15.85).

Use of Physical Force

Threats of applying physical force are communicated to gain subjects' submission by instilling fear in them. This tactic prepares police officers psychologically for the escalation of hostility, yet at the same time seeks to put an end to low-level citizen resistance. Actual physical force is used when no consensus is achieved and the contentious situation is out of control. The number of encounters in which officers used handcuffs or physical force to subdue citizen(s) per 100 shifts is computed for each neighborhood (mean = 26.04, standard deviation = 19.10).

Citizen Demeanor

Police–citizen encounters are a special kind of human contact in which police officers participate with known legal authority, while civilian actors are likely to enter the scene in varying states of emotional agitation: embarrassment, lack of poise, distraction, anger, or fear. Four measures of citizen demeanor during encounters (cursing officers, refusing to answer questions, volunteering information, and describing suspects) are aggregated.

Cursing and Fighting Officers

Citizens denying police legitimacy can sometimes indulge in insults to or fights with officers. Although rare in absolute terms, open challenges to police authorities during encounters are astonishingly explicit and frequent in some neighborhoods. The number of encounters in which citizen(s) cursed or fought officer(s) per 100 eight-hour shifts is estimated to gauge this extreme form of antagonism (mean = 27.74; standard deviation = 17.72).

Citizen Cooperation

Police solve crimes and capture criminals with information supplied by victims, witnesses, bystanders, concerned residents, or even suspects themselves. Fortunately, willing alliance with and the active assistance to encountered police officers are more common than unpleasant confrontations. The numbers of encounters in which citizens volunteered information or provided a description of crime suspects to officer(s) per 100 eight-hour shifts (mean = 390.54; standard deviation = 80.27) is used.

Citizen Attitudes

Given that it requires much less effort to think stereotypically than to think in individual terms, citizens' perceptions of police work are thoroughly weighted by cultural categories accepted as part of the ethnic, social class, and age group affiliations expedited by residential segregation. Two survey measures of citizen attitudes (police mistreatment of citizens and satisfaction with police services) are constructed.

Perceived Police Mistreatment

Even though prejudices and discrimination may not be as pervasive among police officers as among other occupational groups, they are more deleterious and destabilizing because of the authority to use violence and to deprive citizens of their freedom vested in the police. The percentage of respondents who knew someone mistreated by the police during the year prior to the survey is estimated for each neighborhood (mean = 5.07; standard deviation = 3.38).

Citizen Satisfaction

How content are neighborhood residents with the police services they receive? Answers to this question are of concern to the police because an evaluation of police services transcends the ephemeral nature of face-to-face encounters. Although most people are satisfied with the job done by the police most of the time, great dissatisfaction exists in some areas. The mean household rating of overall quality of police services for each neighborhood on a scale of 1 to 5 is estimated (mean = 2.69; standard deviation = .39).

DATA REDUCTION: FACTOR ANALYSIS

The comparatively small size of the sample (n = 60 neighborhoods) creates a serious problem to the multivariate analysis of PSS data. Since

Table 4.2
Factor Loadings for the Four Factors Used as Independent Variables

	SES Factor	Life-Cycle Factor	Crime Factor	Incivility Factor
Household income	.93392	-----	-----	-----
Education	.94883	-----	-----	-----
Home ownership	.65476	-----	-----	-----
Teenage population	-----	.94868	-----	-----
Average age	-----	-.94868	-----	-----
Crime known to police	-----	-----	.87838	-----
Property crime	-----	-----	.81720	-----
Violent crime	-----	-----	.50900	-----
Incivility known to police	-----	-----	-----	.93779
Incivility dealt by police	-----	-----	-----	.93779
Eigenvalue	*2.20119*	*1.87274*	*1.69845*	*1.75897*
Percent of variance	*73.4%*	*62.4%*	*56.6%*	*87.9%*

in multiple regression analysis, the degrees of freedom for the estimates equals the sample size n minus the number of parameters (df = $n - (k + 1)$), the inclusion of all 15 neighborhood variables will reduce the degrees of freedom by more than one-fifth (df = 60 − (15 + 1)). When so many degrees of freedom are lost, it becomes practically impossible for the individual predictors to attain statistical significance. Furthermore, when too many variables are added to the model, the standard error of the estimates of the regression coefficients tends to inflate in value, thus hindering efforts at making inferences. In theory, a perfect specification requires virtually an infinite number of variables, for the social world is co-determined by an unknown number of elements. However, the more predictors there are in the model, the less dependable are the coefficients. Regression with fewer parameters might be desirable for this reason (Achen, 1984).

In order to solve this problem, factor analysis is repeatedly performed to reduce the 11 highly correlated individual indicators of neighborhood structure to four statistically more independent factors that accurately mirror the theorized five dimensions of neighborhood structure (Table 4.2). No factor is extracted for race. The percentage of the nonwhite population is used as the race parameter in the analysis. Principal component analysis provides the solution. All factor loadings are statistically relevant (at least .60).

Average household income, education, and homeownership are positively loaded on the SES factor (.93392, 94883, and .65476, respectively), indicating that the higher the SES score, the higher the SES standing of a neighborhood. As for the life-cycle scale, the teenage population is positively, and the average age of household members negatively, loaded on the life-cycle factor (.94868 and −.94868), showing a correspondence between a higher life-cycle score with a higher number of households with teenage youths and a lower average age of neighborhood residents. Crimes known to the police, property crime, and violent crime are all positively loaded on crime factor (.87838, .87120, and .50900, respectively), which shows that a higher crime score is correlated with a higher proportion of respondents being victims of property and violent crime as well as radio-dispatched patrols involving crimes in progress in the neighborhood. Finally, both dispatches and actual encounters involving incidents of loitering, vagrancy, and loud noise are positively loaded on the incivility factor (.93779 and .93779), which should be interpreted as a direct gauge of the level of disorder and incivility in the neighborhood.

Data reduction allows the empirical testing of ecological hypotheses to conform to the basic rule in statistical modeling that the number of predictors incorporated should not exceed one-tenth of the collection of cases comprising the sample (Agresti & Finlay, 1986). The reduction of independent and dependent variables to a handful of highly interpretable factors has safeguarded the principle of parsimony for good model building, which recommends that no more parameters be introduced than are necessary to adequately represent the basic form of the relationships. Simple and compact models are easier to understand and interpret.

METHODS FOR ANALYZING RELATIONSHIPS

Since all measures used in the testing of the model were continuous variables measured on ratio scales, two basic analytical procedures designed for ratio variables were employed to examine the research hypotheses underlying the current study. I modeled the form of relationship between neighborhood ecology and police–citizen relations with a linear regression function at both the bivariate and multivariate level.

Bivariate Analyses

A Pearson correlation describes how a score on a police practice or citizen behavior relates to a score on a neighborhood variable. Analyses focused on three different, but related, aspects of such relationships. For one, I investigated whether an association existed between a neighborhood characteristic and a given component of police–citizen relations by using a test of the hypothesis of statistical independence. If two variables were correlated, then I would be interested in the next issue: the strength of their association. These first two aspects of bivariate relationships were revealed by the coefficient of determination or Pearson r^2 and its attained level of statistical significance. The third aspect involved the specification of the form and direction of the relationships. The unsquared Pearson correlation coefficient r shows whether the association is positive or negative: if the coefficient is less than 0, the relation is negative, and if it is greater than 0 the association is positive. This ecological model specifies with clarity and precision the direction of its causal propositions. The central proposition of this theory of police–citizen relations is that both nonauthoritative policing styles and community support are inversely and linearly associated with the power and moral marginality of a neighborhood as measured by demographic and deviance variables, thus can be generically represented by the following formula:

$$E(\text{nonauthoritative policing/citizen support}) = \alpha + \beta \text{ neighborhood marginality/disrepute} + \varepsilon$$

The mathematical formula depicts how the mean of the conditional distribution of a dependent variable varies across different values of an independent variable, and expresses the dependent variable "policing style/citizen behavior" as a linear function of the independent factor "neighborhood marginality," with slope β, and Y-intercept α, and error term ε. The ε term in the equation accounts for the fact that the variables will not be perfectly related, which suggests that the relationship of any neighborhood variable to any outcome variable is one that allows variability in the values of the outcome variable for each value of the predictor. Each one of the ten dependent variables reflecting either policing styles or community response will be regressed on each one of the six predictors gauging different aspects of neighborhoods.

Multivariate Analysis

Ordinary least squared (OLS) regression is used to test the hypothesized relationships between independent and dependent variables. These statistical models were probabilistic (as opposed to deterministic), since I modeled the *mean*, not every observed value, of the dependent variable as a linear function of the independent variables. Probabilistic logic argues in terms of "averages" or "tendencies"; therefore, individual exceptions are expected. It also assumes that neighborhood forces laid out in the theory are critical causes of variations in police–citizen interactions, but not that they are *the only* causes of those changes. Ecology hypotheses predict a *direct* relationship between authoritative policing styles and neighborhood power/moral marginality on the one hand, and an *inverse*

Data, Variables, and Analytical Strategy

association between citizen support of police and neighborhood power/moral marginality. The whole theoretical model can be represented in the next seven mathematical formulas:

(i) $E(\text{police proaction}) = \alpha - \beta_1 \text{ SES status} + \beta_2 \text{ ethnic minority} - \beta_3 \text{ life-cycle} + \beta_4 \text{ crime} + \beta_6 \text{ incivility} + \varepsilon$

(ii) $E(\text{police enforcement}) = \alpha - \beta_1 \text{ SES status} + \beta_2 \text{ ethnic minority} - \beta_3 \text{ life-cycle} + \beta_4 \text{ crime} + \beta_6 \text{ incivility} + \varepsilon$

(iii) $E(\text{police coercion}) = \alpha - \beta_1 \text{ SES status} + \beta_2 \text{ ethnic minority} - \beta_3 \text{ life-cycle} + \beta_4 \text{ crime} + \beta_6 \text{ incivility} + \varepsilon$

(iv) $E(\text{citizen hostility}) = \alpha - \beta_1 \text{ SES status} + \beta_2 \text{ ethnic minority} - \beta_3 \text{ life-cycle} + \beta_4 \text{ crime} + \beta_6 \text{ incivility} + \varepsilon$

(v) $E(\text{citizen cooperation}) = \alpha + \beta_1 \text{ SES status} - \beta_2 \text{ ethnic minority} + \beta_3 \text{ life-cycle} - \beta_4 \text{ crime} - \beta_6 \text{ incivility} + \varepsilon$

(vi) $E(\text{citizen dissatisfaction}) = \alpha - \beta_1 \text{ SES status} + \beta_2 \text{ ethnic minority} - \beta_3 \text{ life-cycle} + \beta_4 \text{ crime} + \beta_6 \text{ incivility} + \varepsilon$

(vii) $E(\text{citizen satisfaction}) = \alpha + \beta_1 \text{ SES status} - \beta_2 \text{ ethnic minority} + \beta_3 \text{ life-cycle} - \beta_4 \text{ crime} - \beta_6 \text{ incivility} + \varepsilon$

The obtained coefficients of multiple determination (R^2) signal the goodness of fit of the model and measure the proportion of the total variation in police–citizen interactions by the simultaneous predictive power of all ecological variables. The interpretation of partial regression coefficients is somewhat complicated. Like most macro-level studies, multivariate analyses of PSS aggregate data suffer from strong intercorrelations among independent variables, which is particularly problematic between SES and race parameters ($r = -.7684$). If all parameters were included at once, most regression models would yield highly significant R^2s but nonsignificant partial regression coefficients, which also would have inflated standard errors. The difficulty caused by multicollinearity in conducting t tests for the significance of individual parameters is that it is possible to conclude that none of the individual parameters are significantly different from zero when an F test on the overall multiple regression equation indicates a significant relationship. Thus little faith could be placed in the sign of the individual coefficients. Since regression coefficients lose their meaning when serious multicollinearity exists (preventing effective statistical control), two measures are taken to remedy the problem. First, bivariate correlation coefficients offer helpful information on the strength and direction of partial relationships that might be present. Second, three separate models with different subsets of parameters were estimated for each dependent variable: one partial model would include the SES factor but exclude the race indicator, a second partial model would drop SES and incorporate race, and a full model would include all parameters. Despite the complication that multicollinearity causes to the interpretation of regression coefficients, it does not affect the goodness of fit of the equation (Agresti & Finlay, 1986).

CHAPTER 5

Testing the Theory

POLICING STYLES

Policing styles vary across communities in predictable ways. Place matters. This assertion can be corroborated by observing whether statistically significant differences in the aggregate measures of service delivery exist. The next question to answer would be whether these fluctuations in policing styles are socially purposeful. Ecological theories would posit that the meaning and explanation of policing are found not only in a crime-fighting mandate, but also in its reinforcing effects on the geographic segmentation of fortunes and misfortunes.

As discussed in the previous chapter, the existence of fairly strong multicollinearity between the SES scale and race caused multivariate regression equations to yield individual coefficients with dubious stability when both were simultaneously included in the full model. Therefore, three separate models were built for each dependent variable: an SES partial model with SES but without race, a second with race but without SES, and a third full model with all independent variables. Bivariate correlation coefficients and regression coefficients from partial models supplied additional references to interpret the influence of individual parameters on the dependent variables.

Table 5.1
Neighborhood Ecology and Police Proaction: Residential Security Checks

Independent variables	Zero-order correlation	SES model beta	Race model beta	Full model Beta
SES	.1618(*)	.1437	----	.0802
Race (% black)	-.1352	----	-.1406	-.0808
Age (youths)	.0618	.0945	.1299	.1150
Crime	-.1693	-.2031(*)	-.2135*	-.2043(*)
Incivility	-.0275	.1453	.1290	.1412
R^2		.0595	.0596	.0617
Adjusted R^2		.0089	.0086	.0251
Significance F		.2400	.2433	.3090

(*) p near .10, * p<.10, ** p<.05, *** p<.01, **** p<.001

Police Proaction

In what kind of environment are patrol officers more likely to suspect and initiate investigation?

Residential Security Checks

Measures of police proaction are expected to be positively correlated with neighborhood social marginality and negatively connected to neighborhood moral respectability. Residential security checks are usually conducted at the discretion of individual officers who hold mental schemes prescribed by the occupational culture of police, which includes categories to assess the conventionality and dangerousness of citizens and neighborhoods. Table 5.1 displays the bivariate (zero-order) and regression coefficients found between independent and dependent variables. Given the small sample size, the significance level was chosen as p < .10. Only observed correlations statistically significant at this level were regarded as representing a genuine bivariate association between two variables, discounting the possibility of its resulting from sampling error only. These were one-tailed tests because of the directional hypotheses tested here.

The regression models for residential security checks produced statistically nonsignificant coefficients of multiple determination (R^2s), revealing a very weak association between neighborhood structure and the rate of residential security checks. All three models explained about 6 percent of the total variance in the rate of police checks of civilian residences. Only crime contributed to the explained variance and showed a counterintuitive, negative relationship with the measure of police proaction. Patrol officers were more likely to monitor the safety of residential buildings in areas where residents experienced less criminal victimization.

Table 5.2
Neighborhood Ecology and Police Proaction: On-view Stops

Independent variables	Zero-order correlation	SES model beta	Race model beta	Full model beta
SES	.2696**	.1152	----	.0962
Race (% black)	-.1374	----	.0979	.0249
Age (youths)	.0381	.1003	.0877	.0717
Crime	-.2963**	-.1650*	-.1837*	-.1676(*)
Incivility	-.4967***	-.3963***	-.3865**	-.3965***
R^2		.3325	.3352	.3659
Adjusted R^2		.2718	.3108	.3096
Significance F		.0000	.0000	.0000

(*) p near .10, * p<.10, ** p<.05, *** p<.01, and **** p<.001.

There was also some indication that the rate of proactive checks of residential properties increased in areas where the average income and education of residents was higher. All three remaining parameters behaved in an unexpected direction, although none of them attained or neared the minimum statistical threshold. Proactive residential checks were slightly more likely in neighborhoods with smaller, nonwhite populations, and lower levels of fear and disorder were connected, albeit remotely, to a larger volume of residential security checks. In sum, core and reputable neighborhoods experienced higher levels of property-centered police proaction.

An important observation can be made from these results. The proactive monitoring of citizens' residences was more common in neighborhoods already enjoying greater social influence and a higher standard of public safety. There were surely more manpower and resources available for this kind of proaction in places where patrol officers did not have to respond to a large number of crime-related calls. Police might also have perceived properties in better-off and respectable neighborhoods as attractive targets of criminal elements that deserve extra protection. Overall, all three equations produced determination coefficients of negligible size, indicating that this particular type of police proaction was mostly independent of ecological influences, at least in PSS data.

On-view Nontraffic Stops

The observed R^2s indicated that about one-third of the variance in the dependent variable was accounted for by the ecological model. Despite this satisfactory goodness of fit of the models, the performance of individual parameters completely deviated from the formulated hypothesis (see Table 5.2). Neighborhood characteristics matter, but not in the anticipated way.

Both public safety measures were particularly and consistently influential across analyses. Crime rate emerged as the most powerful predictor of police stopping citizens for nontraffic matters. Police conducted comparatively more proactive on-view stops of citizens in safer and the safest neighborhoods. Contradicting the hypothesis that high crime rates lower neighborhoods' moral standing and invite proactive police activities, proactive field interrogations were more frequent in low crime areas. Incivility and disorder also exhibited very similar patterns of association being negatively correlated with proactive on-view citizen stops. Patrol officers were much more likely to interrupt citizens' routines to conduct field interrogation in highly organized and well-attended communities. Neighborhood SES appeared to have an effect on on-view stops of citizens, but this bivariate association became nonsignificant when other predictors were controlled for in the multivariate equations. Race and life-cycle were not relevant at all.

Two explanations can be given to account for the counterintuitive results from the analysis of proactive stops of citizens. First, the same *organizational* argument made to explain the unanticipated findings on proactive checks of residential properties can be repeated here. More police manpower and resources are on hand for the execution of proactive policing. Logistic exhaustion makes it difficult for the police to devise and implement crime-prevention tactics in areas overwhelmed by a large quantity of citizen calls for help and crime-related dispatches. Second, it is probable that signs of unconventionality and offensiveness are targeted for control only in conventional and exemplary neighborhoods, but ignored or tolerated in marginal and disreputable areas. One of the consequences of residential segregation is the spatial segregation of lifestyles, behaviors, and people that do not conform to the dominant standards of acceptability.

Important conclusions can be drawn from the analysis of police checks of residential properties and on-view stops of citizens. First, proaction characterized the policing of core and respectable neighborhoods, while reactive policing prevailed in marginal and disreputable areas. The rejection of the ecological hypothesis should not come without caution. That police were more likely to stop citizens in better-off and safer communities does not mean that the rich and white were more likely to be intercepted by the police for field interrogation. To the contrary, PSS data demonstrate that residents of nonwhite, youthful, and high-crime neighborhoods were much more likely to report being stopped by the police during the year prior to the research interview. When the same five-variable ecological equation was used to model the percent of survey respondents reported being stopped by the police in an *ad hoc* analysis, an impressive goodness of fit was observed ($R^2 = .4406$). All parameters, three of them statistically significant, were associated with self-reported on-view stops, as the model would predict. Residents of nonwhite, youth-dominated, and high-crime neighborhoods experienced higher rates of police field interrogation. When results from this analysis are read vis-à-vis findings from the observational data, it becomes plausible that core and respectable *neighborhoods* are cast as potential victims, while *residents* of peripheral and discreditable neighborhoods are potential offenders. Security checks were to protect valued properties from being illegally appropriated or damaged, and the stopping of citizens for questioning was aimed at preventing the intrusion of dangerous individuals into core and respectable districts. Potential victims and their possessions are to be protected, while potential offenders are to be controlled. From an ecological perspective, the rejection of the hypothesis of police proaction can be reasonably discounted by the argument that the police pit themselves against threats from the peripheries through the selective delivery of proactive interventions to protect their middle- and upper-class constituencies.

Second, not all police proactive interventions were equally predictable. Residential security checks were far more dissociated from community structures than nontraffic stops, which turned out to be heavily determined by demographic and safety factors (especially when self-reported data were analyzed). This difference should not be overlooked. Since stopping and questioning citizens are extremely intrusive and can easily arouse public hostility, we should be concerned that extra-legal community factors, such as the race and age of respondents, exercise more influence on police behavior than neighborhood safety conditions. The rule of law not only dictates that citizens be equally protected by criminal justice institutions but also that the burden of police intrusion be reasonably and equally shared by different segments of society.

Police Enforcement of Law

Because police do not define similar problems similarly in different neighborhoods, the legal definitions of incidents and the formal processing of citizens vary across areas. Nonlegal alternatives such as mediation, referral, and counseling may be used instead. Communities with social power and enjoying a moral reputation are less likely to be policed with enforcement-oriented tactics, and peripheral districts deprived of social capital and moral respectability are likely to see their behaviors and disputes being legally defined and formally processed.

Arrests

The R^2s evidenced a satisfactory goodness of fit for the regression models. The five ecological indicators accounted for nearly 30 percent of the variation in neighborhood arrest rates (see Table 5.3).

Table 5.3
Neighborhood Ecology and Law Enforcement: Arrest

Independent variables	Zero-order correlation	SES model Beta	Race model beta	Full model Beta
SES	-.4389****	-.3017**	----	-.1575
Race (% black)	.3545***	----	.3010***	.1836*
Age (youths)	-.1079	-.1537(*)	-.2116**	-.1824*
Crime	.3636***	.1510	.1716(*)	.1536
Incivility	.4060****	.1959*	.2291**	.2051**
R^2		.2815	.2850	.2930
Adjusted R^2		.2292	.2330	.2076
Significance F		.0015	.0009	.0008

(*) p near .10, * p<.10, ** p<.05, *** p<.01, and **** p<.001.

All independent variables were statistically significant at either bivariate or multivariate levels and evidenced strong substantive influence on the outcome variable, mostly in the predicted direction. Race and age exerted powerful effects supporting the argument that the demographic characteristics of a neighborhood may boost or curb the degree to which criminal law is applied. The relative number of nonwhite residents was directly proportional to the rate at which police–citizen encounters resulted in some kind of arrest, regardless of the level of crime and disorder. Citizens processed in nonwhite-dominated areas were much more likely to experience police authority to legitimately limit people's liberty. Larger teenage populations significantly and unexpectedly decreased the relative amount of arrests in the community. Contradicting my hypothesis, neighborhoods with lower average ages and larger teenage populations were less likely to have high arrest rates. If this result is unpacked vis-à-vis the findings on proactive policing, it is evident that although patrol activities were singularly proactive and aggressive in areas populated by young families with teenagers, these active encounters did not precipitate a large number of arrests. When there were many youths, tactical choices other than arrest were favored. Police reluctance to arrest may have resulted from the paternalistic tendencies of the police subculture, which prescribes age-appropriate sanctions according to the life-stage characteristics of neighborhoods. SES generated significant bivariate and partial model coefficients in the predicted direction but failed to attain the significance threshold in the full model when race was controlled for. This pattern suggests that arrest rates were higher in poorer neighborhoods because these impoverished areas were mainly inhabited by nonwhite residents.

All public safety indicators were statistically significant in bivariate analyses but only incivility remained statistically influential in regression

Table 5.4
Neighborhood Ecology and Law Enforcement: Report Writing

Independent variables	Zero-order correlation	SES model Beta	Race model Beta	Full model beta
SES	-.1799*	.0151	----	-.1857(*)
Race (% black)	.0008	----	.1172	.2556*
Age (youths)	-.0376	-.1913*	-.1607*	-.1263
Crime	.4582****	.4735****	.4910****	.4698****
Incivility	.2839**	.0268	.0423	.0139
R^2		.2473	.2585	.2697
Adjusted R^2		.1925	.2045	.2020
Significance F		.0018	.0011	.0019

(*) p near .10, * p<.10, ** p<.05, *** p<.01, and **** p<.001.

models. Arrests were common in neighborhoods with serious incivility and disorder. One explanation of this finding could be that incidents of disorder (e.g., loitering, noise, etc.) are more likely than index crimes to remain "hot" when police arrive, which makes an arrest more predictable. This finding can also be interpreted to support the hypothesis that legalistic policing is meant to restore order in disordered neighborhoods; when informal social control breaks down, formal control fills in. Overall, public safety conditions were as significantly influential as demographic forces in determining the level of police enforcement behavior, as measured by arrest rates.

Report Writing

Regression models produced statistically and substantively significant R^2s for the filing of written reports. One-fourth of the variance in the outcome variable was explained by the ecological equation (see Table 5.4).

Mixed findings emerged from the analyses. The most important correlate of official report writing was the neighborhood crime rate, supporting the hypothesis that legalistic policing intensifies in morally disorganized areas. More incidents were officially recognized and recorded by the criminal justice system in high-crime districts. This may simply reflect that filing official incident reports is a routine official response to criminal events, particularly serious ones, and constitutes an essential tool of crime control that initiates the complex legal process. The impact of incivility on report writing was significant at the bivariate level but became nonsignificant when other variables were controlled. It also suggests that the higher rates of arrests observed in places with more incidents of disorder were primarily an indication of police dispensing summary street justice. Crime was the most influential public safety factor that caused the police to react with the formal procedure.

Demographic variables exerted very modest effects on the dependent variable. Neighborhood SES was found to be negatively associated with police filing of written reports at the bivariate level, confirming the hypothesis that formal legality is more commonly used by the police in lower SES places to solve interpersonal conflicts. Although this correlation became nonsignificant in the partial model, it remained moderately strong in the full model, which indicates that the link was present. The impact of life-cycle stage on police report writing paralleled its influence on arrests. Nonsignificant at the bivariate level, life-cycle became statistically significant in both partial models. Police were less enthusiastic about arresting citizens or in filing incident reports and thus were less likely to officially record incidents or disputes that occurred in neighborhoods with lower average ages and larger representations of the teenage population. Formality and legal procedures were preferred in adult or mature neighborhoods. Race emerged significant in the full model when other variables were held constant. Independent of the crime rates, police were more likely to file official reports in minority or immigrant neighborhoods, as predicted.

Ecological theories have been quite useful in explaining variations in law enforcement across neighborhoods. Robust regression models were able to generate strong coefficients of multiple determination and most of the individual neighborhood indicators exercised effects on the dependent variables in the predicted direction. Here, an interesting pattern deserved to be highlighted.

Although arrests and report writing were used to operationalize the theoretical construct of "law enforcement behavior," they displayed differential associations with different aspects of community structure. Altogether, arrest rates were equaly closely correlated with demographic and crime variables, while report writing had stronger ties only with public safety variables. Why didn't a higher volume of arrests result in a greater number of filed reports in lower SES and larger nonwhite population neighborhoods? I propose a possible answer. Arrests were more frequent in poor and minority neighborhoods, regardless of their crime rates, because, unlike arrests made on warrants, on-scene, nonwarrant arrests were not always aimed at the capture of suspects but helped the police to gain control of the encountered citizens. Since deep-rooted tensions have historically been embedded in police–citizen relations in poor and minority neighborhoods, challenges to police authority were more likely to erupt in encounters that occurred in these areas. The result is greater reliance on arrest to subdue the manifestations of insubordination and resistance. If this is actually the dynamic in place, then arrest as a tactical choice will likely in the long run, and in the aggregate, become

Table 5.5
Neighborhood Ecology and Police Coercion: Verbal Coercion

Independent variables	Zero-order correlation	SES model Beta	Race model beta	Full model beta
SES	-.5135****	-.4983****	----	-.1618
Race (% black)	.5526****	----	.5491****	.4285***
Age (youths)	.0587	.0119	-.1269	-.0969
Crime	.3183***	.2073*	.2319**	.2135*
Incivility	.1546(*)	-.1663	-.1200	-.1447
R^2		.2969	.3512	.3597
Adjusted R^2		.2457	.3040	.3004
Significance F		.0003	.0000	.0001

(*) p near .10, * p<.10, ** p<.05, *** p<.01, and **** p<.001.

a strategy of class and race control. Arrest rates were not correlated to crime rates but to SES and race measures because during police–citizen encounters arrests were made more to maintain officers' authority and control and less to apprehend crime suspects. In contrast, report writing was technically and socially a response to criminal offenses already committed; therefore, they were mainly associated with crime rates. However, as crime is more serious in lower SES and minority neighborhoods, the consequence is not different from the concentration of arrests in these same areas: police impose formal legality at a higher rate in marginal and disreputable communities.

Police Coercion

The use of coercive practices by police to elicit citizen compliance and deference is at least partly based on differences in power and reputation conferred to people according to their place of residence. The verbal and physical coercion of citizens is likely to be used in areas that occupy strata inferior to those constituencies to whom police owe their ideological affiliation and political loyalty.

Verbal Coercion

Verbal coercion was measured by the number of encounters in which patrol officers shouted at or threatened to use force against citizens per 100 eight-hour shifts. The observed R^2s indicated that the ecological equation explained about one-third of the total variance in police use of coercive language (see Table 5.5).

Among the demographic factors, race and SES had the strongest impact on police use of verbal coercion. Patrol officers more often used commanding or authoritative language to exact citizen compliance in

Table 5.6
Neighborhood Ecology and Police Coercion: Physical Coercion

Independent variables	Zero-order correlation	SES model beta	Race model beta	Full model Beta
SES	-.5413****	-.4128****	----	-.1447
Race (% black)	.5486****	----	.4491****	.3412**
Age (youths)	.2265**	.1125	.0010	.0258
Crime	.3799***	.0738	.0953	.0787
Incivility	.4382****	.2277**	.2670**	.2448**
R^2		.3664	.3994	.4062
Adjusted R^2		.3203	.3557	.3512
Significance F		.0000	.0000	.0000

(*) p near .10, * p<.10, ** p<.05, *** p<.01, and **** p<.001.

nonwhite and low-SES neighborhoods. As a consequence of their marginalization from the civic life of the larger community, the poor, minority, and immigrants (who as a group had the least participation in political and economic systems) were prime candidates for experiencing the coercive facet of state authority. The life-cycle attributes of a neighborhood did not affect the aggregate rate of verbal coercion by police.

Crime rates exerted decisive influence on the dependent variable. Patrol officers verbally belittled or threatened force against citizens at higher rates in high-crime areas. Incivility was nearly significant in the bivariate analysis but became weaker when crime and demographic characteristics were held constant, showing that their impact on the police use of verbal coercion was largely mediated by crime rates. This finding buttresses the proposition that underlying antagonism toward police and the discredited image of people who live in high-crime areas are likely to prompt police to resort to coercive language to establish order.

Physical Coercion

The application of physical restraints on citizens constitutes one of the most coercive tactics that police officers are legitimately allowed to use under appropriate circumstances. In this analysis, the rate of encounters in which officers used handcuffs or physical force against encountered citizens was used as the dependent variable. The regression equations demonstrated robust goodness of fit by generating large R^2s. This ecological model explained over one-third of the variance in police use of physical coercion (see Table 5.6).

All parameters showed statistically significant effects in the hypothesized direction on the dependent variable. Among demographic measures, SES and race were the most powerful predictors of physical coercion by police. Regardless of the levels of crime or other disturbances, patrol officers used handcuffs and physical force against citizens most frequently in neighborhoods inhabited by poor and minority residents. The life-cycle stage only surfaced as a significant correlate in the bivariate analysis, showing that the observed positive correlation between the youthful population and high rates of physical coercion was due to the larger representation of teenage residents in nonwhite-dominated neighborhoods.

All public safety indicators strongly correlated with the dependent variable at the bivariate level, revealing that comparatively more citizens were handcuffed or physically controlled by the police in areas where crime and incivility were commonplace. Of the two public safety indicators, incivility was the most powerful. The finding that more citizens were handcuffed and subdued in less orderly neighborhoods may be related again to the greater likelihood of encountering trouble-making vagabonds, the mentally ill, or rowdy youths.

PSS data provided powerful empirical backing to the police coercion aspect of ecological theory. The multivariate equations not only achieved admirable goodness of fit but also corroborated most of the hypothetical links between dimensions of neighborhood structure and police coercion, showing that police coercion was mainly distributed along class and racial lines, with high rates of crime and incivility exercising independent effects as well. Officers were particularly rough toward citizens in poor and minority neighborhoods. Residents of high-crime or high-disorder communities were also likely to be disciplined with physical prowess. Core and respectable neighborhoods enjoyed the privilege of being treated with courtesy and politeness, the right to be policed by words and not force.

Ecological hypotheses of police base their conceptualizations on both the political economy of metropolitan places and the historical role of police in preserving the existing order of resources and prestige allocation through differential service delivery. Specifically, police proaction, coercion, and enforcement are predicted to intensify in (1) marginal neighborhoods with higher concentrations of poor, minority, and youth and (2) disreputable communities suffering worse problems of crime and incivility. Six full equations were built to test the hypotheses put forward and their coefficients of multiple determination (R^2s) averaged .2927, explaining nearly one-third of variability in rates of police behavior with just a handful of key predictors. The rejection of the police proaction hypothesis stands out as an exception. The anomalous finding of a positive relationship between police proaction rates and the centrality and respectability of neighborhoods suggests that organizational factors, such as scarce resources, can interfere and distort the influence of community structure on police behavior.

Bivariate and partial correlations generally supported the main hypotheses. With a few exceptions, most measures of neighborhood structure and public safety were statistically significantly correlated with operational indicators of police proaction, enforcement, and coercion. Arrest, official report writing, coercive language, and use of physical force were consistently negatively associated with attributes of neighborhood marginality and positively affected by crime-related conditions. Police did act more coercively and formally in powerless and disorganized communities. The unexpected positive associations between proactive checks of residential properties and on-view stops of citizens and measures of social influence and public safety were reinterpreted within the conceptual framework of ecological analysis by arguing that the perceptions of powerful-citizens-as-potential-victims and powerless-citizens-as-potential-offenders drive the allocation of police manpower and logistics. When coupled with results from an *ad hoc* analysis of self-reported stops, empirical findings showed that while police conducted more intense monitoring of civilian properties and a larger number of field interrogations in core and respectable neighborhoods, more residents of marginal and disreputable areas reported being spontaneously intercepted by the police when they are walking or driving in wealthy areas they do not live or work in. In the ultimate instance, proactive policing serves to remind people of their right *place* in a stratified and segregated society.

CITIZEN DEMEANOR AND ATTITUDES

In the aggregate, what citizens do during their encounters with the police and how they feel about the quality of police work not only result from the stratified and segregated structure of social life but also constitute a part of this organization of fortunes and misfortunes. Police face indifference and enmity in powerless places, while influential areas greet patrol officers with respect and appreciation on their streets. The same differential display of antagonism and recognition also occurs in people's minds. Public opinion on police and policing is more favorable in core and respectable neighborhoods, and more unpropitious in peripheral and discredited communities.

Citizen Hostile Demeanor

The powerlessness and helplessness of marginal and disreputable communities are converted into visible antagonism when residents meet the frontline guardians of the perceived unfair social order face-to-face. In this analysis, the rate of citizens cursing or fighting officers was estimated as the dependent variable. The equations produced R^2s and accounted for between 39 percent and 46 percent of the total variance in citizen hostility toward police during encounters (see Table 5.7).

Testing the Theory

Table 5.7
Neighborhood Ecology and Citizen Demeanor: Citizen Hostility

Independent variables	Zero-order correlation	SES model beta	Race model beta	Full model beta
SES	-.5816****	-.4798****	----	-.1239
Race (% black)	.6056****	----	.5455****	.4531****
Age (youths)	.0688	.0240	-.1411	.0912
Crime	.4310****	.2170**	.2377**	.2235***
Incivility	.3505***	.0321	.0738	.0549
R^2		.3856	.4509	.4559
Adjusted R^2		.3409	.4110	.4055
Significance F		.0001	.0000	.0000

(*) p near .10, * p<.10, ** p<.05, *** p<.01, and **** p<.001.

All individual parameters attained important statistical and substantive significance levels in either bivariate or multivariate analyses, or both. A minimum of voluntary submission is generally present in core and respectable neighborhoods, but often lacking in the opposite extremes of the continuum. Racial composition played the most prominent role in determining citizens' hostile demeanors during encounters. Patrol officers were remarkably more likely to be verbally abused or physically attacked in districts with a larger nonwhite population. The same kind of hostile behavior was extremely rare in white neighborhoods. The powerful effects of neighborhood SES in the bivariate analysis and the partial model dissipated in the full model when racial composition was held constant, suggesting that poorer neighborhoods offered higher levels of hostile demeanor toward patrol officers not so much because of their socioeconomic standing, but because there were disproportionately more nonwhite residents in these areas. Life-cycle stage became significant after racial composition was held constant; citizen aggression against police increased in areas with lower average age and larger youth groups, as predicted.

Crime and incivility all positively correlated with citizens' hostile demeanor at the bivariate level as hypothesized, showing that the breakdown of community order had turned citizens against law enforcement agents. In high-crime neighborhoods, patrol officers encountered more crime suspects who were more likely to offer resistance to police intervention. This commonsensical argument, however, could only be a partial explanation because most of the crime-related encounters involved "cold" offenses for which the suspects had already left the scene. Ecological argument holds that a high level of crime not only increases the number of police–suspect encounters (which will always be tense and hostile) but also alienates neighborhood residents from the police, who

Table 5.8
Neighborhood Ecology and Citizen Demeanor: Provision of Information

Independent variables	Zero-order correlation	SES model beta	Race model beta	Full model Beta
SES	.0962	.2743**	----	.0319
Race (% black)	-.2396**	----	-.3660***	-.3898**
Age (youths)	-.0617	-.0747	.0185	.0244
Crime	.2170**	.2089*	.2069*	.2032*
Incivility	.2349**	.2327*	.2180*	.2131*
R^2		.1310	.1827	.1830
Adjusted R^2		.0678	.1232	.1074
Significance F		.0484	.0117	.0237

(*) p near .10, * p<.10, ** p<.05, *** p<.01, and **** p<.001.

are supposed to protect them from criminal victimization. Crime undermines trustful interactions between police and citizens.

Citizen Cooperative Demeanor

I hypothesized that citizens encountered in marginal and disreputable neighborhoods tend to refrain from assisting or cooperating with police work. Although some support for the hypothesis was found, part of the hypothesis was refuted by the PSS data. These unanticipated results, however, illuminated an important dilemma in police–community relations by accentuating the subordination and dependency that characterize peripheral neighborhoods in their relationship to governmental bureaucracies. To begin with, the multivariate models produced moderate goodness of fit by explaining 13 percent to 18 percent of the total variance in citizen cooperative behavior (rate of citizens' providing descriptions of crime and volunteering assistance) (see Table 5.8).

All predictors were significant at either the bivariate or multivariate level, or both. Demographic characteristics associated with social influence facilitated citizen cooperation with the police. Higher rates of citizen cooperation were found in neighborhoods with higher SES, smaller nonwhite populations, and more mature households. The declined impact of SES and life-cycle in the full model points out again that although these structural features maintained descriptive associations with citizen cooperation, only race (proportion of nonwhite population) could have exercised substantial causal influence. All else constant, residents of neighborhoods with a larger white population were much more likely to willingly supply officers with the information they needed.

Findings on the effects of public safety conditions falsified this part of the hypothesis. Unexpectedly, albeit not incomprehensibly, citizens living in high-crime and high-incivility neighborhoods were more likely to provide the police with information about crimes and criminals. To put it another way, police received more cooperation from citizens who are more directly affected by crime and disorder. Does it mean that residents of high-crime neighborhoods shared a stronger sense of mutual obligation or common will to safeguard community order? If so, these findings would contradict the traditional sociological view that crime and disorder undermine the formation of effective community control by isolating residents from each other. A solution may be found if we put the quagmire in a utilitarian perspective: people cooperate with the police to maximize their own benefits. Assisting officers in solving crimes and apprehending criminals in crime-ridden neighborhoods was a self-protection measure rather than a manifestation of civic altruism. That many victims and bystanders of criminal incidents offered assistance to police officers, whom they normally despise, showed how desperate residents of high-crime areas were in trying to survive in the urban jungle. When people from core neighborhoods collaborate with the police because they *want* to (just as they participate in other civic affairs), residents of disreputable neighborhoods do so because they *have* to.

A "double bind" situation exists in disreputable communities where perceived "underprotection" can effectively lead to "overpolicing" if disorganized neighborhoods tired of crime and disorder resort to police assistance to keep their dangerous streets a little bit cleaner and safer. In crime-stricken neighborhoods, the source of people's fear and pain are their own neighbors. Therefore, the willingness of residents of high-crime neighborhoods to volunteer intelligence and to describe suspects to the police may in fact make police work more effective, although it does not necessarily strengthen their own communities. The real danger of the cycle of "underprotection" and "overpolicing" is found in the stretched social contract between the police and the policed. Residents of high-crime areas surrender their right to use force and loan that right to the police to use it in the name of community welfare and security. Unfortunately, the sacrifice of these individual rights does not result in a real freedom to live with minimal fear of victimization by others or by the police.

Negative Citizen Perceptions

Theoretically, there would be a widespread dissatisfaction with police services in marginal and disreputable neighborhoods whose residents tend to view police work as an unfair or ineffective enterprise. The dependent variable in the following analyses was the percentage of survey respondents who knew people who had been mistreated by the police in the year before the interview. The R^2s supported the theory, in that almost half of the total variance in citizen negative attitudes toward police could be explained. The equation not only yielded an impressive

Table 5.9
Neighborhood Ecology and Citizen Attitudes: Perceived Police Mistreatment

Independent variables	Zero-order correlation	SES model beta	Race model beta	Full model beta
SES	-.5614****	-.4652****		-.1278
Race (% black)	.6462****	----	.5248****	.4295****
Age (youths)	.3259***	.3109***	.1781**	.2018**
Crime	.3392***	.0000	.0214	.0068
Incivility	.3925***	.2030*	.2441	.3346**
R^2		.4424	.5003	.5056
Adjusted R^2		.4019	.4639	.4598
Significance F		.0000	.0000	.0000

(*) p near .10, * p<.10, ** p<.05, *** p<.01, and **** p<.001.

coefficient of determination but also completely corroborated the ecological hypothesis of public perception of police behavior (see Table 5.9).

All five independent variables showed significant bivariate and/or regression correlations in the predicted direction. Racial composition was the strongest predictor of negative perceptions of police services. Most residents of white-dominated neighborhoods did not know of people mistreated by the police, while in communities with large concentrations of nonwhites, knowledge of police misconduct was common. When looking at life-cycle characteristics and SES, perceptions of police mistreatment of citizens were more deeply rooted in poorer and younger neighborhoods, while in better-off and more mature areas such beliefs were extremely infrequent. However, their effects again seem to be largely mediated by racial composition.

Both public safety indexes were positively correlated with negative perceptions of police as hypothesized. Crime and disorder increased perceptions of police mistreatment. Mistrust and suspicion of police activities were more often shared in places where residents felt more vulnerable to predatory crime and suffered more serious problems of disorder and incivility. In contrast, in areas where the perceived likelihood of becoming a crime victim was low and community order was intact, police enjoyed popular trust and a better public image. Clearly, the citizenry rated the quality of police services through the subjective evaluation of personal safety and the visibility of neighborhood disorder.

PSS data were amply supportive of the hypothesis that police are feared and suspected in marginal and disreputable areas, and trusted and respected in core and respectable neighborhoods. When this outcome was read vis-à-vis the unanticipated findings from the analysis of citizen cooperative demeanor, the double bind that ensnared both the

Table 5.10
Neighborhood Ecology and Citizen Attitudes: Public Satisfaction

Independent variables	Zero-order correlation	SES model Beta	Race model beta	Full model beta
SES	.6160****	.5021****	----	.5042****
Race (% black)	-.4877****	----	-.3732***	.0026
Age (youths)	-.1184*	-.0681	.0247	-.0688
Crime	-.4765****	-.2531**	-.3106**	-.2531**
Incivility	-.3691***	-.0221	-.0989	-.0220
R^2		.4462	.3636	.4461
Adjusted R^2		.4059	.3173	.3949
Significance F		.0000	.0000	.0000

(*) p near .10, * p<.10, ** p<.05, *** p<.01, and **** p<.001.

police and the policed in a relational paradox becomes even clearer. The same high-crime neighborhoods that were more likely to provide police with useful information thought of police as dishonest and not trustworthy. By the same token, the low-crime neighborhoods that were less involved with the police held the police at higher esteem. These findings render plausible the assumption that community perceptions of police and policing are a product of macro-level forces as well as the result of actual interactions between individual police and citizens.

Positive Citizen Attitudes

Favorable attitudes toward police are held by residents of core and respectable neighborhoods, while people living in peripheral and disreputable areas are less likely to hold friendly thoughts about police. The dependent variable used in this analysis was the percentage of survey respondents who were satisfied with police services in their community. Ecological equations produced powerful R^2s, showing that the six parameters included in the model were responsible for more than half of the total variance in residents' satisfaction with police services (see Table 5.10).

All five parameters displayed partial associations with the dependent variable in the expected direction. Neighborhood SES had the strongest effect, indicating that the percentage of respondents who were satisfied with police services was higher in places where residents had higher incomes, more years of schooling, and owned their homes. These favorable attitudes were foreign in lower SES neighborhoods. Racial composition also had an important and positive impact on attitudes. While a greater percentage of whites in the neighborhood increased the level of supportive attitudes, the existence of a large number of nonwhite residents decreased public endorsement of police work. The fact that minority group members had lesser stakes in the established social order was, in part, materialized into less friendlier perceptions of police work. The life-cycle stage, measured as larger representations of teenage residents and lower average ages, maintained a significant negative relationship with supportive attitudes, as predicted. It appeared quite difficult for police to develop a friendly and trustful relationship with youths.

The most influential public safety variable associated with citizens holding positive perceptions of police was crime. Lower crime led to higher levels of satisfaction with the police and of perceived police responsiveness, whereas neighborhoods with more fear of crime experienced less satisfaction and were less likely to feel police were delivering what they needed. Incivilities that undermine local morale also damage the public image of the police. Feelings of defenselessness and fear of crime, which are in a large part sustained by vicarious accounts, media representations, and a general sense of impotence and vulnerability, can undermine the formation of a healthy and constructive police–community partnership.

The outcomes of this analysis strongly support the hypothesis that residents of core and respectable neighborhoods were more likely than residents of marginal and disreputable communities to exhibit positive attitudes toward police. On top of exposing firsthand experiences with the police, perceptions of police effectiveness and rectitude reflected a neighborhood's standing in the current arrangement of social power and moral respectability. People in neighborhoods that had a lesser stake in the prevailing system of material rewards and in dangerous neighborhoods were annoyed by the way police delivered services, while residents of areas with greater social influence and safer communities were overwhelmingly content with how police work was conducted.

Four full models with different measures of citizen demeanor and attitudes as dependent variables were tested. Their coefficients of determination (R^2) averaged .3974, which implied that 40 percent of the variance in different aspects of citizen demeanor and attitudes were explained by the ecological theory. Furthermore, most individual correlation coefficients were statistically and substantively significant in the anticipated direction. These results provide an important empirical basis to the citizen response aspect of the theory and highlight the usefulness of examining citizen behavior and beliefs within the ecological framework of analysis. Although all six independent variables performed very well in these analyses, the racial and ethnic identities of neighborhoods were the most fundamental determinants of whether residents would have consonant or dissonant relationships with the police, suggesting class and race bias in citizens' demeanor and attitudes toward police.

The next critical issue that has already been repeatedly emphasized and discussed is the apparent inconsistency that existed in the policing of high-crime neighborhoods. On the one hand, these places were more likely to exhibit hostility toward patrol officers and less likely to have positive views of police work. On the other hand, they were among the most cooperative communities in terms of volunteering information and suspect descriptions. This apparent contradiction further emphasized a desperate helplessness in these disreputable neighborhoods. Crime-ridden settlements could not depend on their own family, schools, and voluntary associations to mediate disputes or regulate behaviors, therefore, they had to resort to official representatives of the status quo that had created their plight in the first place, to bring order and safety back to their communities. The ambivalent nature of this double bind further increased the odds of clashes between the police and the policed in these areas. The underlying discontent and the collective feelings of oppression fostered a powerful distrust toward police, yet the deprivation of resources obliged citizens to interact with the police at higher rates. Not surprisingly, PSS data showed that encounters produced in these areas were emotionally charged situations spotted with citizen co-operation as well as dotted with incidents of open hostility. Relying on officials who they dislike and do not trust for assistance represents another problem for those segregated in poor and dangerous environments.

DISCUSSION OF FINDINGS

Findings from the analysis of the PSS data reported above help us to address three empirical questions: (1) How well did this theory as a conceptual framework perform in interpreting police behavior and citizen response? (2) what are the most revealing patterns of police–citizen interactions detected in the study? and (3) what can we learn from the results to improve our theory and advance our understanding of the problem?

Judged by the observed explanatory power of the 10 full multivariate models built to test the theory, it can be concluded that an ecological analysis of police–citizen relations is empirically viable and useful to the interpretation of PSS data on policing styles and citizen behavior toward police. Almost all multivariate equations attained the statistical significance level of at least .01 and their coefficients of multiple determination range from .10 to .55, yielding an average R^2 of .36, and demonstrating that the six demographic and public safety variables accounted for more than one-third of the total variance in police–citizen relations. Overall evidence pointed out that, like policing styles, citizens' responses are highly "classed" and "raced," and somewhat "aged." The social distance that separates core neighborhoods from peripheral communities has ensured that residents of core communities benefit from a more informal and noncoercive style of policing with approval and appreciation, while a more authoritative style of policing that relies on legalism and coercion and stirs suspicion and mistrust among residents prevails in marginal neighborhoods. Equally important were the lenses formed by crime, fear, and disorder through which police and citizens obtain information to evaluate and act toward each other. The breakdown of public safety turns policing into a highly legalistic and coercive enterprise and insidiously antagonizes the policed against the police.

Findings on police proaction and citizen cooperation were counterintuitive, yet even these unanticipated outcomes has shed new light on the issue. The large volume of crime-related demands seem to have stretched police manpower and other resources to a point where conducting proactive crime prevention becomes logistically implausible in disreputable neighborhoods. Also, police proaction could mean control of potential criminals or protection of potential victims, depending on the context. *Ad hoc* analysis provided additional information indicating that residents of safe and respectable places were not the prime targets of police proactive tactics; they were mainly protected as potential victims of crime, while residents of marginal and high-crime neighborhoods reported being the preferred candidates of police field interrogation. If citizens only get to meet the police when they are being perceived as crime suspects in foreign areas or when they have become crime victims on their own turf, resentment and frustration will grow. This view of police neglect and the perception of police reliance on law and force to subdue citizens are used to construct the social reality of "underprotection" and "overpolicing" in marginal high-crime neighborhoods.

Despite the more authoritative policing style and the general discontent toward police, citizens living in marginal and disreputable neighborhoods demonstrated higher levels of collaboration with the police during encounters. Strangely, the most cooperative neighborhoods are those in which a number of time bombs—police coercion, frequent confrontations between police and citizens, lack of empathy, and widespread mistrust and suspicion—are ticking. The fact that the police are needed does not make them loved. If these communities that suffer more than their share of crime do not come to the police for protection, to whom can they turn? Too often, the same police officers that arouse a strong sense of alienation among local residents are desperately needed as parents, social workers, or judges of last resort in these places, although they avowedly dislike performing such social service functions, for fear of becoming a repository for diffuse and distasteful tasks shed by other agencies and being tainted by the low esteem in which the social services are held.

Here, police–community relations are made tense by inherent centrifugal and centripetal forces. Residents of downtrodden neighborhoods verbally and behaviorally express their aversion to the police, yet, at the same time, they have no choice but to count on the legal authority and the around-the-clock availability of the police to make their lives viable in an adverse environment. The same is true for the police. The police occupational subculture holds that only "true cop work" is worth pursuing, and that "true cop work" deals with the control of felonious events and crime-prone individuals, both of which concentrate in marginal and disreputable neighborhoods. By aggressively enforcing the law and forcefully applying coercion on encountered citizens in disorganized neighborhoods, police reaffirm their position on the "thin blue line." Such is the entwined ambivalence of the symbiotic repulsion between police and the policed in marginal and notorious communities.

In contrast, core and respectable districts populated by middle- or upper-class, white, and more mature households maintain a congenial although somewhat detached relationship with the police. The minimum level of police–citizen interactions in these areas does not dissipate the deep identification that tightly binds them together. In fact, the reality that citizens do not have to request services from their officers with frequency cements their satisfaction with the functioning of this political institution. Few contacts make for good relations. Through stout political support and favorable opinions, residents of these influential areas extend their recognition and allegiance to the police, who in turn reward their constituents with a service-oriented and noncoercive style of policing.

CHAPTER 6

Conclusion and Discussion

FUTURE DIRECTIONS OF THE THEORY

During the course of police research, social scientists are regularly criticized for a lack of theoretical development and exploration. There are few theories of police or policing that are adequate and comprehensive for the task of explaining police–citizen interactions. At this stage of development of criminal justice into a "young" and yet distinct scientific discipline, our job is primarily to invent theories, and only secondarily to test them.

A great deal has been learned in the elaboration and evaluation of this ecological theory of police–citizen relations. The structural analysis of police–community relations emphasizes the ordering of social positions and networks of social relationships that are based on the arrangement of mutually dependent institutions (economy, polity, education, etc.) of society. It takes into consideration that although individual officers and citizens co-produce the thousands of small face-to-face encounters that shape their relations, the social reality of inequality and segregation exists prior to and outside of individual experiences. An evaluation of the theory with PSS data corroborated most of the proposed hypotheses, thus renders the theory plausible with substantial explanatory power. Police did act more legalistically and coercively in lower class, minority, and youthful neighborhoods as well as in higher fear and higher disorder communities. Proactive policing was found in marginal areas but not in disreputable areas as first anticipated. The large volume of crime-related demands appeared to have exhausted police resources and greatly reduced their capacity to launch proactive activities. Citizen hostility and negative attitudes toward police were much less frequent in core and respectable neighborhoods, where recognition and approval of police work were widely shared. A very illuminating yet unexpected finding was the high rate of citizen cooperation in the very peripheral and discreditable places where citizen antagonism was highest. It showed how extreme social deprivation has forced these neighborhoods into a symbiotic dependence on police interventions to maintain a minimum level of peace and order. The quality of police–citizen relations in a stratified and segregated society seems highest in areas where the need for direct police services is minimal and to deteriorate in places where intense police–citizen interactions occur.

Despite the success of matching this conceptual skeleton with real-world data, some fine-tuning of the theory may further improve its correspondence with the empirical reality. Based on an examination of the findings from the PSS data, I sketch out some possible directions for further development of the theory.

The Role of Intraneighborhood Structure

That residential segregation defines the demographic landscape of American metropolises implies that in terms of demographic statistics, between-neighborhood variance is much more important than within-neighborhood variance. As a matter of fact, the internal homogeneity that distinguishes urban and suburban residential areas was the main justification for the use of neighborhood as the unit of analysis. Accordingly, my formulations on and assessment of ecological factors were also limited by their singular focus on the change in the *level* or *rate* of determined demographic variables. An additional question concerns a possible change in the *dispersion*, or *variance*, of the same structural features within neighborhoods. Economic inequality and racial heterogeneity stick out as the two key measures of within-neighborhood dispersion that dominate the research on community control. The existence of income inequality and racial heterogeneity in a bounded geographic unit is frequently portrayed as a destabilizing pressure and is associated with the relative deprivation and group competition that breed grievances and antipathy among residents. This negative depiction of demographic diversity points to its potentially destructive effects on police–citizen relations. But the reality may be more complicated than this simplistic inference.

In fact, policing may develop in two opposing directions in economically unequal and ethnically diverse communities, depending on the de-

Conclusion and Discussion

gree of residential stability and long-term migration trends that characterize these places. The most researched heterogeneous neighborhoods are those transitional districts undergoing massive white flight that usually suffer animosity and sparse acquaintanceship networks among residents, attenuated control of public space, and low participation in community activities (Bursik & Grasmick, 1993; Sampson & Groves, 1989). The problem in these transitional areas are caused not by the absolute lack of resources that wreaks marginal neighborhoods, but by the residential instability fueled by fear or indifference that undermines the social organization needed for the control of crime and violence. Therefore, police work is likely to be more proactive, enforcement oriented, and coercive to counterbalance the anarchical state of community disarray. If conducted without local political support, this more authoritative style of policing can be inflammatory in neighborhoods already tensed by class or racial differences.

But if the significant economic inequality and ethnic diversity of a neighborhood are accompanied by softened racial prejudices and sustained private and public investment in the institutional infrastructure (e.g., school, hospital, housing, playground, etc.), the elusive goal of residential stability may become a reachable reality. Stereotypical categorizations of neighborhood worthiness dissipates as residents of varying income levels and cultural backgrounds engage in meaningful interactions. The skills, education, and voluntary associations that better-off families bring to their communities can help their less wealthy neighbors to "free ride" in these stable, integrated neighborhoods. Past research has found that because of practical needs and better position, those families of larger size or higher income are more likely to spend money on housing improvements and to participate in community organizations, which increases the livability of the entire community (Taub, Taylor, & Dunham, 1984). The open environment, thus created, can turn the ethnic heterogeneity of residents from being a source of tension and conflict to a source of cultural enrichment and social capitalization. The objective is to create collective interests and a shared destiny in the system so that neighbors of different class and race backgrounds can identify with each other and work together toward common goals. Effective and democratic policing strengthens under these ecological conditions. Moreover, the stabilization and development of thriving, integrated communities are the main policy prescriptions that can be derived from an ecological theory for the long-term progress of police–citizen relations.

The Nonrecursive Nature of Police Behavior and Citizen Response

The strong correlations found between independent and dependent variables in the multivariate models hint that it is very likely that equally

Figure 6.1
The nonrecursive ecological model

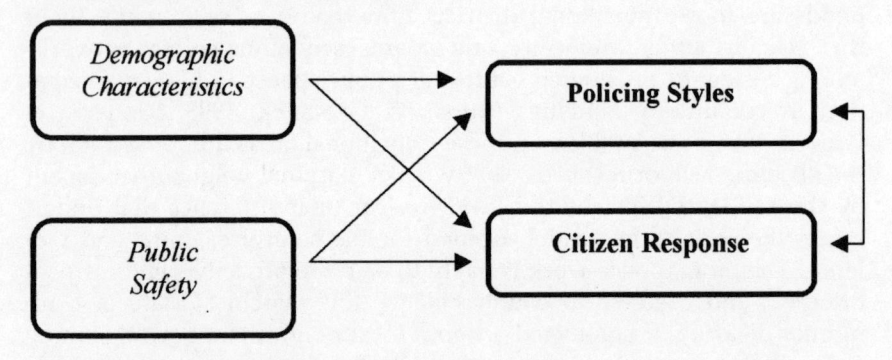

```
  Demographic
  Characteristics  ─────────▶  Policing Styles  ◀─┐
         ╲       ╱                                │
          ╲     ╱                                 │
           ╳                                      │
          ╱     ╲                                 │
         ╱       ╲                                │
  Public          ─────────▶  Citizen Response ◀──┘
  Safety
```

important correlations exist among the dependent variables. The acceptance of this possibility would lead to a more dynamic view of police–community relations, in which nonrecursive and reciprocal causal influences between policing styles and citizen response are formally hypothesized. Certain methods of service delivery produce determined types of citizen response, and vice versa. The explicit formulation of police and citizens' mutual determination in accounting for the relationships between them adds some flexibility to an ecological theory that never means to embrace a static structural absolutism that describes both parties only as passive objects manipulated by structural forces.

At the individual encounter level, citizen demeanors were found to be among the most important determinants of officers' tactical choices (Worden & Shepard, 1996). It is reasonable to assume that the same reverse impact of police behavior on citizen conduct also exists at this micro level of analysis. However, at the neighborhood level, the reciprocal effects of prevailing policing styles and aggregate citizen response occur within the confines of the power structure and moral hierarchy of the larger society. Even though both parties actively, and sometimes creatively, engage in purposeful interactions, the stage of their drama has already been set by historical patterns of social stratification and residential segregation before individual encounters actually occur. Therefore, if included, policing styles and citizen responses will have to be specified as *endogenous* variables caused by neighborhood structure characteristics and never as *exogenous* variables of the ecological model. The interactions between police and the policed do not dilute the effects of stratification and segregation on the relationships of the citizenry to the state, but only reinforces the power differentials and geographic segmentations that define urban and suburban neighborhoods. Figure 6.1 shows the model that is likely to result from the consideration of reciprocal influences. In the diagram, policing styles and citizen response

Conclusion and Discussion

maintain a mutually reinforcing relationship. This reciprocal relationship could be significant, but is not self-sustained and is heavily dependent on exogenous structural factors.

Despite the interpretive improvements that may derive from the inclusion of demographic dispersion within neighborhoods and the consideration of the reciprocal effects of police–citizen interactions, the macro-dynamics of social stratification and residential segregation will considerably restrict the statistical effects of intraneighborhood variations and those of volitional behaviors of individual actors on the direction of police–citizen relations. While situational factors were found to be associated with the tactical behavior of *individual* officers in past research (Worden, 1996; Worden & Shepard, 1996), the proposed ecological theory assumes the fundamental supremacy of structural factors that operate across neighborhoods over local conditions and individual efforts in determining *aggregate* modes of policing styles and citizen response.

As the nation's cities are transformed through complex processes of industrial restructuring and fragmenting political jurisdictions, the factual legitimacy of state policing is eroding rapidly in the outer segments. Police and other criminal justice institutions will continue having difficulty getting disenfranchised members to follow instructions during face-to-face encounters and to approve the police role and work in society. Particularly at risk for rejecting police legitimacy are young adults and adolescents, whose life-choice decisions regarding marriage, work, and education are restricted by their geographic environments. As urban areas become more spatially differentiated in terms of resources and social conditions, a growing cadre of inner-city youth perceive little opportunity for advancement and, on this presumption, make decisions that ultimately lock them into a permanent state of confrontation with the status quo. This disjunction of power structure has direct consequences for American policing and police reform.

POLICE REFORM: A VIEW FROM AN ECOLOGICAL PERSPECTIVE

Although community policing has been a catch word for American policing, it is still in the conceptualization phase of development (Rosenbaum, 1998). Among the multitudes of definitions, some elements stand out as fundamental: a renewed attention on disorder and incivility, an emphasis on the involvement of community not only as a client but also as a partner, and the restructuring of police organizations. At the heart of this new model of policing is the mobilization of neighborhood residents and local institutions to create self-regulating communities where people become more territorial by increasing their surveillance of suspicious behavior, providing greater supervision of local youths and involvement in common activities. This grand vision of police–community partnership calls for a transformation of citizen behaviors and attitudes toward police through radical changes in police philosophy and practices. Although the rhetoric of change is strong at the top levels of executive government and law enforcement agencies, many attempts at reinventing police services have been courageously experimented with (Greene, 2000; Mastrofski, 1998), and some have even announced that a "democratic revolution" is now taking place in inner-city policing (Meares & Kahan, 1999), the reality is still less than encouraging as the focus moves away from "sound bite" discourses (Brodeur, 1998). Lack of quality control, uneven citizen participation, and resistance within police departments are only some of the downstream obstacles in the attempted transformation of policing. The occupational isolation of the police and the geographic segregation of the policed have poisoned American law enforcement. The extensive and intensive separation of one neighborhood from another, and of the police from the policed, have distorted and damaged any chance for a meaningful civic partnership.

This ecological approach situates police–community relations in the political and social context of police work; more specifically it explains policing styles and citizen behaviors and attitudes as the result of interaction between the power stratification and moral differentiation of neighborhoods. People who have bought into the same neighborhood share a mode of police services; and through the collective consumption of these services, residents have a common stake in the area's policing. Structural conditions determine cultural dispositions of police and the policed, and these cultural dispositions dictate actual interactions. Sustained improvements in police–community relations require a more permanent source of pressure to change both the contextual structure of policing and the content of value and belief systems. To engage the community, that is, to create a meaningful community partnership, has been and should always be an ideal in democratic policing. The following sections are intended to reflect on past difficulties as well as to look for realistic solutions.

Community and Policing

Recent police reform initiatives have struggled to restore the principles of community to American life, to give the term "community" a substantive meaning, and to recover the idea of locality as a basis for civic participation. Partnerships between neighborhoods and government have been advocated to alleviate the hardship resulting from societal neglect and the exclusion of poor people and minority districts. Working against the tide, they have kept alive the dream of participatory democracy through face-to-face cooperation in which people can reason with

Conclusion and Discussion

each other and search for common interests. Community policing programs time and again have managed to create top-down pressure to induce openness and imagination in police departments as well as to provide outlets for civic activism and lay leadership development. The growing managerialism within law enforcement agencies, which invites the police to think of the public as consumers of police services and to pay attention to customers' wishes and concerns, has sometimes fostered modest redistribution of governmental investment in marginal neighborhoods (Skogan, 1998).

Nonetheless, the historic experience with community policing suggests that it is, at best, an ameliorative, not a transforming, problem-solving strategy. Research has shown that in areas most in need of police–community partnerships, there exist not only important gaps in the quality of service provided by the police but also huge gaps in the quality of service provided by the public to the police (Bennet, 1998). In terms of peripheral neighborhoods' interests, partnership efforts have been constrained by the fact that while they could set up a new negotiating table and bring genuine concerns to that table, citizens from these neighborhoods have always been negotiating from a position of vulnerability. They come to the table with less political leverage and fewer resources to start with and are restricted also by the fact that policing often is intimately connected to rigid political processes that determine how different neighborhoods are categorized and how they should be policed.

Residential Segregation as a Critical Impediment to Police–Community Partnerships

Experiences of law and order have been strongly interwoven with, and constrained by, practices and attitudes toward class, racial, and age groups. The dynamics of neighborhood formation have always been in the direction of the concentration of resources and security on the one hand, and the seclusion of poverty and decay on the other hand. Antidiscrimination housing regulations and governmental urban planning have done little to reverse the persistence of extreme metropolitan residential segregation. When the proportion of white and middle-class residents of urban neighborhoods steadily decreases as the metropolitan population rises, four-fifths and one-third of high poverty neighborhoods are minority citizens and children, respectively (Jargowsky, 1997). What accounts for this growing residential polarization? A housing market sanctioned by the state. Since nearly all housing in the United States, and therefore most housing decisions and actions, are private, urban residential segregation has evolved in the minds of homebuyers from a social problem to a self-justifying fact of capitalist existence. The free market supports the notion that people like to live with their own kind.

Given that the principle only works for the included, those with power and choice, residential segregation is subtly and profoundly coercive for the excluded. Location establishes a special destiny for its residents. The standing of a neighborhood vis-à-vis other neighborhoods creates fortunes or misfortunes that its residents experience in common. Each place occupies a very unique political position in relation to the police amidst current extreme segregation, which structurally precludes the formation of interracial and interclass coalitions, undermining the emergence of pluralistic police constituencies.

In this highly unequal society, distancing and exclusion serve to remove the underlying problems of our market society further and further from daily experiences and immediate consciousness. Social distancing and physical exclusion might help to ameliorate the chronic sense of insecurity that middle-class households feel about their place and status, and to actually perpetuate their advantageous position. Maintaining isolated islands of powerlessness and disrepute exacts heavy social costs. The deterioration of neighborhoods costs the entire society in terms of the restricted ability to come and go freely as well as limiting access to sections of the city that are of cultural, social, and even economic importance. Those who are left in urban ghettos, as the analysis of PSS data showed, give up hope of changing public service agencies, and become angrier and more desperate. Detached from the market and politics, many of them and their neighbors have become more willing to threaten and harm than to try to compete and succeed in the mainstream. Ultimately, further exclusion becomes a tool for containing the worst effects of prior exclusion.

By looking for the causes of and solutions to problems of crime and disorder within the boundaries of local neighborhoods, community policing has tried to build a renewed sense of belonging among the peripheral communities on the back of exclusion from nonlocal centers of power and resources. "The police are going to help the poor and the excluded to solve their own problems," it is said. Police are to be embraced by the community while proactively penetrating every street and every corner of the neighborhood to get rid of disorder and incivility. Once the broken windows are fixed, the garbage is collected, and the junkies are kicked out of the neighborhoods, healthier social institutions will flourish. Yet, more often than not, policing remains business as usual. Enforcing civil codes and directing more police resources to high-crime areas have resulted in the greater probability of a fine, court citation, stop and search, and arrest for people living there who already receive the most police attention. The decentralization of police functions has never increased community control of the police; sometimes it only leads to the diffusion of responsibility and accountability.

Community policing initiatives have been far more shaped by beliefs than by an understanding of the social dynamics of and policymaking habits in American urban centers. Principal among these has been the stubborn tendency to bound urban disorder and its correlates, to locate their causes and solutions in the people who are experiencing them, and to interpret them in ways that do not require adjustment by those who live outside the social margins. In spite of evidence to the contrary, like the name-contaminating application of legalistic and intrusive controls in lower-SES and minority-dominated neighborhoods, the belief persists that people carelessly perpetuate their own hardships. We continue to view marginal and disreputable neighborhoods as if they were autonomous entities—not really part of a societal reward system—ruined by residents who were responsible for their own fate. Yet, there is abundant evidence that the market forces and political interests of outside people and institutions have had an important role in undermining the quality of life within disadvantaged neighborhoods, and thus constraining residents' possibilities to change the legalistic and coercive styles of policing to a true police–neighborhood partnership. Too often, police attempts to engage the community ended up destroying the very fabric that they wanted to repair. Disappointing experiences in civic cooperation and aggressive disinfecting strategies in the streets inadvertently reduced the future supply of trust for collaborative actions (Duffee, Fluellen, & Roscoe, 1999).

The idea that the police can mobilize resources and capacities in marginal and disreputable neighborhoods for their own regeneration has often been used to promote self-policing without the requisite external support and linkages. However, even under the best of circumstances, only a few residents act as neighborhood guardians, and fewer still as neighborhood organizers (Skogan, 1998; Skogan & Hartnett, 1997). Propositions and findings from ecological theory suggest that while the ideal of police–community partnerships is a genuine choice for core neighborhoods, it can become a false choice for poor and minority communities. In a society given to economic and racial segregation, focusing on the separate policing of individual neighborhoods implies a degree of acceptance of the permanent nature of one's exclusion. It is simply not possible for the deprived and distrusted to end their disorganization by setting up mini police states in inner cities, where people do not have adequate control over the police. Even when police innovations help to establish a sense of connection and solidarity within a peripheral neighborhood, that is not the same as a sense that one's community is vitally associated with and valued by the larger society. While participation nurtures democracy, it does not necessarily lead to increased opportunity or resources for one's neighborhood.

The history of police–community partnerships also reflects more subtle contradictions. Police have not only asked the powerless to solve problems that they did not cause, but have distrusted their capacity to do so or the motives of the indigenous leadership (the "loud mouths" and "gimmie-guys" known to the police) that emerged with self-help efforts (Skogan, 1998). The police also have often disliked the consequences of community mobilization, whether articulation of specific demands or expression of anger and frustration. In fact, police are more often the targets of neighborhood protests than allies in these civic mobilizations. Such confrontations sometimes have yielded victory against further injustices, but they rarely have done anything significant to improve community well-being. The history of police–community partnerships is not just one of deliberation and negotiation, but of expectations engendered and then betrayed by police failure to meet these demands. Just as the poor and the minorities are blamed for their own plight, citizens, media, and political authorities point their fingers at police incompetence to account for the unfulfilled promises. Very few have seriously questioned the axiom that neighborhood residents and local police, and they alone are the co-producers of social order (or disorder). Because of the perceived betrayal, each generation of police–community partnerships has found that it is harder and harder to marshal the motivation and trust needed to achieve its objectives.

It is reasonable to postulate the existence of an inverse relationship between residential segregation by race, class, and age and problematic policing. A less segregated metropolitan region tempers police–citizen conflict by creating common interests and encouraging integration among different social groups. The propensity to diminish intergroup prejudice is a function of face-to-face interaction. A socially polarized metropolitan region has a high potential for the development of coercive and legalistic policing and deep discontent toward police in its poor and minority sections.

Police Innovations in Societal Context

It is inevitable that the delivery of police services is caught up in larger social dilemmas. If the legitimacy of police action must be founded on consensual laws impartially enforced, then it will always be problematic in a social order premised on the unequal distribution of wealth and influence. The environment in which police departments have been forced to operate has made it difficult for them to successfully implement programs aimed at citizen mobilization and empowerment. A natural implication for an ecological theory is that the logic of community policing becomes irrational under conditions of community neglect and exclusion, and the lack of political determination to address these structural failures. It is the very existence of firmly segregated metropolises and profoundly depleted and isolated neighborhoods that is problematic

Conclusion and Discussion 143

and destructive. We cannot continue to move quickly past the idea and simply focus on addressing its consequences. Each time we do so, the stakes are much higher, and the tasks much more difficult.

I am not arguing that we should disavow community policing. Assuring responsive services and public participation in marginal neighborhoods is beneficial to those who live there. Police–community partnerships aspire to motivate neighborhood residents to renounce and seek mastery over their own insecurity and depredation. But when we focus our attention inside the neighborhood, on dilapidated and abandoned buildings, idle youths, graffiti, gangs, and fear, we must remember to look to causes and solutions beyond those conditions immediately linked to these problems. Current police reform vows to venture upstream to investigate the source of these problems, but upstream is as far away as the unreachable horizons. The most basic reasons for the prevalence of crime and fear, as well as the concentration of police–community animosity in poor and minority neighborhoods, are not found in police ineffectiveness, population indifference, nor even in the breakdown of community organization. It would be equally naive to attribute competence to the police and moral worthiness to the public in areas enjoying positive police–community relations. The causes of police–community relations are found in the primacy of the *marketplace* in defining people's worth and entitlement, and in shaping relations of subordination, in a limited sense of social obligation (particularly toward the poor, the young, and minorities), in the continued sanctioning of exclusionary housing segregation, and in the resulting feelings of helplessness and exclusion. Building a police reform agenda primarily on initiatives that address what has not yet been done by the local residents only masks the underlying threat of organizations and institutions whose routine functioning requires some spaces be ignored in order for the exchange value and profits of other places to be maximized (Logan & Molotch, 1987).

Police and citizens' inability to create a somewhat larger frame of mutual interest and mutual responsibility leaves them with little room to effectively address fundamental determinants of turbulent police–community relations. Police cannot continue to base their crime control efforts on the assumption that American culture and its system of distribution and redistribution are basically sound and just need some fine-tuning. The control of marginal neighborhoods and the surveillance of their residents are not exceptions to American policing, but are important elements of it. In the 1960s, police work was characterized as a form of state penetration in civil society to exercise permanent, coercive supervision over the "dangerous classes," and at the same time a constant manipulation of appearances to evoke, establish, and sustain the moral assent of the civilized majority (Silver, 1967). This observation will remain valid in the 2000s because inequality and segregation have not been significantly reduced yet. Of all the constraints on police–community partnership, it has been residents' sense of exclusion, physical and social, that has been the most difficult to address. What little common ground—in beliefs, experiences, identities, and aspirations—once existed between residents of peripheral neighborhoods and the larger society is now already gone. No strategy tried by the police has worked to eliminate the feeling of being oppressed. That is because the heart of the problem is not about underpolicing, but about the denial of social membership.

What about the Future?

Addressing the collapse of law and order does not primarily mean trying to bring large numbers of well-trained, courteous police officers into the inner city. Doing so without reconstructing the social and political sites in which policing takes place is conducive to the creation of a police state. The major barrier to a healthy police–community partnership in marginal neighborhoods is not the police occupational subculture that so often accommodates prejudices against the powerless and the disreputable, but the occupational field at the street level where the showdown between state coercion and societal neglect occurs. Advocates who believe in the transforming power of community policing or of any other police innovation underestimate the devastation that current practices in the market and the political decision making has caused in the lives of millions of citizens.

The key to building positive police–community relations does not lie in the hands of the criminal justice system. The citizenry can legitimately demand "more of the same," that their police catch more criminals and solve more crimes, that their prosecutors get more convictions, or their correction systems house more inmates. As a matter of fact, experts agree that the American criminal justice system has been doing very well in accomplishing these objectives (Walker, 1988). What the criminal justice system cannot fix are those social conflicts rooted in the miscarriage of distributive justice.

Experiences with the police are geographically determined. Unless the ecology of exclusion is gradually replaced by an ecology of inclusion in American metropolises, fundamental improvements will never occur in police–community relations. Neighborhood decline and disorder cannot be solved with programs in ghettos and barrios alone. More substantive improvements in police–community relations will not be realized by the geographically isolated groups alone, without massive participation from the traditional middle-class constituencies of the police. Public policy has to address structural obstacles to individual choice in residential mobility as well as encourage residential integration. In the long run, inner-city residents should be politically and economically empowered to move to and stay wherever they choose, whereas white and middle-class groups should be rewarded with high-quality public services if they choose to disperse into diversified and integrated communities. Residential segregation by race and class provides no basis for police–community partnership because it forces all issues of crime and policing to cleave along these two demographic lines. Police reform exclusively based on either middle-class stereotypes of the inner city or the grievances of the disenfranchised neighborhoods is not large enough or cohesive enough to carry through more significant and lasting changes. Only geographic diversification of class and race can create a situation in which households of different backgrounds necessarily share a common stake in neighborhood safety and democratic policing. Given the growing diversification within neighborhoods, informal controls and neighborhood organization provided by the most able groups yield benefits for others as well. Therefore, macro policies that increase productivity and reduce inequality are fundamental to doing so in the long run because history has shown they are the most effective tools to affect the spatial organization of residents and interests. Police initiatives that aim to alter the consciousness and behavior of disadvantaged neighborhoods' residents are unlikely to make much difference without larger changes in the metropolitan economy and in rates of segregation (Jargowsky, 1997; Wilson, 1987). Bad neighborhoods defeat good programs. But when actual improvements take place in the opportunity and residential structures, police initiatives to engage the community may do more good and help more individuals.

Is the creation of stable neighborhoods with equality and heterogeneity a utopian dream? Some empirical findings suggest that it is a viable, albeit difficult, enterprise. After examining the process of neighborhood change, Taub and colleagues concluded that "people tolerate a high level of threat if they find other aspects of the community to be a sufficiently gratifying compensation [...]. In certain circumstances, neighborhood amenities raise tolerance levels and thus maintain high levels of satisfaction even when the neighborhood is perceived as a comparatively threatening place to live" (1984, p. 170).

Ethnically integrated neighborhoods would diffuse police identification with the values and interests of larger, varied portions of the population, converting police officers into impartial *public* servants of a more diverse and tolerant society. Segregated niches of marginality can at best become recipients of legalistic and coercive police services that constrict the freedom of the citizenry without effectively enhancing public safety and liberty. Only by teaming up with better-off and more influential neighbors can less powerful citizens have realistic chances of turning into *constituents* of the police. Residential integration supports intergroup coalitions, whose concerns are more likely to be attended to by the police and to shape other related policies. Research has shown that both police behavior and citizen attitudes toward them are very sensitive to changes in the sociodemographic characteristics of area residents. Urban police crackdowns on drug trafficking, for example, were found to be more successful in gentrifying neighborhoods than in rundown areas because some new residents with higher incomes and better education began to set up new standards of acceptable conduct (Worden, Bynum, & Frank, 1994).

A tragic example of how a segregation-producing housing policy can become a structural prescription for poor police–community relations would be the construction of high-rise public housing buildings funded by the federal government during the late 1950s and early 1960s. To qualify for these residential projects, most nonelderly public housing applicants were usually single, unemployed, and had children. As a direct consequence of the selection criteria, many female-headed, minority households moved into these units. A huge flock of transient males frequented these places as uncommitted lovers and fathers of children born out of wedlock; more importantly, not a few of these commuting visitors were drug traffickers who adroitly developed public housing facilities into flourishing marketplaces for drug dealing. This picture decidedly impacted on how police conduct their business. "Public housing residents appeared to them [the police] to occupy the lowest rung on the drug distribution ladder. As a result, drug and cash seizures there rarely equaled the statistical standards set in other areas. In both cities [Denver and New Orleans], PHA [Public Housing Authorities] residents were frequently viewed with scorn by police officers, who perceived signs of encouragement for their efforts in public housing areas" (Skogan & Annan, 1994, p. 134).

When the police became convinced that occupants of public housing were often the problem rather than the solution, relations with the policed residents soured.

On their side, the poor often fear the police and resent the way they exercise their authorities. They may be interested in monitoring police misconduct and pressing for police accountability as they are in increasing police presence in their community. Many residents of poor and minority neighborhoods have had antagonistic encounters with the police. The police are another of their problems; they frequently are perceived to be arrogant, brutal, racist, and corrupt. Groups representing these neighborhoods will not automatically look to the police for legitimacy and guidance in preventing drug abuse, or extend a welcome hand of cooperation if the police just appear at the door. (Skogan & Annan, 1994, p. 142)

Conclusion and Discussion

Wounded trust and cynicism cannot be healed with public relations programs alone because neither the police nor the citizens can significantly alter the neighborhood's position in the social power structure. Social isolation in high poverty neighborhoods helps to maintain an oppositional culture whose values and norms prepare its bearers to antagonize against deliverers of public services, making it difficult for police to successfully engage the residents or for children to succeed in school (Anderson, 1990, 1997). The desire for police protection and the fear of losing control of the police create a dilemma that neither the police nor the policed are able to solve.

Circumstances and endeavors promoting productivity and income generation have had the most dramatic impact on socioeconomic inequality and segregation in the past (Jargowsky, 1997). Macroeconomic policies that would significantly improve police–community relations and reduce crime in the long run are those measures that stimulate productivity growth without "exaggerating the perils of inflation" or "underestimating the virtues of low employment" (Blinder, 1987, p. 33). Productivity growth should be pursued because it is the key to rising living standards. Although both inflation and unemployment generate economic inefficiency, they could have quite different effects on crime and policing. While the costs of inflation are more or less equally distributed across various segments of society, unemployment increases inequality, thus residential segregation and poorer quality of life in marginal neighborhoods, by striking hardest at the lowest end of the income distribution. Full employment makes significant inroads against poverty and discontent. Police will appreciate that.

Social policies ought to enhance the human capital of those who now have the least by investing in the quality of education and opportunities for training and retraining. The goal should exceed that of improving the academic performance of public school students, but strive to connect the preparation of children from disadvantaged neighborhoods with industries producing knowledge-based goods. Active assistance of inner-city residents to obtain, remain in, and commute to gainful, skilled jobs is crucial to the betterment of police–community relations because economic assimilation leads to stable spatial assimilation. The increase of the middle class in general, and of the minority middle class in particular, facilitates the eventual dispersal of peripheral neighborhoods.

Equally important are maneuvers that seek the full enforcement of fair housing and equal employment regulations, enabling people to leave marginal areas if they choose, for example, through housing voucher programs. In order to accelerate residential mobility, not only should choices be made available to inner-city residents but also the *controlled* revitalization and gentrification of once declining neighborhoods should be undertaken in order to attract human talents, financial resources, and political leverage from core residential areas and business districts. These programs will have to be carefully planned and closely monitored for them to resuscitate the physical places and, more importantly, the people already living in those places.

What can police do amid all these macro-politics? They can start to understand that the improvement of neighborhood quality of life is dependent on the course of changing economic, social, and political structures. Police have to recognize that their priorities have often been dictated by the wishes of the respectable establishment, favoring the enhancement of internal controls in neighborhoods over political actions that sustain the livability of those neighborhoods. But they should also be commended by the public for performing the arduous task of confronting and processing crime and disorder in many of our embattled streets. Their hard work and creativity have sometimes had a positive short-term impact on neighborhood crime rates (Kelling & Coles, 1996), and current efforts at devising innovative community-based programs have the prospects for jump-starting the rebuilding of neighborhood institutions (Duffee, Fluellen, & Roscoe, 1999). All these endeavors are noble and valuable in themselves. But crime reduction, community building, and neighborhood sustainability will not endure if left to the police without support from economic, housing, tax, and education policies made by federal, state, and local governments.

Harangued and funded by the federal government, many police departments are heroically engaging in collaborative projects to import external organizations, human talents, and financial assistance into local institutions of social organization to compete with gangs, drug trade, police control, and welfare dependency as bases for community preservation. The costs of the current basis for community organization in peripheral neighborhoods, as adaptive and acceptable as it may be, are simply too high. Families, schools, and churches now operate in a survival mode, expecting the police to hold the front line with verbal threats, batons, handcuffs, guns, sirens, and arrests. Nevertheless, the public must frankly accept the fact that the police do not control internal actors and external resources crucial to the success of multiagency actions or the mobilization of external resources, and do not even have control over their own budgets, strategic philosophy, and top leadership. Therefore, until residents of marginal neighborhoods truly become constituents of their own political governance, police should only be evaluated on how well they perform traditional police tasks, and not on whether multiagency actions effectively take place or neighborhoods improve. It comes as no surprise that voices are heard urging police managers to give up the idea of engaging the community, which risks ignoring the end product of policing in favor of the means. According to this thread of thinking, problem-solving policing should instead be embraced because it focuses on the mandate of crime reduction and stresses the role of the police rather than the role of community (Brodeur, 1998).

Until not long ago the American economy had experienced unprecedented growth. Everything that should be down was down—unemployment, inflation, interest rates, and crime. Everything that should be up was up—GDP, capital spending, incomes, the stock market, employment, exports, consumer confidence, and public satisfaction with the performance of government at all levels. Experts differ greatly in their interpretations of the vibrant paradise we saw and lived in. Some optimistically found the pathway leading to another coming American century in the lower crime rates, sharp reductions in the welfare rolls, booming entertainment industries, and record numbers of teens entering college (Zuckerman, 1998). Others believed that, rather than an unchangeable trend toward sustained prosperity supported by a revolutionary growth in national productivity, the optimism was dangerously founded on one of the many upward bounces that together with other downward fluctuations make up the complete economic cycle (Krugman, 1998). This economic debate may sound foreign to police reform, but it should not be ignored by students of crime and justice because of its serious implications for social conditions, demographic changes, and social deviance and its control.

Recent Gallup poll data suggest that this historic economic boom that started in 1992 also uplifted American perceptions of police services, at least in the aggregate. Sixty-two percent of the respondents are confident in the ability of the police to protect them from violent crime, and a comparable 60 percent say they have respect for their local police (Chambers & Newport, 2000), both measures at their historical peaks. Yet a disturbing and inconsistent finding somewhat taints this rose-colored picture. As many as 32 percent of the respondents still believe there is police brutality in their neighborhoods, when the same indicator rarely exceeded 10 percent in the tumultuous years of the 1960s. Another Gallup study also found that while 74 percent of whites say that blacks are treated by the police the same way that whites are, only 36 percent of blacks feel that this is the case in their own community (Ludwig, 2000). Why do black people see increases in police brutality and perceive unequal treatment in *their own* neighborhoods? Lower tolerance for this kind of police misconduct has probably led to heightened awareness, but cannot explain this increasing divergence of experiences with the police. When a growing majority of the population is enjoying satisfying police services as part of their improved general well-being, a growing minority of citizens are feeling mistreated by the police. These discrepancies in experiences with and perceptions of the police are geographically distinguished. In fact, poll analysts have observed that "nonwhites and those living in urban areas are overwhelmingly more likely to say there is police brutality in their area than are whites and those living in the suburbs and in rural areas. Only 28% of whites say yes to this brutality question, compared to 50% of nonwhites. Similarly, 46% of those living in urban areas say yes, compared to just 15% of those in rural areas" (Chambers & Newport, 2000). Attitudes motivate behavior. The rates of assaults against law enforcement officers in cities with a population of 50,000 or above average 17.3 per 100 officers, while the rates for the suburban counties and rural counties are 13 and 6.2 per 100 officers, respectively (Federal Bureau of Investigations, 1999). Communities mired in conflicts with the police are increasingly likely to delegitimize police as a respectful institution.

Despite, and because of, the economic miracle powered by the information revolution and global integration, the process of social marginalization has continued to accelerate and to fracture post-industrial cities (Body-Gendrot, 2000). Deindustrialization, a service economy, and financial globalization have increased and continue to contribute to growing class polarization and racial differentiation by employing more high-wage and low-wage workers and fewer in the middle range. The result is the perpetuation of the hierarchical clustering of residential space, with protective citadels and enclaves on the one end and constraining ghettos on the other (Logan, 2000; Marcuse & van Kempen, 2000). Policing will remain fragmented in this context, with its legitimacy firmly established in and sanctioned by the centers of power, while contested among and by people who must endure its social and physical consequences. Based on ecological theory, I will indulge myself in a mental experiment envisioning what would happen to American policing in a different socioeconomic scenario.

The consequences of an economic slowdown are straightforward. If America is bogged down by worldwide depression and suffers a serious economic recession with high unemployment, the spatial and political isolation of traditional urban ghettos makes them extremely vulnerable to fiscal austerity. To the politicians and their middle-class constituents who do not have immediate self-interest in the welfare of marginal areas, trimming social programs servicing the less powerful, who are basically unable to inflict political damage, is economically sound and politically safe in times of declining resources.

A weak economy multiplies peripheral neighborhoods in size and number. A depressed job market unleashes new breeds of "chronic losers," which heightens racial intolerance and thickens residential segregation as a form of social control. Tougher preventive controls from the police and protracted frustration and anger among the haveless because of social stagnation would discourage the police and the policed to reciprocate civility. Given the deeper fragmentation of the current social fabric, the memories of high-unemployment-but-low-crime from the

Great Depression will not be repeated. Existing networks of illegal economy revolving around the drug trade, the trafficking of arms and illegal immigrants, prostitution, gambling, and money laundering will quickly expand in the hardest-hit urban neighborhoods, supplying money and jobs to the cornered residents and corrupting law enforcement agents. The deterioration of public safety, coupled with rising racial tension and xenophobia, will surely encourage a more repressive and punitive approach to crime control and turn police–community relations in desperate inner cities into a ticking time bomb.

What if the current expansion of the economy continues for a while? If we do not dismantle present practices of segregation and exclusion, or if we pursue an inner-city improvement strategy that combines governmental financial assistance to poor areas with continuing segregation, the fragmentation of policing will not change. Real long-term solutions to this problem will only come when the surplus from a strong economy is coupled with comprehensive fiscal, housing, and transportation policies to reconnect residents of marginal neighborhoods to higher education and remunerative jobs in the context of policy-induced residential integration. Without the determination to achieve prosperous integration, even a sustained economic growth at the national level can bring about new strains in police–community interactions through two related residential movements. In times of prosperity, the flight of the thriving minority middle-class families from minority communities and the gentrification of poor areas by the inflow of middle-income groups will hurt the least resourceful.

Education and material well-being have acted as effective solvents of racial prejudices and allowed the growth of the black middle classes and their movement into stable suburban neighborhoods, which further consolidated their new class status. Intolerance toward racial minorities has steadily declined among educated middle-class whites, who have been somewhat more likely to accept middle-class black neighbors than have been working-class whites to accept black neighbors of their own class (Taub et al., 1984). Although the exodus of new middle-class, minority families into stable, more integrated suburbs would not negatively affect police–community relations in these areas, their absence from inner-city neighborhoods harms police–community relations there in two basic ways. On the one hand, their presence in the area provides positive role models to children and boosts linkages with external opportunities, both effects help to organize the residents around conventional activities, thus prevent the neighborhood from becoming prime targets of aggressive crime-control policing. On the other hand, past activism has equipped many educated blacks and Hispanics with acute civic consciousness as well as leadership skills to influence and work with governmental agencies, including the police, for the benefits of their communities.

In addition to the out-migration of middle-class black households, the gentrification of central districts also often accompanies the economic growth of the city. When historic neighborhoods are rediscovered and renovated by bohemian artists, gays, and childless young professionals, they become substantially upgraded, and attractive for more settled middle-class families. Because of the unusually high degree of tolerance within this risk-taking population, gentrifying communities are generally racially integrated, socioeconomically inclusive (Taub et al., 1984), less densely populated, and have a smaller young male population (McDonald, 1986). Like some of the ethnically integrated suburbs, gentrified areas are training grounds for the development of fresh relationships of mutual trust and respect between police and minority citizens. Self-regulatory capacities in gentrified districts are restored (McDonald, 1986) and closer cooperation between the police and the public ensued (Worden et al., 1994). Evidence suggests that not only does gentrification improve police–citizen relations because of demographic changes, but effective policing can also stir residential movements leading to the revitalization of areas. Operation Pressure Point launched by the NYPD in 1984 to disrupt the drug market and to improve the quality of life was judged so successful that rent and land value started to soar after the crime drop, attracting professionals from nearby areas (Kleiman & Smith, 1990). Nevertheless, the gentrification of decaying neighborhoods quietly introduces another formidable demographic challenge to good policing.

Unlike "incumbent upgrading" where the housing stock is renovated for existing residents with little or no population change, gentrification improves police–community relations by simply displacing police suspicion and citizen distrust to adjacent disadvantaged zones. Although the in-migration of largely white and middle-class households that often resuscitates the economic and political vitality of a neighborhood can quickly foster a strong alliance between police and new residents, the concomitant relocation of original residents to nearby marginal areas simply creates new focuses of tension and resentment. Such a pseudo-progression toward democratic policing enhances the civic appearance of the place without genuinely promoting the self-governance of the less fortunate, and thus should not be sought, openly or tacitly, as a policy choice. There will be no good policing without the sociopolitical emancipation of the policed.

Even the most sensible policies and investment, if limited to police reform or police engagement of the community without attention to societal context, will have only minimal impact. In spite of it all, the community policing movement remains strangely powerful, even in its vulnerability. Perhaps I was wrong when I argued earlier that community policing is not a transforming strategy. There is a certain intrinsic transformative value in mobilization and collective action. More than any other police reform, community policing has struggled to fuse the visionary with the actual, and translate the result into measurable action. That, in part, is why police efforts to engage the community seem so new each time, even though they follow well-worn paths and face long-standing hurdles.

As we enter this new century, will the American people and their police treat each other with a stronger sense of concern and responsibility for the interests of the common good? How can the policing of 21st-century America become a civic enterprise of the people, by the people, and for the people? An ecological theory of police–citizen relations offers a useful theoretical framework from where we can depart to think about these questions.

References

Achen, C. H. (1984). *Interpreting and using regression.* Newbury Park, CA: Sage.
Adams, K. (1999). What we know about police use of force. In National Institute of Justice (Ed.), *Use of force by police: Overview of national and local data* (pp. 1–14). Washington, DC: National Institute of Justice.
Agresti, A., & Finlay, B. (1986). *Statistical methods for the social sciences.* San Francisco: Dellen Publishing Co.
Albrecht, S., & Green, M. (1977). Attitudes toward the police and the larger attitude complex: Implications for police–community relationships. *Criminology, 5,* 67–86.
Alpert, G. P., & Dunham, R. G. (1988). *Policing multi-ethnic neighborhoods: The Miami study and findings for law enforcement in the United States.* Westport, CT: Greenwood Press.
Anderson, E. (1990). *Street wise: Race, class, and change in the urban community.* Chicago: University of Chicago Press.
Anderson, E. (1997). Violence and inner-city street code. In J. McCord (Ed.), *Violence and childhood in inner-city violence* (pp. 1–30). New York: Cambridge University Press.
Arthur, J. A., & Case, C. E. (1994). Race, class and support for police use of force. *Crime, Law and Social Change, 21,* 167–182.
Bachman, R. (1992). *Elderly victims.* Washington, DC: U.S. Department of Justice.
Banerjee, W. C., & Baer, W. C. (1984). *Beyond the neighborhood unit: Residential environments and public policy.* New York: Plenum.
Banton, M. (1963, April). Social integration and police. *Police Chief,* 10–12.
Bayley, D. H. (1985). *Patterns of policing: A comparative international analysis.* New Brunswick, NJ: Rutgers University Press.

Bayley, D. H. (1986). The tactical choice of police patrol officers. *Journal of Criminal Justice, 14*, 329–348.
Bayley, D. H. (1994). *Police for the future*. New York: Oxford University Press.
"A beating in Brooklyn." (1997, August 25). *Time*, p. 38.
Bennet, T. (1998). Police and public involvement in the delivery of community policing. In J. P. Brodeur (Ed.), *How to recognize good policing? Problems and issues* (pp. 107–122). Thousand Oaks, CA: Sage.
Billy, J. O. G., & Moore, D. E. (1992). A multilevel analysis of marital and nonmarital fertility in the United States. *Social Forces, 70*, 977–1011.
Bittner, E. (1967). The police on skid row. *American Sociological Review, 32*, 699–715.
Bittner, E. (1970). *The functions of the police in modern society*. Washington, DC: National Institute of Mental Health.
Bittner, E. (1974). Florence Nightingale in pursuit of Willie Sutton: A theory of the police. In H. Jacob (Ed.), *The potential for reform in criminal justice* (pp. 17–44). Beverly Hills, CA: Sage.
Bittner, E. (1975). The impact of police–community relations. In D. P. Geary (Ed.), *Community relations and administration of justice* (pp. 291–310). New York: Wiley.
Bittner, E. (1976). Policing juveniles: The social context of community practice. In M. K. Rosenheim (Ed.), *Pursuing justice for children* (pp. 69–93). Chicago: University of Chicago Press.
Bittner, E. (1982). Emerging police issues. In B. L. Garmire (Ed.), *Local government police management* (pp. 1–12). Washington, DC: International City Management Association.
Bittner, E. (1983). Urban police. In S. H. Kadish (Ed.), *Encyclopedia of crime and justice* (Vol. 3, pp. 1135–1139). New York: Free Press.
Black, D. J. (1970). Production of crime. *American Sociological Review, 35*, 736–748.
Black, D. J. (1971). The social organization of arrest. *Stanford Law Review, 23*, 1087–1111.
Black, D. J. (1976). *The behavior of law*. New York: Academic Press.
Black, D. J. (1980). *The manners and customs of the police*. New York: Academic Press.
Black, D. J. (1989). *Sociological justice*. New York: Oxford University Press.
Blau, J., & Blau, P. (1982). Metropolitan structure and violent crime. *American Sociological Review, 47*, 114–128.
Blinder, A. S. (1987). *Hard heads, soft heads: Tough-minded economics for a just society*. Reading, MA: Addison-Wesley.
Block, R. L. (1974). Why notify the police?: The victim's decision to notify the police of an assault. *Criminology, 11*, 555–569.
Block, R. L. (1979). Community, environment, and violent crime. *Criminology, 17*, 46–57.
Body-Gendrot, S. (2000). *The social control of cities?: A comparative perspective*. Oxford: Blackwell.
Boggs, S. L., & Galliher, J. F. (1975). Evaluating the police: A comparison of back street and household comparison. *Social Problems, 22*, 393–406.
Boydstun, J. H. (1975). *San Diego field interrogation: Final report*. Washington, DC: The Police Foundation.
Brandl, S. G., Frank, J., Worden, R. E., & Bynum, T. S. (1994). Global and specific

attitudes toward the police: Disentangling the relationship. *Justice Quarterly, 11*, 119–134.
Bratt, R. G. (1983). People and their neighborhoods: Attitudes and policy implications. In P. L. Clay & R. M. Hollister (Eds.), *Neighborhood policy and planning* (pp. 133–150). Lexington, MA: Lexington Books.
Brewster, K. L., Billy, J. O. G., & Grady, W. R. (1993). Social context and adolescent behavior: The impact of community on the transition to sexual activity. *Social Forces, 71*, 713–740.
Brodeur, J.-P. (1998). The assessment of police performance: Conclusions. In J. P. Brodeur (Ed.), *How to recognize good policing? Problems and issues* (pp. 215–222). Thousand Oaks, CA: Sage.
Brown, M. K. (1988). *Working the street: Police discretion and the dilemmas of reform.* New York: Russell Sage Foundation.
Buerger, M. E. (1994). A tale of two targets: Limitations of community anticrime actions. *Crime and Delinquency, 40*, 411–436.
Bureau of Justice Statistics. (1991). *Law enforcement management and administrative statistics 1990.* Washington, DC: U.S. Department of Justice.
Bureau of Justice Statistics. (2000). *Criminal victimization 1999: Changes 1998–99 with trends from 1993–99.* Washington, DC: Author.
Burgess, E. W. (1925). The growth of the city. In Robert E. Park & Ernest W. Burgess (Eds.), *The city* (pp. 47–62). Chicago: University of Chicago Press.
Bursik, R. J., & Grasmick, H. G. (1993). *Neighborhood and crime: The dimensions of effective community control.* San Francisco: Lexington Books.
Cao, L., Frank, J., & Cullen, F. T. (1996). Race, community context and confidence in the police. *American Journal of Police, 15*, 3–22.
Chambers, C., & Newport, F. (2000). Americans rate their police [Online]. Princeton, NJ: Gallup Organization. Available: http://www.gallup.com/poll/release/pr000911.asp [2000, September 20]
Chira, S. (1989, July 16). Programs to ease social problems burden New York's poorest areas. *New York Times*, p. 1.
Clarke, R. V. (1995). Situational crime prevention. In M. Tonry & D. P. Forrington (Eds.) *Building a safer society: Strategic approaches to crime prevention* (pp. 91–150). Chicago: University of Chicago Press.
Clemente, F., & Kleiman, M. (1976). Fear of crime among the aged. *Gerontologist, 16*, 207–210.
Cohen, L. E., & Felson, M. (1979). Social change and crime rate trends: A routine activity approach. *American Sociological Review, 44*, 588–608.
Covington, J., & Taylor, R. B. (1991). Fear of crime in residential neighborhoods: Implications of between- and within-neighborhood sources for current models. *Sociological Quarterly, 32*, 231–249.
Cox, S. M., & Fitzgerald, J. D. (1996). *Police in community relations: Critical issues.* Dubuque, IA: Brown & Benchmark.
Crank, J. P. (1990). The influence of environmental and organizational factors on police styles in urban and rural environments. *Journal of Research in Crime and Delinquency, 27*, 166–189.
Crank, J. P. (1998). *Understanding police culture.* Cincinnati, OH: Anderson.
Curry, G. D., & Spergel, I. A. (1988). Gang homicide, delinquency and community. *Criminology, 26*, 381–405.

Davis, J. R. (1990). Comparison of attitudes toward the New York City police. *Journal of Police Science and Administration, 17,* 233–243.

Davis, R. C. (2000). *Perceptions of the police among members of six ethnic communities in central Queens, NY.* Rockville, MD: National Institute of Justice.

Decker, S. H. (1981). Citizen attitudes toward the police: A review of past findings and suggestions for future policy. *Journal of Police Science and Administration, 9,* 80–87.

DuBow, F., McCabe E., & Kaplan, G. (1979). *Reactions to crime: A critical review of literature.* Washington, DC: Government Printing Office.

Duffee, D. E. (1990). *Explaining criminal justice: Community theory and criminal justice reform* (2nd ed.). Prospect Heights, IL: Waveland Press.

Duffee, D. E., Fluellen, R., & Roscoe, T. (1999). Constituency building and urban community policing. In R. H. Langworthy (Ed.), *Measuring what matters: Proceedings from the policing research institute meetings* (pp. 91–119). Rockville, MD: National Institute of Justice.

Durkheim, E. (1964 [1895]). *The rules of sociological method.* New York: Free Press.

Eck, J. E., Maguire, E. R. (2000). Have changes in policing reduced violent crime? An assessment of the evidence. In A. Blumstein & J. Wallman (Eds.), *The crime drop in America* (pp. 207–265). New York: Cambridge University Press.

Edmonston, B., & Guterbock, T. M. (1984). Is suburbanization slowing down? Recent trends in population deconcentration in U.S. metropolitan areas. *Social Forces, 62,* 905–925.

Elliston, F. A., & Feldberg, M. (1985). Authority, discretion, and the police function. In F. A. Elliston & M. Feldberg (Eds.), *Moral issues in police work* (pp. 11–13). Lanham, MD: Rowman & Littlefield.

Entwisle, D. R., Alexander, K. L., & Olson, L. S. (1994). The gender gap in math: Its possible origins in neighborhood effects. *American Sociological Review, 59,* 822–838.

Ericson, R. V. (1982). *Reproducing order: A study of police patrol work.* Toronto: University of Toronto Press.

Federal Bureau of Investigations. (1999). *Law enforcement officers killed and assaulted 1998.* Washington, DC: Author.

Fernandez, R. M., & Kulik, J. C. (1981). A multilevel model of life satisfaction: Effects of individual characteristics and neighborhood composition. *American Sociological Review, 46,* 840–850.

Ferraro, K. F. (1995). *Fear of crime: interpreting victimization risk.* Albany: State University of New York Press.

Fielding, N. G. (1991). *The police and social conflict: Rhetoric and reality.* London: Athlone Press.

Fischer, C. S. (1982). *To dwell among friends: Personal networks in town and city.* Chicago: University of Chicago Press.

Flanagan, T. J., & Vaughn, M. S. (1996). Public opinion about police abuse of force. In W. A. Geller & H. Toch (Eds.), *Police violence: Understanding and controlling police abuse of force* (pp. 113–128). New Haven, CT: Yale University Press.

Free, Jr., M. D. (1995). *African Americans and the criminal justice system.* New York: Garland.

Friedrich, R. J. (1980). Police use of force: Individuals, situations, and organizations. *Annals of the American Academy of Political and Social Science, 452,* 82–97.

Furstenberg, F. F., & Wellford, C. F. (1973). Calling the police: The evaluation of police services. *Law and Society Review, 7,* 394–406.

Gale, D. E. (1983). Middle-class resettlement in older urban neighborhoods: The evidence and implications. In P. L. Clay & R. M. Hollister (Eds.), *Neighborhood policy and planning* (pp. 35–53). Lexington, MA: Lexington Books.

Garner, J. H., & Maxwell, C. D. (1999). Measuring the amount of force used by and against the police in six jurisdictions. In National Institute of Justice (Ed.), *Use of force by police: Overview of national and local data* (pp. 25–44). Washington, DC: National Institute of Justice.

Garofalo, J., & McLeod, M. (1989). The structure and operations of neighborhood watch programs in the United States. *Crime and Delinquency, 35,* 326–344.

Goldstein, H. (1979). Improving policing: A problem-oriented approach. *Crime and Delinquency, 25,* 235–258.

Gove, W. (1985). The effect of age and gender on deviant behavior: A biopsychological perspective. In A. Rossi (Ed.), *Gender and the life course* (pp. 115–144). Hawthorne, NY: Aldine.

Green, L. (1996). *Policing places with drug problems.* Thousand Oaks, CA: Sage.

Greenberg, S. W. (1983). *External solutions to neighborhood-based problems: The case of community crime prevention.* Paper presented at the annual meeting of the Law and Society Association.

Greene, H. T. (2000). Understanding the connections between race and police violence. In M. W. Markowitz & D. D. Jones-Brown (Eds.), *The system in black and white: Exploring the connections between race, crime, and justice* (pp. 73–84). Westport, CT: Praeger.

Greenfeld, L. A., Langan, P. A., & Smith, S. K. (1997). *Police use of force: Collection of national data.* Washington, DC: Bureau of Justice Statistics.

Greenwood, P. W. (1995). Juvenile crime and juvenile justice. In J. Q. Wilson & J. Petersilia (Eds.), *Crime* (pp. 91–120). San Francisco: ICS Press.

Grinc, R. M. (1994). Angels in marble: Problems in stimulating community involvement in community policing. *Crime and Delinquency, 40,* 437–468.

Guyot, D. (1991). *Policing as though people matter.* Philadelphia: Temple University Press.

Habermas, J. (1981). *The theory of communicative action* (Vol. 1). London: Heinemann.

Hagan, J. (1994). *Crime and disrepute.* Thousand Oaks, CA: Pine Forge Press.

Hagan, J., Gillis, A. R., & Chan, J. (1978). Explaining official delinquency: A spatial study of class, conflict, and control. *Sociological Quarterly, 19,* 386–398.

Hahn, H. (1971). Ghetto assessment of police protection and authority. *Law and Society Review, 6,* 183–194.

Harcourt, B. E. (1998). Reflecting on the subject: A critique of the social influence conception of deterrence, the broken-window theory, and order maintenance policing New York style. *Michigan Law Review, 97,* 291–389.

Harris and Associates. (1978). *The 1978 HUD survey on the quality of urban life.* Washington, DC: Government Printing Office.

Hearn, F. (1997). *Moral order and social disorder: The American search for civil society.* New York: Aldine de Gruyter.

Hening, J., & Maxfield, M. G. (1978). Reducing fear of crime: Strategies for intervention. *Victimology, 3,* 297–313.

Hepburn, J. R. (1978). Race and the decision to arrest: An analysis of warrants issued. *Journal of Research in Crime and Delinquency, 15,* 54–73.

Homant, R. J., Kennedy, D. B., & Fleming, R. M. (1984). The effect of victimization and the police response on citizens' attitudes toward police. *Journal of Police Science and Administration, 12,* 323–332.

Human Rights Watch. (1998). *Shielded from justice: Police brutality and accountability in the United States.* New York: Author.

Hunt, J. (1985). Police accounts of normal force. *Urban Life, 13,* 315–341.

Hunter, A. (1983). The urban neighborhood: Its analytical and social context. In P. L. Clay & R. M. Hollister (Eds.), *Neighborhood policy and planning* (pp. 3–20). Lexington, MA: Lexington Books.

Hurst, Y. G., & Frank, J. (2000). How kids view cops: The nature of juvenile attitudes toward the police. *Journal of Criminal Justice, 28,* 189–202.

Jackson, P. I. (1986). Black visibility, city size, and social control. *Sociological Quarterly, 27,* 185–203.

Jackson, P. I., & Carroll, L. (1981). Race and the war on crime: The sociopolitical determinants of municipal police expenditures in 90 non-southern U.S. cities. *American Sociological Review, 46,* 290–305.

Jacob, H. (1971). Black and white perceptions of justice in the city. *Law and Society Review, 5,* 69–89.

Jacobs, D. (1979). Inequality and police strength: Conflict theory and coercive control in metropolitan areas. *American Sociological Review, 44,* 913–925.

Jacobs, D., & O'Brien, R. M. (1998). The determinants of deadly forces: A structural analysis of police violence. *American Journal of Sociology, 103,* 837–862.

Jargowsky, P. A. (1997). *Poverty and place: Ghettos, barrios, and the American city.* New York: Russell Sage Foundation.

Jaynes, G., & Williams, R. M. (Eds.). (1989). *A common destiny: Blacks and American society.* Washington, DC: National Academy Press.

Johnston, R. J. (1976). Residential area characteristics. In D. T. Herbert & R. J. Johnston (Eds.), *Social areas in cities. Vol. I: Spatial Processes and Form* (pp. 193–235). New York: Wiley.

Kelling, G. L., & Coles, C. M. (1996). *Fixing broken windows: Restoring order and reducing crime in our communities.* New York: Free Press.

Kelling, G. L., Pate, A. M., Dickman, D., & Brown, C. E. (1974). *The Kansas City preventive patrol experiment: A summary report.* Washington, DC: Police Foundation.

Kelly, R. D. G. (1994). *Race rebels: Culture, politics, and the black working class.* New York: Free Press.

Kleiman, M. A. R., & Smith, K. D. (1990). State and local enforcement: In search of a strategy. In M. Tonry & J. Q. Wilson (Eds.), *Drugs and crime* (pp. 69–108). Chicago: University of Chicago Press.

Klinger, D. A. (1994). Demeanor or crime? Why "hostile" citizens are more likely to be arrested. *Criminology, 32,* 475–493.

Klinger, D. A. (1996). More on demeanor and arrest in Dade County. *Criminology, 34,* 61–82.

References

Klinger, D. A. (1997). Negotiating order in patrol work: An ecological theory of police response to deviance. *Criminology, 35*, 277–306.

Lanza-Kaduce, L., & Greenleaf, R. G. (1994). Police–citizen encounters: Turk on norm resistance. *Justice Quarterly, 11*, 605–623.

LeBeau, J., & Coulson, R. (1996). Routine activities and the spatial-temporal variation of calls for police services: The experience of opposites on the quality of life spectrum. *Police Studies, 19*, 1–14.

Lipset, S. M., & Schneider, W. (1983). *The confidence gap: Business, labor and government in the public mind.* New York: Free Press.

Liska, A. E. (1992). Introduction to the study of social control. In A. E. Liska (Ed.), *Social threat and social control* (pp. 1–29). Albany: State University of New York Press.

Liska, A. E., & Chamlin, M. B. (1984). Social structure and crime control among macrosocial units. *American Journal of Sociology 90*, 383–395.

Liska, A. E., Lawrence, J. J., & Benson, M. (1981). Perspectives on the legal order: The capacity for social control. *American Journal of Sociology, 87*, 413–426.

Logan, J. R. (2000). Still a global city: The racial and ethnic segmentation of New York. In P. Marcuse & R. van Kempen (Eds.), *Globalizing cities: A new spatial order?* (pp. 158–185). Oxford: Blackwell.

Logan, J. R., & Molotch, H. L. (1987). *Urban fortunes: The political economy of place.* Berkeley: University of California Press.

Logan, J. R., & Schneider, M. (1984). Racial segregation and racial change in American suburbs, 1970–1980. *American Journal of Sociology, 89*, 874–888.

Ludwig, J. (2000). *Perceptions of black and white Americans continue to diverge widely on issues of race relations in the U.S.* [Online] Princeton, NJ: The Gallup Organization. Available: http://www.gallup.com/poll/releases/pr000228.asp [2000, September 20]

Lundman, R. J. (1980). Police patrol work: A comparative perspective. In R. J. Lundman (Ed.), *Police behavior: A sociological perspective* (pp. 52–65). New York: Oxford University Press.

Lundman, R. J. (1994). Demeanor or crime? The Midwest City Police–Citizen Encounters Study. *Criminology, 32*, 631–656.

Lundman, R. J. (1996). Demeanor and arrest: Additional evidence from previously unpublished data. *Journal of Research on Crime and Delinquency, 33*, 306–323.

Lurigio, A. J., & Skogan, W. G. (1994). Winning the minds and hearts of police officers: An assessment of staff perceptions of community policing in Chicago. *Crime and Delinquency, 40*, 315–353.

Manning, P. (1997). *Police work: The social organization of policing.* Prospect Heights, IL: Waveland Press.

Marcuse, P., & van Kempen, R. (2000). Introduction. In P. Marcuse & R. van Kempen (Eds.), *Globalizing cities: A new spatial order?* (pp. 1–21). London: Blackwell.

Marshall, I. H. (1997). Minorities, crime, and criminal justice in the United States. In I. H. Marshall (Ed.), *Minorities, migrants, and crime* (pp. 1–35). Thousand Oaks, CA: Sage.

Massey, D. S. (1985). Ethnic residential segregation: A theoretical synthesis and empirical review. *Sociology and Social Research, 69*, 315–350.

Massey, D. S., & Denton, N. A. (1993). *American apartheid: Segregation and the making of the underclass*. Cambridge, MA: Harvard University Press.

Mastrofski, S. D. (1998). Community policing and police organization structure. In J.-P. Brodeur (Ed.), *How to recognize good policing? Problems and issues* (pp. 161–191). Thousand Oaks, CA: Sage.

Mastrofski, S. D., Parks, R. B., Reiss, Jr., A. J., & Worden, R. E. (1998). *Policing neighborhoods: A report from Indianapolis*. Washington, DC: National Institute of Justice.

Mastrofski, S. D., Parks, R. B., Reiss, Jr., A. J., & Worden, R. E. (1999). *Policing neighborhoods: A report from St. Petersburg*. Washington, DC: National Institute of Justice.

Mastrofski, S. D., Parks, R. B., Reiss, Jr., A. J., Worden, R. E., DeJong, C., Snipes, J. B., & Terrill, W. (1998). *Systematic observation of public police: Applying field research methods to policy issues*. Washington, DC: National Institute of Justice.

Mayhall, P. D., Barker, T., & Hunter, R. D. (1995). *Police–community relations and the administration of justice*. Englewood Cliffs, NJ: Prentice Hall.

McDonald, S. C. (1986). Does gentrification affect crime rates? In A. J. Reiss & M. Tonry (Eds.), *Communities and Crime* (pp. 163–201). Chicago: University of Chicago Press.

Meagher, M. S. (1985). Police patrol style: How pervasive is community variation? *Journal of Police Science and Administration, 13*, 36–45.

Meares, T. L., & Kahan, D. M. (1999). When rights are wrong: The paradox of unwanted rights. In T. L. Meares & D. M. Kahan (Eds.), *Urgent times: Policing and rights in inner-city communities* (pp. 3–30). Boston: Beacon Press.

Messner, S. F., & Tardiff, K. (1985). The social ecology of urban homicide: An application of the routine activities approach. *Criminology, 23*, 241–267.

Mollen Commission. (1994). *Commission to investigate allegations of police corruption and anti-corruption procedures of the police department*. New York: Author.

Monkkonen, E. H. (1992). History of urban police. In M. Tonry & N. Morris (Eds.), *Modern policing* (pp. 547–580). Chicago: University of Chicago Press.

Moore, M. H. (1992). Problem-solving and community policing. In M. Tonry & N. Morris (Eds.), *Modern policing* (pp. 99–158). Chicago: University of Chicago Press.

Muir, W. K., Jr. (1977). *Police: Streetcorner politicians*. Chicago: University of Chicago Press.

Murray, C. (1995). The physical environment. In J. Q. Wilson & J. Petersilia (Eds.), *Crime* (pp. 346–361). San Francisco: Center for Contemporary Studies Press.

Myers, D. (1983). Population processes and neighborhoods. In P. L. Clay & R. M. Hollister (Eds.), *Neighborhood policy and planning* (pp. 113–132). Lexington, MA: Lexington Books.

Newman, O., & Franck, K. (1980). *Factors influencing crime and instability in urban housing developments: Summary report*. Washington, DC: U.S. Department of Justice.

Petersilia, J. (1983). *Racial disparities in the criminal justice system*. Santa Monica, CA: RAND.

References

Police Foundation. (1981). *The Newark foot patrol experiment.* Washington, DC: Author.

Radelet, L. A., & Carter, D. L. (1994). *The police and the community.* New York: McMillan.

Reisig, M. D., and Parks, R. B. (2000). Experience, quality of life, and neighborhood context: A hierarchical analysis of satisfaction with police. *Justice Quarterly, 17,* 607–630.

Reiss, A. J., Jr. (1971). *Police and the public.* New Haven, CT: Yale University Press.

Reuss-Ianni, E. (1983). *Two cultures of policing: Street cops and management cops.* New Brunswick, NJ: Transaction.

Riksheim, E. C., & Chermak, S. M. (1993). Causes of police behavior. *Journal of Criminal Justice, 21,* 353–382.

Roncek, D. W. (1981). Dangerous places: Crime and residential environment. *Social Forces, 60,* 74–96.

Rosen, J. (2000, April 10). Why Patrick Dorismond didn't have to die. Excessive force. *New Republic.*

Rosenbaum, D. P. (1998). The changing role of the police: Assessing the current transition to community policing. In J. P. Brodeur (Ed.), *How to recognize good policing? Problems and issues* (pp. 3–29). Thousand Oaks, CA: Sage.

Russell, B. (1969). *Power.* New York: Norton.

Sampson, R. J. (1985). Race and criminal violence: A demographically disaggregated analysis of urban homicide. *Crime and Delinquency, 31,* 47–82.

Sampson, R. J. (1986a). Effects of socioeconomic context on official reaction to juvenile delinquency. *American Sociological Review, 51,* 876–886.

Sampson, R. J. (1986b). Crime in cities: Formal and informal social control. In A. J. Reiss, Jr., & M. Tonry (Eds.), *Communities and Crime* (pp. 271–311). Chicago: University of Chicago Press.

Sampson, R. J. (1995). The community. In J. Q. Wilson & J. Petersilia, *Crime* (pp. 193–216). San Francisco: ICS Press.

Sampson, R. J., & Bartusch, D. L. (1999). Legal cynicism and subcultural tolerance of deviance: The neighborhood context of racial differences. *Law and Society Review, 32,* 777–804.

Sampson, R. J., & Cohen, J. (1988). Deterrent effects of the police: A replication and theoretical extension. *Law and Society Review, 22,* 163–189.

Sampson, R. J., & Groves, W. B. (1989). Community structure and crime: Testing social-disorganization theory. *American Journal of Sociology, 94,* 774–802.

Sampson, R. J., & Laub, J. H. (1993). *Crime in the making: Pathways and turning points through life.* Cambridge, MA: Harvard University Press.

Sampson, R. J., & Wilson, W. J. (1995). Toward a theory of race, crime, and urban inequality. In J. Hagan & R. D. Peterson (Eds.), *Crime and inequality* (pp. 37–54). Stanford, CA: Stanford University Press.

Sampson, R. J., Raudebush, S. W., & Earls, F. (1997). Neighborhoods and violent crime: A multilevel study of collective efficacy. *Science, 277,* 918–924.

Schuman, H., & Gruenberg, B. (1972). Dissatisfaction with city services: Is race an important factor? In H. Hahn et al. (Eds.), *People and politics in urban society* (pp. 369–392). Beverly Hills, CA: Sage.

Shaw, C. R., & McKay, H. D. (1942). *Juvenile delinquency and urban areas.* Chicago: University of Chicago Press.

Sherman, L. W. (1980). Causes of police behavior: The current state of quantitative research. *Journal of Research in Crime and Delinquency, 17,* 69–100.

Sherman, L. W. (1992). Police and crime control. In M. Tonry & N. Morris (Eds.), *Modern policing* (pp. 159–230). Chicago: University of Chicago Press.

Sherman, L. W., & Rogan, D. P. (1995). Effects of gun seizures on gun violence: "Hot spots" patrol in Kansas City. *Justice Quarterly, 12,* 673–693.

Sherman, L. W., Gartin, P. R., & Buerger, M. E. (1989). Hot spots of predatory crime: Routine activities and the criminology of place. *Criminology, 27,* 27–55.

Shevsky, E., & Bell, W. (1955). *Social area analysis.* Stanford, CA: Stanford University Press.

Short, J. R. (1996). *The urban order: An introduction to cities, culture, and power.* Cambridge, MA: Blackwell.

Silver, A. (1967). The demand for order in civil society: A review of some themes in the history of urban crime, police, and riot. In D. J. Bordua (Ed.), *The police: Six sociological essays* (pp. 1–24). New York: Wiley.

Skogan, W. G. (1990). *Disorder and decline: Crime and spiral of decay in American neighborhoods.* New York: Free Press.

Skogan, W. G. (1998). Community participation and community policing. In J. P. Brodeur (Ed.), *How to recognize good policing? Problems and issues* (pp. 88–106). Thousand Oaks, CA: Sage.

Skogan, W. G., & Annan, S. O. (1994). Drugs and public housing: Toward an effective police response. In D. L. MacKenzie & C. D. Uchida (Eds.), *Drugs and crime: Evaluating public policy initiatives* (pp. 129–148). Thousand Oaks, CA: Sage.

Skogan, W. G., & Hartnett, S. M. (1997). *Community policing, Chicago style.* New York: Oxford University Press.

Skogan, W. G., & Maxfield, M. G. (1981). *Coping with crime: Individual and neighborhood reactions.* Beverly Hills, CA: Sage.

Skolnick, J. H. (1967). *Justice without trial: Law enforcement in democratic society.* New York: Wiley.

Skolnick, J. H., & Bayley, David H. (1986). *The new blue line: Police innovation in six American cities.* New York: Free Press.

Skolnick, J. H., & Fyfe, J. J. (1993). *Above the law: Police and the excessive use of force.* New York: Free Press.

Slovak, J. S. (1986). *Styles of policing: Organization, environment, and police styles in selected American cities.* New York: New York University Press.

Smith, D. A. (1986). The neighborhood context of police behavior. In A. J. Reiss, Jr., & M. Tonry (Eds.), *Communities and crime* (pp. 313–341). Chicago: University of Chicago Press.

Smith, D. A. (1987). Police response to interpersonal violence: Defining the parameters of legal control. *Social Forces, 65,* 767–782.

Smith, D, A., & Jarjoura, G. R. (1988). Social structure and criminal victimization. *Journal of Research in Crime and Delinquency, 25,* 27–52.

Sparrow, M. K., Moore, M. H., & Kennedy, D. M. (1990). *Beyond 911: A new era for policing.* New York: Basic Books.

Stahura, J. M. (1986). Suburban development, black suburbanization and the black Civil Rights Movement since War World II. *American Sociological Review, 51,* 131–144.

References

Stark, R. (1987). Deviant places: A theory of the ecology of crime. *Criminology, 25,* 893–909.
Steffensmeier, D., & Allan, E. A. (1995). Age-inequality and property crime: The effects of age-linked stratification and status attainment processes on patterns of criminality across the life course. In J. Hagan & R. D. Peterson (Eds.), *Crime and inequality* (pp. 95–115). Stanford, CA: Stanford University Press.
Stinchcombe, A. L. (1987). *Constructing social theories.* Chicago: University of Chicago Press.
Sykes, R., E. & Clark, J. P. (1975). A theory of deference exchange in police–civilian encounters. *American Journal of Sociology, 81,* 587–595.
Taub, R., Taylor, D., & Dunham, J. (1984). *Paths of neighborhood change.* Chicago: University of Chicago Press.
Tittle, C. R. (1994). The theoretical bases for inequality in formal social control. In G. S. Bridges & M. A. Myers (Eds.), *Inequality, crime, and social control* (pp. 21–52). Boulder, CO: Westview Press.
Trojanowicz, R. C. (1983). An evaluation of a neighborhood foot patrol. *Journal of Police Science and Administration, 2,* 410–419.
Trojanowicz, R. C., & Smyth, P. R. (1984). *A manual for the establishment and operation of a foot patrol program.* East Lansing, MI: National Neighborhood Foot Patrol Program.
Turk, A. (1969). *Criminality and legal order.* Chicago: Rand McNally.
Vala, J., Monteiro, M., & Leyens, J. (1988). Perception of violence is a function of observer's ideology and actor's group membership. *British Journal of Social Psychology, 27,* 231–237.
Van Maanen, J. (1978). The asshole. In P. K. Manning & J. Van Maanen (Eds.), *Policing: A view from the streets* (pp. 228–238). Pacific Palisades, CA: Goodyear Publishing Company.
Venkatesh, S. A. (1997). The social organization of street gang activities in an urban ghetto. *American Journal of Sociology, 103,* 80–111.
Verba, S., & Nie, N. H. (1972). *Participation in America.* New York: Harper & Row.
"A veteran chief: Too many cops think it's a war." (1997, September 1). *Time,* pp. 28–29.
Waddington, P.A.J., & Braddock, Q. (1991). Guardians or bullies? Perceptions of the police among adolescent black, white and Asian boys. *Policing and Society, 2,* 31–45.
Waegel, W. B. (1981). Case routinization in investigative police work. *Social Problems, 28,* 263–275.
Waegel, W. B. (1984). How police justify the use of deadly force. *Social Problems, 2,* 144–155.
Walker, D., Richardson, R. J., Denyer, J., Williams, O., & McGaughey C. (1972). Contact and support—an empirical assessment of public attitudes toward the police and the court. *North Carolina Law Review, 51,* 43–79.
Walker, S. (1988). *Sense and nonsense about crime: A policy guide* (2nd ed.). Pacific Grove, CA: Brooks/Cole.
Walker, S. (1992). *Police in America: An introduction* (2nd ed.). New York: McGraw-Hill.
Walker, S., Spohn, C., & De Leon, M. (1996). *Color of justice: Race, ethnicity, and crime in America* (S. Horne, Ed.). Belmont, CA: Wadsworth.

Walsh, W. F. (1986). Patrol officers arrest rates: A study of the social organization of police work. *Justice Quarterly, 3,* 271–290.

Warner, B. D. (1997). Community characteristics and the recording of crime: Police recording of citizens' complaints of burglary and assault. *Justice Quarterly, 14,* 631–650.

Webb, V. J., & Marshall, C. E. (1992). *Relative importance of race and ethnicity on citizen attitudes toward the police.* Rockville, MD: National Institute of Justice.

Weiler, C. (1983). Urban euthanasia for fun and profit. In P. C. Clay & R. M. Hollister (Eds.), *Neighborhood policy and planning* (pp. 167–175). Lexington, MA: Lexington Books.

Weisheit, R. A., Falcone, D. N., & Wells, L. E. (1999). *Crime and policing in rural and small town America* (2nd ed.). Prospect Heights, IL: Waveland Press.

Weitzer, R. (1999). Citizens' perceptions of police misconduct: Race and neighborhood context. *Justice Quarterly, 16,* 819–846.

Weitzer, R. (2000). Racialized policing: Residents' perceptions in three neighborhoods. *Law and Society Review, 34,* 129–156.

Weitzer, R., & Tuch, S. A. (1999). Race, class, and perceptions of discrimination by the police. *Crime and Delinquency, 45,* 494–507.

Whitaker, G. P., Phillips, C. D., & Worden, A. P. (1983). *Aggressive patrol: A search for side-effects.* Washington, DC: National Institute of Justice.

White, M. J. (1987). *American neighborhoods and residential differentiation.* New York: Russell Sage Foundation.

Wiley, M. G, & Hudik, T. L. (1974). Police–citizen encounters: A field test of exchange theory. *Social Problems, 22,* 119–127.

Wilson, J. Q. (1968). *Varieties of police behavior: The management of law and order in eight communities.* Cambridge, MA: Harvard University Press.

Wilson, J. Q. (1978). *Varieties of police behavior: The management of law and order in eight communities* (2nd ed.). Cambridge, MA: Harvard University Press.

Wilson, J. Q., & Kelling, G. L. (1982, March). Broken windows. *Atlantic Monthly,* pp. 29–38.

Wilson, W. J. (1987). *The truly disadvantaged.* Chicago: University of Chicago Press.

Wilson, W. J. (1997). *When work disappears: The world of the new urban poor.* New York: Knopf.

Worden, R. E. (1996). The causes of police brutality: Theory and evidence on police use of force. In W. A. Geller & H. Toch (Eds.), *Police violence: Understanding and controlling police abuse of force* (pp. 23–51). New Haven, CT: Yale University Press.

Worden, R. E., & Shepard, R. L. (1996). Demeanor, crime, and police behavior: A reexamination of the Police Services Study data. *Criminology, 34,* 83–105.

Worden, R. E., Bynum, T. S., & Frank, J. (1994). Police crackdowns on drug abuse and trafficking. In D. L. Mackenzie & C. D. Uchida (Eds.), *Drugs and crime: Evaluating public policy initiatives* (pp. 95–113). Thousand Oaks, CA: Sage.

Worrall, J. L. (1999). Public perceptions of police efficacy and image: The "fuzziness" of support for the police. *American Journal of Criminal Justice, 24,* 47–66.

Zuckerman, M. B. (1998). A second American century. *Foreign Affairs, 77,* 18–31.

Index

Age. *See* Life cycle
Arrest, 13, 19–22, 24, 25, 27, 28, 30–32, 33, 34, 37, 38, 65, 75, 77–79, 85, 91, 94, 103, 115–17, 140, 148

Bayley, David H., 30, 77
Bittner, Egon, 29, 43, 75, 77–78
Black, Donald J., 11–12, 33–34, 36, 77, 79
Blacks, 8, 22, 27, 28, 33, 34, 45, 47–48, 61, 63, 76, 79, 82, 86, 87–90, 95 n.3, 100, 149–50, 151–52. *See also* Race and ethnicity
Brutality, police, 19, 27–28, 29, 32, 86, 87, 149–50

Citizen attitudes toward police, 27, 31–32, 38–40, 87–90, 125–29, 149–50; age and, 88–89; measurement of, 105; negative, 105, 125–27; positive, 105, 127–29; race and ethnicity and, 87–90, 91, 149–50; research on, 39–40, 149–50; socioeconomic status and, 89–90
Citizen demeanor toward police, 37–38, 83–87, 122–25; age and, 84–86; cooperative, 105, 124–25; hostile, 104–5, 122–24; measurement of, 104–5; socioeconomic status and, 83–84
Coercion, police, 9, 11, 24, 25, 29–32, 35, 40, 64, 75–76, 78, 81, 82, 85, 93, 119–22, 144; measurement of, 104; physical, 30–31, 104, 120–21; and public hostility, 31–32, 75, 88–89; tactics of, 30; verbal, 30, 104, 119–20
Community, policing, 1–2, 3, 4–7, 8, 9, 19, 137–44
Corruption, police, 5–6, 19
Crime: age and, 55–56; control as police mission, 20, 64, 74, 79–80, 93; as determinant of community response, 90–93, 123–25, 126, 128; as determinant of police behavior, 79–83, 112–13, 114, 117–18; ecological determinants of, 53–56; measurement of, 101–2; race and ethnicity, 54–55; socioeconomic status and, 54

Disorder: age and, 61–62; as determinants of community response, 123–

125, 126, 128; ecological determinants of, 56–62; measurement of, 102; policing of, 2, 5, 25, 74, 116–18; race and ethnicity and, 5, 60–61; and social stigma, 63; socioeconomic status and, 58–60

Fear: age and, 61–62; of crime, 2, 26, 50, 56–59, 61–62, 63, 64–65, 80–82, 93–94, 98, 113, 125, 128, 130, 133, 135, 143; of police, 28, 31, 35, 78, 104, 126, 146, 147; police-induced 56–57; race and ethnicity and 60–61; of strangers, 5, 45, 48, 57, 60, 83, 125
Field interrogation, 26–25, 41 n.1, 103, 113–15

Goldstein, Herman, 26

Hispanics, 27, 28, 34, 49, 88, 100, 151. *See also* Race and ethnicity
Hypothesis (hypotheses), 3, 38, 54, 69, 77, 93–94, 107, 108, 112, 113, 114–15, 116, 117, 118, 121–22, 124, 126, 128, 133; benefits diffusion, 29; "class-bias," 59; kind-of-people, 8

Immigrants, 47–48, 86; police treatment of, 5, 28, 78–79
Incident report writing, 103, 117–19
Incivility. *See* Disorder
Inequality, 4, 26, 43, 55–56, 64. *See also* Stratification

Kansas City Police Department, 14, 27–28
Klinger, David A., 2–3, 6–7

Law enforcement, 32–35, 65, 76–79, 115–19; measurement of, 103
Legitimacy, of *status quo*, 1, 6, 19–22, 25, 27, 35–37, 52, 72, 75, 76
Life cycle, 48–50, 55–56; and crime, 55–56; and disorder, 61–62; measurement of, 100–101; and policing, 27–28, 74, 75–76, 84–86, 88–89, 116, 118, 120. *See also* Crime; Segregation

Los Angeles Police Department (LAPD), 21–22, 32
Lundman, Richard J., 12

Market, 2, 4, 28–29, 44, 45–47, 48, 51, 53, 54, 55–56, 62, 66, 71, 77, 92, 93, 139–40, 141, 143, 144, 146, 149, 150, 152
Middle classes: cultural and political dominance of, 51–52, 63, 71, 77, 141; and fear of crime, 58–59, 63; police identification with, 52–53, 77, 86, 91, 131
Moore, Mark H., 26
Moral hierarchy of neighborhoods, 62–66, 66–67, 80, 94–95, 125
Multicollinearity, 109–10, 111

Neighborhood: homogeneity, 45, 58–59, 81, 135; in social theory and policy, 3–4, 7–9, 13, 46; as unit of analysis, 3, 13, 17. *See also* Community, policing; Segregation
New York City Police Department (NYPD), 6, 27, 28, 71, 78, 91

Police: brutality, 19, 27–28, 29, 32, 86, 87, 149–150; corruption, 5–6, 19; history, 5–6, 20–21; identification with middle classes, 52–53, 77, 86–87, 131; legitimacy, 1, 6, 19–22, 25, 27, 35–37, 72, 75, 76; public image of, 35, 38; societal role, 2; subculture of isolation, 6, 20; use of stereotypes in, 6, 8, 28, 54, 80, 81, 122, 135, 146
Police behavior: ecological determinants of, 69–83; as a macro-level phenomenon, 9–14; psychological analysis of, 9–10; sociological analysis of, 10–13. *See also* Coercion, police; Law enforcement; Proaction, police
Police Services Study (PSS), 3, 15–17, 97–98, 133
Police work: organization, 6–7, 43–44; role of criminal law in, 24, 32–33. *See also* Policing

Index

Policing, 22–24; community, 1–2, 3, 4–7, 8, 9, 137–44; styles of, 10, 24

Poverty, 46–47, 49, 59–60, 71–72, 78, 89–90, 91–92, 114–15. *See also* Socioeconomic status

Power stratification of neighborhoods. *See* Stratification

Proaction, police, 24–29, 73–74, 112–15; and crime reduction, 25, 27–28; measurement of, 102–3; and public hostility, 27, 41 n.1

Quality of life, 4, 32, 59

Race and ethnicity, 15–16, 17, 26, 27, 47–48, 50–51, 54–55, 60–61, 78–79, 86, 116, 118–21, 123–24, 126–28; measurement of, 100. *See also* Segregation

Reaction, police. *See* Proaction, police

Reform, 1–2, 5–6, 20–21, 137–53

Reiss, Albert J., 8

Research methods, 9, 107–10

Residential security checks, 102–3, 112–13

Russell, Bertrand, 35–36

Sampson, Robert J., 56, 67 n.2

Segregation, 5, 16, 26, 44–67, 134, 138, 139–42; by age, 44, 48–50; by race and ethnicity, 44, 47–48, 50–51; by socioeconomic status, 44, 45–47, 49, 50–53

Sherman, Lawrence W., 3

Skogan, Wesley G., 57, 60–61, 62, 142, 146

Social: mobility, 46–48; stigma, 8, 63–66, 80–81, 92

Socioeconomic status, 15–16, 17, 45–47, 50–53, 54, 70–72, 73–74, 78–79, 83–84, 89–90, 91–92, 113, 118–21, 123–24, 126–27; measurement of, 98–100. *See also* Poverty

State, 2, 19, 20, 21, 25, 31, 35, 36, 39, 41, 52, 60, 65, 71, 76, 93, 136, 137, 139, 143–44

Stratification: of neighborhoods, 50–53, 62, 66–67, 70–72, 80–81, 83–84, 94–95, 114–15, 139–40; social, 5, 26

Theory, need for, 2–3, 8–9, 14–15, 40

Unemployment, 50–51, 54, 147, 149–51

Urban political economy, 3, 44–45, 48, 83–84, 90, 93, 121

Urbanization, 5

Wilson, James Q., 10–13

Youth. *See* Life cycle

About the Author

HUNG-EN SUNG is the Research Director for the Drug Treatment Alternative-to-Prison program at the Kings County District Attorney's Office in New York. His research interests include the study of crime and social control, drug abuse and its treatment, and comparative criminology. He completed his doctorate in criminal justice at SUNY Albany and has published journal articles on migration and crime and drug issues.